Judicial Reputation

Judicial Reputation

A Comparative Theory

NUNO GAROUPA AND
TOM GINSBURG

The University of Chicago Press   Chicago and London

The University of Chicago Press, Chicago 60637
The University of Chicago Press, Ltd., London
© 2015 by The University of Chicago
All rights reserved. Published 2015.
Paperback edition 2017
Printed in the United States of America

26 25 24 23 22 21 20 19 18 17   2 3 4 5 6

ISBN-13: 978-0-226-29059-1 (cloth)
ISBN-13: 978-0-226-47870-8 (paperback)
ISBN-13: 978-0-226-29062-1 (e-book)
DOI: 10.7208/chicago/9780226290621.001.0001

Library of Congress Cataloging-in-Publication Data
Garoupa, Nuno, author.
  Judicial reputaion : a comparative theory / Nuno Garoupa and
Tom Ginsburg
      pages cm
  Includes bibliographical references and index.
  ISBN 978-0-226-29059-1 (cloth : alk. paper)—ISBN 978-0-226-29062-1
(e-book)   1. Judges. 2. Judicial process—Public opinion. 3. Judicial
ethics.   I. Ginsburg, Tom, author.   II. Title.
  K2146.G374 2015
  347'.01401—dc23
                                                        2015011458

To our five daughters

It takes many good deeds to build a good reputation, and only one bad one to lose it.

—BENJAMIN FRANKLIN

Reputation is character minus what you've been caught doing.

—MICHAEL IAPOCE

Contents

Preface

This book is an effort to understand the structure of judicial systems around the world. Such systems exhibit the range of similarities and differences that motivates comparative inquiry in many fields. While there is no shortage of other accounts in comparative law trying to explain the various facts that we observe, most of these draw very heavily on history, tradition, and culture. Our account, however, starts in a different place: the economics of information and the powerful agency model that has become central to modern law and economics. We show that this very simple model can explain a good deal of the variation that we observe around the world. Judicial organization, it turns out, shares a lot with what economists sometimes call industrial organization.

This volume integrates into a common framework a number of themes that have appeared in our earlier work. These articles include "Hybrid Judicial Career Structures: Reputation vs. Legal Tradition," *Journal of Legal Analysis* 3 (2012): 1–38; "Building Reputation in Constitutional Courts: Political and Judicial," *Arizona Journal of International and Comparative Law* 28 (2011): 539–68; "Reputation, Information and the Organization of the Judiciary," *Journal of Comparative Law* 4 (2011): 226–54; "Judicial Audiences and Reputation: Perspectives from Comparative Law," *Columbia Journal of Transnational Law* 47 (2009): 451–90; "Guarding the Guardians: Judicial Councils and Judicial Independence," *American Journal of Comparative Law* 57 (2009): 201–32; "The Comparative Law and Economics of Judicial Councils," *Berkeley Journal of International Law* 27, no. 1

(2008): 53–83; "Gobierno judicial y consejo judiciales: una mirada desde el derecho y law economía," in *Reforma al poder judicial: gobierno judicial, corte suprema y gestión*, ed. José Francisco García et al., 41–75 (Santiago, Chile: Universidad Adolfo Ibáñez, 2007). We are grateful to the publishers for permission to draw on these articles, though each has been substantially modified and updated in this book.

Ginsburg is especially grateful to Dean Michael Schill of the University of Chicago Law School for his continuing support. Ginsburg would also like to thank the Russell Baker Scholars Fund of the University of Chicago Law School and the American Bar Foundation for research support, as well as the Fulbright Commission and the University of Trento for hosting the final stage of drafting. David Pervin at the University of Chicago Press was very helpful in shaping the project from an early stage. We also thank the many audiences in law schools who have heard versions of the chapters here. Of particular importance for serial comments on the work are Mitu Gulati, David Law, Eric Posner, Mark Ramseyer, Steven Shavell, Larry Solum, and Tom Ulen. We owe special debts to Eyal Benvenisti, Shai Dothan, Sam Ginsburg, and Mila Versteeg, who reviewed our draft book manuscript and provided insightful suggestions that substantially improved the final product. Thanks also to César Alonso Borrego, Omri Ben-Shahar, Wen-chen Chang, Luciana Gross Cunha, Paul Diehl, Matt Finkin, Vic Fleischer, Martin Gelter, Emilio Gerelli, Fernando Gómez Pomar, James Gordley, Gillian Hadfield, F. Andrew Hanssen, Sarah Harding, Stefan Van Hemmen, Dan Klerman, Richard McAdams, James Melton, Tom Miles, Michael Palmer, Anthony Ogus, Maria Ângela Oliveira, Daniela Piana, Ariel Porat, Weijia Rao, Limor Riza, Jairo Saddi, (the late) Luis Schuartz, Lydia Tiede, and Decio Zylbersztajn. We indemnify their individual reputations for our many errors.

Our various research assistants who worked on parts of this project include Eric Alston, Sofia Amaral Garcia, Carolina Arlota, Taimoor Aziz, Sonja Bunijevac, Rebecca Crouse, Yeny C. Estrada, Galina Fom, Arushi Garg, Nuria González, Alex Hearn, Sonali Maulik, Christopher Minelli, Lauren Morris, Leila Morshed Mohseni, Antônio Porto, and Guilherme Vasconcelos Vilaça. We owe each of them a debt of gratitude. And special thanks to Christopher Rhodes of the University of Chicago Press for seeing the project to fruition.

Introduction

In the summer of 2012, Chief Justice John Roberts surprised many observers with his opinion in the most widely anticipated Supreme Court case in many decades.[1] In providing the crucial fifth vote to uphold the Affordable Care Act—popularly known as Obamacare—Roberts ensured that the signature policy of President Barack Obama's first term would remain in place, even as the election season was heating up. Conservatives were outraged, and many called him a traitor or worse. An unprecedented leak by someone with very close knowledge of the decision—probably another justice on the court—revealed that Roberts had changed his mind at a very late stage in the process.[2]

Why did Roberts change his mind? The conventional wisdom is that Roberts was worried about the damage to the reputation of the court were it to go the other way. The president had expressed great confidence that the decision on his signature first-term policy would be favorable, and Roberts himself had repeatedly articulated a theory of judicial modesty and restraint at his confirmation hearings. The news media had predicted a huge backlash against both Roberts and the court were it to strike down the Obamacare system and suggested that Obama would likely have "run against the court" in the fall 2012 election (meaning that he would use an attack on the court for political gain). On balance, it is believed, Roberts decided to uphold the law for strategic reasons, while including some language in the decision to allow future decisions limiting federal power. Response was swift: while many legal scholars and some liberals applauded Roberts's judicial statesmanship, conservatives labeled him a traitor to the cause. Roberts's reputation was surely affected by his decision, as was that of the court.

Reputation is crucial in any endeavor, but it is particularly important for courts, which famously lack the purse or the sword.[3] Armed only with pens, judges can only be effective if they are persuasive and authoritative to the parties before them, the legal community, and the public as a whole. To be authoritative requires, at bottom, a reputation for good decision making. This reputation may vary across audiences—for instance, legal elites may have a different perception than politicians or the general public—but reputation before some audience is *always* important for judges. We develop the idea that reputation is instrumental to ensure compliance, to secure material resources, and to protect the court from various forms of backlash. The starting point for our perspective is the simple observation that courts are governmental institutions and that judges are agents of society. They are not demigods who shape public policies from on high but are actors situated within broader political structures. Courts make decisions within these broader contexts: they are constrained by what is possible and by the preferences of others whose action, or at least acquiescence, is required to effectuate judicial decisions. Furthermore, in the policy spaces in which other officials *cannot* act, or which politicians intentionally leave open for judicial action, judges have power that they can wield. Courts that enjoy a positive reputation may enjoy more degrees of freedom than those that do not and can use their power to advance the goals and preferences of the individual judges.[4]

As we will explain in more detail, we are not suggesting that all judges and courts should have a reputation for the same specific attribute. Any judicial system seeks to balance multiple goals, and so judges may value a reputation for, among other things, speedy decision making, creativity, accuracy, and independence from or deference toward the administration. There is no universal formula that captures the optimal balance among these goals, and so no universal formula for judicial reputation. What we do argue is that courts need to establish some type of reputation with their audiences in order to facilitate compliance, influence, and legitimacy. In some countries, a reputation for being deferential toward the administration might be important to enhance the influence and effectiveness of the judiciary; in other countries, such a reputation might have the exact opposite effect. And even within countries, the reputation for being deferential could be welcomed by some groups and disliked by other groups. It all varies with the particular configuration of what economists call the agency model.

A brief review of the agency model is in order. The agency model postulates a principal, which for the moment we will assume is the public or a governmental actor at the center of the political system. The principal has certain tasks that she needs accomplished that for various reasons—mainly in relation to expertise but also due to time constraints—she prefers to delegate to someone else. The agent is selected from a pool of potential agents to accomplish these tasks and given instructions at a certain level of detail. Once hired, the agent may or may not follow these instructions and so requires monitoring by the principal. These tasks of selecting, instructing, and monitoring agents are key points of institutional design, and we will spend a good deal of time exploring them.

We treat judges as the agents and society as the ultimate principal, on whose behalf the judges exercise power. The standard problem that arises in principal-agent models is produced by what is called information asymmetry: as the agent's expertise increases, her potential effectiveness increases as well, but her accountability decreases because the principal has difficulty understanding the agent's effort. There is thus a risk that the agent will act in accordance with her own preferences rather than those of the principal. For this reason, the principal must spend resources monitoring the agent.

A word is in order about the principal in our model. "Society" is obviously not a unified actor but an aggregate of individuals and groups with varied interests and preferences. Much work in constitutional and political theory explains how these diverse actors select agents—politicians—to exercise power on their behalf. These politicians then play a role in selecting and monitoring judges, but judges are also viewed in many cases as agents of the public to help monitor the politicians. The precise relationships among the public, politicians, and the courts are complicated and varied, and our analysis will help clarify them. But for now, for expository purposes, we can think of society as the ultimate principal, even if it is simply an analytic construct.

The difficulty of monitoring is especially profound when the "product" the agent is generating is something as abstract as law. If someone hires a taxi driver to take her to the airport, it is fairly easy to determine whether or not the driver has accomplished the task. Similarly, if someone orders a cup of coffee in a café, she can fairly easily determine whether or not the beverage handed to her is coffee (though she may have more trouble determining if it is truly a skinny decaf latte with an extra shot!). The product produced by judges is more complex: it includes resolving particular disputes, applying general norms to individual cases, making new laws, and monitoring other officials. Legal disputes are especially complex because we expect that only the most difficult problems will be worth taking all the way to court. Whatever their task, judges are exercising what is called human capital: they use their brains, and it is not easy to determine if they are exercising full effort or perfectly producing the desired product. The audience that holds itself up as being best situated to evaluate judges—namely, law professors who study judicial output full time—regularly disagree about case outcomes, suggesting that academics may not be such good monitors after all (or perhaps that their "monitoring" varies with their own preferences). One practically needs to *be* a judge to tell if a case is rightly or wrongly decided, and even among judges, there are disagreements about close cases. This exacerbates the agency problem.

In such an environment, judges can exercise power by deviating from the instructions of the principal. From our perspective, the fact that agents do not perfectly perform the actions expected of them is hardly a reason to abandon the agency model. Indeed, policy drift, slack, and other forms of nonperformance are central to it. It is also possible that the agents can become so liberated from the constraints of the principal that they in turn "capture" the principal and become the driving force in producing outcomes.[5] In our view, much of judicial organization is designed to help reduce the agency costs of judges and to ensure that the principal—society—gets the maximum benefit out of them. The key factors driving institutional design are the tasks that society wants of judges, which range from routine processing of administrative claims to mediation to the very creation of law itself.

Consider next the concept of reputation. As described in chapter 1, we define reputation simply as the stock of judgments about an actor's past behavior (which may or may not be used to predict future behavior).[6] This obviously requires information on past performance, and judges help generate that information. Information and communication are essential to resolving the agency problems inherent in judging. Whatever it is that motivates judges (and the literature is not clear on this question), judges must have the ability to communicate with certain audiences that react to decisions: the media, politicians, lawyers and law professors, and the public itself. Through their decisions, judges acquire a reputation with these audiences. A judge with a good reputation will enjoy the esteem of friends and colleagues and may be able to advance to a higher court; a judge with a bad reputation with colleagues is less likely to advance in her career. A judge with a good reputation before lawyers and law professors will be likely to have a more enduring legacy and may be more effective in shaping the law.

Reputation, however, is also a collective quality of the judiciary as a whole. A judiciary that operates effectively will be able to secure resources and enhance its political and social influence, which benefits judges individually. A high-quality judiciary may also become more visible internationally. The global "conversation of courts" means that there are important new audiences for judicial output, and judiciaries may earn prestige through citation by courts of other countries.[7] A judiciary might become a model for judicial reform programs abroad, providing opportunities for travel and exchange for judges. A judiciary with a poor reputation, by contrast, will find itself starved of both resources and respect.

Consider the Italian judiciary, which has gained a good deal of recent notoriety in the United States because of the legal saga of Amanda Knox. Knox was an exchange student in Italy in 2007 and was convicted with her Italian ex-boyfriend of the murder of her British roommate in a sensational case of a sex game gone wrong. An Italian appeals court overturned the verdict, but the Supreme Court ordered a retrial, and she was again found guilty in 2014. But in 2015 the Supreme Court reversed and declared her innocent. The topsy-turvy case highlighted the dysfunction of the Italian judiciary, which has a backlog of eight million cases and takes about five years to resolve criminal cases; civil cases are even slower, at seven years.[8] This poor reputation and the limited effect of earlier reforms recently prompted the International Monetary Fund to call for an overhaul of the court system.[9]

Another recent case is revealing: in 2014, the Bolivian Congress suspended two constitutional judges and indicted them for noncompliance with norms of judicial restraint. These two judges had raised serious doubts about a recent law regulating the notaries in Bolivia. While this kind of decision is standard fare for a constitutional court, it obviously harmed the reputation of the two judges before an important political audience and led to a significant infringement on judicial independence.[10] Still, the generally poor reputation of the Bolivian judiciary has not been affected by this news (and, in fact, this episode received very little coverage outside of Bolivia). The actions taken by these two judges might have resulted in enhancing their reputation in a different country but seemed detrimental for the relevant audiences in Bolivia.

Individual and collective reputations seem to matter intuitively, but we do not have a good understanding of how they develop or change over time. We use the concept of audience to help give a bit more precision to the idea of reputation. Reputation is produced by the interaction of an agent and audiences; one can think of the judge as an actor and the audience as responding to the actor's performance by bestowing a level of esteem. In technical terms, an audience is similar to the principal in that it lacks information to evaluate all aspects of the agent's performance. Most audiences are part of the principal at some level. But, in our conception, an audience is different in that it does not directly produce the contract with the agent. Continuing the performance analogy, the producer of a play is the principal of the actors; the producer is constrained by the audience, but the actor's ability to interact directly with the audience gives him a degree of freedom vis-à-vis the principal. A producer who does not like an actor's performance will have more difficulty firing the actor if he is wildly popular. For much of what follows, one can think about the government as the producer, constrained by the responses of the audiences for judges.

Our approach distinguishes "internal" from "external" audiences for judging. By internal audiences, we mean audiences within the judiciary itself; by external, we mean audiences such as lawyers, the media, or the general public. Some judiciaries are essentially dominated by internal audiences: socialization occurs *within* the profession, and judges are insulated from audiences other than their own colleagues and superiors. These judiciaries develop internal mechanisms to evaluate the performance of judges and thus emphasize the internal reputation of the individual judge while promoting the collective reputation of the judiciary as a whole before external audiences. In such systems, of which the Italian system used to be a paradigm example, individual judges may be well known within the profession but are anonymous to the outside world.

Other judiciaries are much more attentive to external audiences. Judges sign individual opinions that attract media attention; some may write for the public on issues of the day and may garner wide readership. Such judges are likely to have a higher profile as individuals and may be more well known than judges in systems that emphasize collective reputation.

Consider Justice Sonia Sotomayor, who some have taken to calling the "People's Justice." In early 2013, she was asked by Vice President Joseph Biden to administer his oath of office for his second term, which one might characterize as a nonjudicial act. She agreed but asked that the oath be administered early in the day so she could attend a sold-out book signing of her new memoir in New York.[11] The memoir ended up selling millions of copies. Sotomayor has made a point of appearing in popular settings, including the daytime interview show *The View*, *The Today Show*, and the comedy shows hosted by Jon Stewart and Stephen Colbert. As the nation's most prominent Latina official, with a particular reputation for empathy, she has gained a profile that few other judges have achieved. Her concern for the public audience has been reflected in her opinions, such as her dissent in the 2014 case of *Scheutte v. Coalition to Defend Affirmative Action*, which is written in clear, everyday language.[12]

Reputation is important for the entire judiciary as well as for individual judges. Reputation can be segmented across different audiences, and the configuration of audiences may condition judicial incentives. For example, while Justice Sotomayor has developed a particularly strong reputation among the general public in her brief time on the court, her colleague Justice Stephen Breyer is a former professor who seems to spend more time cultivating academic audiences. Supreme Court history also contains examples of judges who had a reputation for political decisions that did not exhibit much legal skill. Two of President Harry Truman's Supreme Court appointments, for example, were old friends of his from the Senate, and they remained popular in Congress though none proved to be a particularly distinguished jurist. In short, reputations can vary among different audiences, and the overall reputation of the judiciary is a product of its reputation with various audiences. Depending on the relative weight of each audience, judges will respond to some incentives more than to others.

It is our view that a complete institutional analysis of the judiciary requires attention to such considerations. The object of our book is to explain how judges respond to the incentives provided by different audiences and how legal systems design their judicial institutions to calibrate the locally appropriate balance between audiences. We do not address whether or not certain audiences *should* prevail over others. We do not have a strong normative theory that judges should, for example, pay more attention to the public rather than the legal profession or superior judges. Nor do we assert there is a universal optimum that applies across countries. Our concern in this book is rather to understand how different institutional configurations facilitate different modes of judicial production, which impact professional norms and the organization of the judiciary.

We will demonstrate that our view is quite different from the traditional approach in comparative law, which emphasizes legal history, especially the common law–civil law distinction, as the driving factor in understanding contemporary institutions. Comparative legal scholars have frequently contrasted the "career" and "recognition" models of judicial organization.[13] *Career judiciary* usually refers to the system prevalent in Europe and civil law jurisdictions in which judges spend their careers in a bureaucratic hierarchy and change jobs periodically. *Recognition judiciary* is frequently associated with the United States and other common law jurisdictions and features judges who are selected relatively late in life after a previous legal career. Judges in the recognition system tend not to move jobs, but their appointments usually involve a political mechanism and hence are high profile and sometimes politicized.

Each system of judicial organization produces different incentives for judges, embodied in the precise design of mechanisms for judicial appointment, assessment, and removal. The incentive structure tends to be reinforced by other aspects of the judicial system, including the possibility of separate opinions and dissents, discretion in sentencing and procedure, the scope of appeals (for example, de novo review), the use of citations, the court's powers to select cases, the management and budget of the court system, and the size of the courts. Not surprisingly, career and recognition judiciaries have very different institutional configurations, responding to different constitutional and political environments, but there are also many hybrid models, as we show in chapter 2.

Our project seeks to go beyond the common law–civil law divide, or the overall categorization of judiciaries into the career or recognition models, to unpack more precisely the institutional structure of judicial organization. Although these models may have had some purchase historically, they do not capture the current configuration of judicial organization, nor do they provide much insight into the direction of change. We suggest that current institutional arrangements are more complex and are better explained by our reputation approach. We know that, for example, the US federal judiciary is quite different from the higher judiciary in the United Kingdom, notwithstanding their shared origins and tradition. Even within the United States, the variation across states is significant, with some states electing their judges and others appointing them. Similarly, career judiciaries in Germany, France, Italy, and Japan differ among themselves in important ways.

Another influential theory in comparative law and economics, associated with a group of prominent economists, emphasizes the enduring impact of what are called "legal origins."[14] Their controversial theory argues that the quality of law adopted at the outset of a country's establishment will have enduring, path-dependent consequences for corporate organization, finance, and economic growth. These scholars divide up legal systems according to the dominant model of the civil code adopted in the country, being of German, French, English, or Scandinavian origin. Like the traditional view of comparative lawyers, this view emphasizes family relationships among systems and a relatively static and stylized conception of judicial structure.[15]

We provide an alternative account of variation in institutional structures. Our departing point is the principal-agent model of the judiciary, described above.[16] Society hires judges as agents to accomplish a certain set of tasks. We assume that these tasks include, in every legal system, some amount of judicial lawmaking, as well as a degree of routine social control and dispute-resolution functions. The task for the principal can be seen as hiring a set of judicial agents involving a mix of high skills and lower level skills. The high-skill agents have more human capital and hence are more expensive, though they may also find it easier to get around the demands of the principal. Low-skill agents may be more malleable and less expensive. There are therefore some trade-offs between hiring large numbers of low-skill agents and a smaller number of high-skill agents. Functional demands, not just tradition, will dictate the mix.

The agents need to provide information to various audiences through the cultivation of reputation. Consider in this light the problem of judicial appointments. The career system involves judges entering a judicial bureaucracy at a young age and spending an entire career as a judge, the process of socialization occurring essentially within the ranks of the profession. Reputation plays a minor role in selection, if any. In a recognition system, judges are appointed later in life, usually after the candidate has established her excellence as a practicing lawyer, prosecutor, or academic. The recognition system involves fewer opportunities for promotion because judges spend less time in the judiciary before retirement. Judicial appointments in recognition systems are based on the individual reputation of the candidate, as assessed by the relevant external constituency. For example, in the United States, the president appoints federal judges, with the advice and consent of the Senate, after the candidates have developed a stellar reputation in other spheres. The external screening of the agent helps compensate for the absence of a vertical hierarchy in the judiciary, which decreases the incentives to comply with rigid internal professional norms. The appointment by external agents dilutes the importance of internal controls and the collective identity of the judiciary but increases the relevance of external assessment. Finally, the lack of a promotion system seriously weakens internal mechanisms of control. Therefore, in recognition judiciaries, individual reputation as perceived by external mechanisms is the dominant factor in judicial appointments.

In contrast, a career judiciary is selected and promoted based on internal judicial assessments of individual merit. Relatively little information is available to the public about individual judges, but the judiciary itself develops and uses internal performance measures to inform decision making related to promotions. Compliance with internal mechanisms makes individual reputation within the profession more important while also reinforcing the role of collective reputation vis-à-vis external constituencies. The external credibility of a given judge does not depend on her individual merit but more on the collective reputation of the entire judiciary. Such systems tend to emphasize the anonymity of the law and the myth that there is a single correct answer for legal questions that, in principle, is invariant to the individual judge making the decision.

The interaction between internal and external constituencies is dynamic, and so tradition alone cannot explain the configurations that we observe. We are in an era of nearly continuous institutional tinkering with judicial structures that goes far beyond what was found in earlier eras. Countries are reforming judicial administration, legal procedure, and even constitutions at a rapid rate.[17] In 2009, for example, the United Kingdom abolished the function of the House of Lords in hearing judicial appeals, while lay decision making has been introduced into criminal trials in civil law countries like Japan, South Korea, and Spain. Such judicial reforms cannot be explained by ancient origins but instead are subject to particular quirks of local politics that might reflect the relative importance of different audiences. For example, expanding or limiting the powers of a multimember judicial council (a board-like body discussed in chapter 4) might increase or reduce the importance of the internal audience of judicial peers. Constitutional reforms that alter the mechanism of judicial appointment might have dramatic effects on incentives for judicial action. However, other changes exogenous to the law might also be relevant. For example, the growing importance of media exposure could enhance the importance of external audiences within judicial systems traditionally dominated by internal individual reputation and external collective reputation. Economic and social changes that reshape the nature of litigation may affect the balance among different external groups and lobbies.[18]

Our institutional approach offers a new lens for understanding judicial organization and behavior. The most important factor is not legal tradition but the interaction between judges and other actors in the political system, as mediated by institutional structures. Each particular system has its own logic, but it is also subject to pressures for change as different audiences become more or less important as a result of exogenous or endogenous change. Our bottom line is that the economics of information and reputation are more important than legal tradition in understanding judicial organization in any given context.

It is also worth thinking about the reputation of the judicial branch in general across countries. Global surveys of various professions indicate that there has been an increase in the population's trust of judges in many countries. In one cross-national survey, judges received an average trust rating of 71 percent in 2014, up nine points from 2010. But there was significant variation in the survey: trust was highest in Canada, and also high in many northern European countries, but low in Argentina, in which only 35 percent of people indicated that they trust judges.[19] This matches other cross-national surveys.[20] The World Justice Project, a large effort to measure perceptions of the rule of law in various countries, has showed some improvement on several dimensions of judicial performance since its inception in 2010.[21] In short, there is the intriguing possibility (discussed in chapter 6) that national judicial reputations may be linked across countries, implying a global production of judicial reputation.[22] This naturally enhances the incentives of high-status judiciaries to invest in the quality and reputation of their colleagues in other countries. Reputation sheds new light on the "global conversation of courts," a process through which judges read and cite each other's opinions.[23]

The remainder of this volume is organized as follows. Chapter 1 introduces our theory of judicial reputation, defining the concept and explaining many aspects of judicial organization—from the structure of opinion writing to the mechanisms of appeal—from the reputation perspective. As noted above, many scholars have contrasted judicial organization along the lines of the common law–civil law divide. We take this as our starting point; the two historical traditions *do* have distinct models of judicial organization. However, in keeping with our emphasis on function rather than tradition as the primary driver of judicial organization, we show that tradition is not destiny. Rather, in countries from both traditions, there are particular hybrid models that exist in specific places. Chapter 2 argues that these "pockets of exception" tell us a good deal about the fundamental forces at work in determining judicial organization.

An interesting and understudied phenomenon in comparative judicial studies is the exploration of the roles judges play in exercising nonjudicial functions. In recent years, judges have led commissions of inquiry, worked on legislation, and in some cases even served as acting heads of state. How these functions affect the core judicial role is fascinating and a source of great contention in many systems. Our particular concern is the impact of these roles on judicial reputation. We argue in chapter 3 that nonjudicial functions can, within certain limits, enhance judicial reputation, but there are also risks that come from too much judicial involvement in nonjudicial functions. As in so many areas, the task is one of optimization within a local context, rather than maximizing a single abstract value like "judicial independence."

Chapter 4 takes up the specific issue of the selection of judges, focusing special attention on a new institution, the judicial council, which has spread around the world in recent decades and helps the judiciary deal with management issues. Chapter 5 uses the reputation perspective to consider an important issue in constitutional design: competition among high courts within a given legal system. In recent years, the spread of designated constitutional courts has meant that there are, in many systems, multiple apex courts. For example, France has long had a supreme court for ordinary cases, the Cour du Cassation, alongside a Conseil Constitutionnel (which adjudicates constitutional questions) and a Conseil d'État (which performs administrative adjudication functions among other tasks). South Korea, Indonesia, and many other countries have a supreme court but also a designated constitutional court. The relations among these bodies are complicated, and we explain how the idea of reputation illuminates the different dynamics identified by scholars who study the local conflicts that arise.

Finally, chapter 6 takes up the impact of globalization on courts, through consideration of the global rule of law movement and the expansion of the international judiciary. The rule of law movement, in which outside actors spend resources to promote judicial reform and independence, obviously expands the external audiences for judicial activity, creating new opportunities to invest in reputation. And recent years have seen a significant proliferation of international courts—now numbering more than twenty-five by some definitions. These courts are interesting environments for testing our theory because they are somewhat free of historical traditions. While judges on such courts of course come from particular backgrounds in common law and civil law countries, they have from the very beginning sought to merge elements of these traditions in defining procedures and such. Legal traditions cannot completely account for this newly emergent phenomenon. The international judiciary provides an ideal environment to test whether our concept of reputation has explanatory power to explain structure.[24]

At this point, we should add a methodological note. In this book, we combine case studies with cross-country descriptive statistics and regression analysis. In our view, these multiple approaches help us avoid some of the standard criticisms about cross-country regression analysis and allow us to more fully explore the institutional varieties across jurisdictions.

Many of our chapters include examples from a small number of jurisdictions, chiefly Japan, the United States, the United Kingdom, Germany, France, and various Latin American countries. In thinking about which countries to focus on, we sought to be systematic in including influential jurisdictions at the core of the common law–civil law divide, as well as countries at various stages of economic development. We also wanted to include countries with different "legal origins," using the economists' categorization (which we do not particularly endorse): We have at least two countries of German "legal origin" (Germany and Japan) and two with English origin (the United Kingdom and the United States). The remainder have been characterized (in some cases mistakenly in our view) as being of French legal origin. This wide set of cases helps demonstrate that our theory is one of general application and not an artefact of the particular cases we select. We also include a number of simple empirical tests of our hypotheses using large-n data, where available, but the nature of our argument is not easily susceptible to rigorous testing. Instead, we see our primary contribution as explanatory, illuminating dynamics in the comparative study of legal systems that have heretofore remained invisible.

ONE

A Theory of Judicial Reputation and Audiences

In 2013, reflecting on the controversial decision in *Bush v. Gore* in which the Supreme Court effectively awarded the presidency to George W. Bush, former justice Sandra Day O'Connor reflected, "Maybe the Court should have said, 'We're not going to take it, goodbye.'" Her reasoning was that the decision "gave the Court a less than perfect reputation."[1] The dissenters in the case had predicted as much; Justice Stephen Breyer warned that the decision might become a "self-inflicted wound."[2] In fact, however, the reputation of the court largely survived the controversial case, in part because different audiences reacted differently: perhaps unsurprisingly, views of the court improved among Republicans and declined among Democrats.[3]

Reputation is crucial in many arenas, and judging is no exception. A judge with a good reputation will enjoy the esteem of his friends and colleagues and may have chances for advancement to higher courts. He might become internationally renowned, such as former Israeli Supreme Court Justice Aharon Barak or US Appeals Court Judge Richard Posner. If particularly well known, he will have a legacy that endures long after death, like US Supreme Court justices John Marshall, Earl Warren, or Oliver Wendell Holmes. A judiciary that operates effectively will earn respect within its own political system and internationally and may become a model for other countries, providing opportunities for judges to travel. A judiciary with a poor reputation, in contrast, will find itself starved of both resources and respect.

Despite the sense that reputation is important, we know very little about how judicial reputation is produced. We understand that some judges and judiciaries are viewed as successful and others are not, but we do not really have any theories about how reputation is developed and sustained. In this chapter, we use economic analysis to provide a theory of judicial reputation and provide evidence of the institutional consequences from a range of legal systems.

We define reputation as the stock of assessments about an actor's past performance. The object of our analysis is to explore how reputation is formed or produced, the mechanisms by which reputation is achieved, and the institutional incentives that reinforce or harm judicial reputation. We do not discuss whether reputation is a good or a bad thing, whether individual reputation is better or worse than group reputation, or whether individual visibility and exposure enhance creativity and legal change in more appropriate ways than group-focused professional environments. Nor is our analysis normative. Our concern in this chapter is to understand how different institutional configurations facilitate different modes of producing reputation, which impact professional norms and the position of judges in society.

Reputation matters because, in the real world, there is imperfect information about judicial performance.[4] In an environment without information asymmetries, reputation would play no role since everyone would be able to observe performance accurately. Under time and informational constraints (which may grow over time as law becomes increasingly complex), a reputation becomes a kind of shortcut to help audiences figure out how to react to judges and their decisions. This implies that every judiciary must consider reputation, because many relevant audiences cannot directly observe certain attributes that they wish to know about.

Reputation requires assessments about performance. These assessments are made by audiences with varying degrees of information. One particularly important audience is the judiciary itself. We refer to the judiciary as the internal audience for judging. All other audiences are lumped together into what we call external audiences, meaning that they are external to the judicial branch. These audiences might be relatively informed about judicial performance, say if they are made up of lawyers or academics, or relatively uninformed, if they are laymen. At the same time, the strategies used by the judiciary have to be based on a set of consistent beliefs (for example, due to sophisticated mechanisms such as Bayesian updates)[5] by those who have less accurate information. The main consequence is that the performance by the judiciary at any given moment might be driven by strategic efforts to build reputation to generate future payoffs (that is, gains for the judiciary).

This chapter focuses on the structures that facilitate judicial production of the raw materials of reputation. Here "raw materials" are things like legal decisions, opinions, talks, other writings, procedural rulings, and oral questioning. We do not discuss the processing of these raw materials by audiences, which might take the form of legal analysis, media reporting, and commentary.

Judicial reputation plays two important roles. First, it conveys information to the uninformed general public about the quality of the judiciary (and, more generally, about the legal system) as perceived by the relevant audiences. Second, reputation fosters esteem for the profession and for the individual judge—both self-esteem and esteem in the eyes of others. A judiciary with high esteem is likely to be able to garner more material resources and to be more insulated from other political actors who might expropriate such resources (whether monetary or social).

The reputation of the judiciary, individually or as a whole, determines its status in any given society and its ability to compete effectively for resources within the government. We do not specify a universal reputation function for judges, and we recognize that judges in different systems will seek reputations for different qualities—such as predictability, wisdom, or efficiency—that might not be valued in other systems. Whatever the definition of judicial quality in a particular legal system, reputation emerges as a relevant factor and plays an important role.

We make three claims. First, reputation matters. Virtually every theory of judicial power is dependent, ultimately, on perceptions of judges and their abilities. A judge's decisions will be respected and complied with only if she has a reputation for high quality, as determined by the relevant audiences. Without compliance, judges cannot accomplish their social functions of resolving disputes, articulating rules, and serving as vehicles for social control.[6] Thus reputation is essential from an instrumental perspective.

Our second claim is that reputation can be divided into individual and collective components. Individual reputation reveals information about individual performance, whereas collective reputation reflects information about the quality of the judiciary in general. At the same time, each member of an institution cares about his individual reputation but also about the reputation of the group as a whole. Collective reputation determines the status of the judiciary, but individual reputation influences the relative perception of an individual judge against their fellow judges (as a group). It follows that not all reputation building is necessarily socially beneficial; it is possible that some internal status dynamic might lead judges to overinvest in aspects of their individual reputations to impress each other. Such internal competition might result, for example, in a particularly complex or technical jurisprudence that is unintelligible for the average citizen, deviating from the social optimum.

The bifurcated nature of reputation between individual and group components creates interesting institutional challenges, which we analyze below using the economic concept of team production.[7] If judicial performance was purely the result of individual effort and the quality of the judiciary could be easily disaggregated into its individual components, individual reputation should prevail as the most important mechanism to provide information. But, crucially, it is often difficult to monitor or differentiate the separate individual contributions to the production of justice or judicial decisions; in technical terms, the judicial product is "nonseparable." Because of this, we also need information about the aggregate performance of the judiciary; the whole is more than the sum of individual contributions. Consequently, an important task of institutional design is to incentivize the optimal balance of investments into the different components of reputation to match the needs of any given society.

Our third claim is that different legal systems configure institutions in different ways in order to address the problems of information and reputation. The classical understandings of the common law and civil law judiciaries can be seen as sets of linked institutions that are mutually reinforcing in addressing the problems of information and reputation. We describe these institutions from the perspective of information and reputation and explain how they interrelate. Judiciaries that emphasize collective reputation utilize institutions to limit publicly available information about the performance of the individual judge. Those that emphasize individual reputation, on the other hand, facilitate the disclosure of such information. In both cases, the disclosure or nondisclosure of private information about individual performance reinforces the kind of reputation that prevails in the judicial system.

Our discussion of institutional arrangements is fundamentally positive in that we are not trying to identify a single universal optimum for all countries. We explain how institutions favor the production of individual or collective information but also assume that the optimal balance may vary across jurisdictions, depending on local preferences, historical events that determine the allocation of human capital, and political economy. Although, from an economic perspective, we might expect that information about individual performance would always be valuable to the relevant audiences (other judges, lawyers, economic and political agents, and the general public), it could well be that the political context makes disclosure of information about individual performance harmful. For example, a judiciary that is concerned about threats to its independence may prefer to mask individual judicial contributions out of concern that politicians may seek to remove judges who decide cases against them.

Judges in different societies play different social functions. Judges everywhere play an important role in dispute resolution.[8] Some courts are primarily engaged in social control, serving as part of the state's apparatus to govern citizens and limit abuse by low-level government officials. Other courts are primarily engaged in lawmaking, articulating norms for the society. As we shall explain, we believe that collective reputation dominates when the legal system emphasizes social control: hierarchical systems reduce agency costs by allowing superior levels to supervise lower levels. On the other hand, when judges are delegated with the task of lawmaking, individual reputation is necessary to ensure accountability. We tend to observe great emphasis on ex ante screening of judges in such environments. In our view, these observations help explain why we observe a dominant structure within any particular legal system but also help explain pockets of exception found in many systems.

Our effort is consistent with a recent body of work in comparative law that looks at the actual institutional structures of different legal systems.[9] This approach contrasts with the deductive approach that starts with legal origins and assumes that ancient institutional distinctions are enduring and consequential.[10] We believe that institutions matter but also emphasize that institutional structures can change over time, and suggest that minor institutional reforms can have major and unintended consequences on the production of reputation. This perspective, we argue, is more helpful for understanding judicial behavior than the simple categorization of legal origins.

Our chapter is organized as follows: The first section lays out why reputation matters. The second and third sections describe our theory, treating judicial reputation from the perspective of the economics of team production. The fourth section identifies how particular institutions affect reputation and suggests that institutional configurations fall into two clusters, roughly but not exclusively corresponding to the common law and civil law judicial systems. We find that the former system favors the production of individual reputation and the latter collective reputation. We illustrate the contrast with a discussion of the United States and Japan in the final section.

Why Reputation Matters

To begin, we should define reputation with some precision. As mentioned above, we think of the reputation of any particular agent as the stock of private assessments of past behavior. This involves information on past performance (if directly observable), as well as signals given by the agent herself (when there is an information asymmetry). Assessment of reputation may be based on public information or private information, depending on the relevant audience. It is possible, but not at all necessary, to imagine that reputation includes an esteem component, so that reputation is granted by a particular audience on the basis of some interdependent production function involving both the judicial "producer" and the outside "consumer." Further, some definitions rely on the idea that reputation is used to predict future performance, but in our context, this is not required: we can speak of the reputation of a long-dead judge.[11]

Reputation has two components. Individual reputation conveys information about the individual performance of a given judge, whereas collective reputation reveals information about the performance of the judiciary as a whole. But judges produce the law collectively, so it is difficult to determine whether any individual decision results from qualities of an individual judge or the judiciary as a whole. Due to the nonseparable nature of judicial production, collective reputation is not simply the aggregation of individual reputations. If it were, then collective reputation would be trivial. In other words, collective information may differ from the sum of assessments about individual performance. Notice that our distinction is not merely explained by cognitive limitations, such as the idea that the general public cannot recall the individual names of judges and therefore uses the perception of an average performance as a proxy. Our distinction is driven by our understanding of judicial production as teamwork.

Judges, like most everyone, care about their reputation to the extent that reputation is an important social and economic asset.[12] No doubt judges care somewhat about monetary rewards, and therefore reputation is important to the extent that those monetary payoffs vary with reputation.[13] If information about individual performance determines salaries, then judges will care about individual reputation. If information about the collective performance and quality of the judiciary determines salaries, then judges may change their behavior accordingly to invest in collective reputation.

Judges also care about nonmonetary rewards, and in this respect, reputation is an important professional asset. Reputation is a credible signal of high quality, which allows judges to fulfill professional duties and achieve career goals.[14] The ability of judges to influence society is shaped by the individual and collective information conveyed to relevant audiences.

The significance of reputation extends far beyond the welfare of an individual judge. The reputation of the judiciary as a whole is dependent on the reputation of its component judges. The reputation of the judiciary has a crucial impact on its ability to accomplish its goals. Judicial decisions, after all, are not self-enforcing but instead require real-world institutions and individuals to take action to ensure compliance.

There are a variety of theories that attempt to explain why people obey the pronouncements of courts. One traditional set of arguments focuses on the legitimacy of judicial decisions; this has been supplemented by social psychological work on procedural legitimacy.[15] Another set of arguments emphasizes enforcement by other state officials, but this only begs the question—for one must have an account of why other officials have an incentive to obey the courts. A third view sees judicial decisions as facilitating the coordination of parties' expectations by providing focal points.[16] In this view, parties obey the judges because they expect *other* parties to play certain strategies in response to the court decision. But regardless of which theory one adopts to explain why judges are obeyed, reputation matters. A better reputation will be correlated with an increased likelihood of compliance, whether the mechanism of compliance involved relies on legitimacy, enforcement, or coordination. As judicial decisions are complied with, they provide further feedback in the form of an improved reputation.

Recently, Aharon Barak, the former chief justice of Israel, has explained in detail why individual judges care about collective reputation and the extent to which it influences their decisions.[17] Barak identifies collective goals: in his view, the judiciary is the "junior partner" in the legislative process, in the sense of playing an important role in helping the law respond to change in social reality; he sees the judiciary as the "senior partner" in the creation and development of the common law within the limitations of the legal system. In order to achieve these goals effectively as a collective, the judiciary needs consistency and credibility.

From this perspective, separate opinions might weaken the force of the judgment if they undermine consistency, hinder compliance, and induce uncertainty. But a robust collective reputation, once developed, allows courts to occasionally make flawed decisions, since there is confidence in individual and collective independence, fairness, and impartiality. In sum, individual judges are confronted with the need to balance their incentives to issue individual opinions, which may advance their personal goals, against the costs of nonunanimity in terms of consistency and credibility. Too many individual opinions may create uncertainty within the legal system and hurt all judges' prestige and ability to shape the law.[18] The production of reputation is thus a collective action problem.

One can get a sense of how important reputation is by considering the situation of judges in some developing countries. Despite a recent consensus among development agencies that law plays a crucial role in economic development, real-world reforms are difficult to implement, and we have little evidence that billions of dollars of investment in improving judicial performance has actually paid off.[19] In many countries, the judiciary has a reputation for corruption.[20] Sometimes individual judges may not work hard enough; others may work hard but do not act in line with the collective judiciary. In such environments, collective action has failed, and individual judges seek to maximize their own wealth or reputation at the expense of their collective reputation. It is hard to pin one's hopes for reform on institutions that have poor reputations to start out with.

Judicial reputation is especially important in such environments. Many believe that a high-quality judiciary can improve the anticipated enforcement of property rights, security of contract, and investment, all of which should contribute to economic growth. Without good formal legal institutions, people move toward informal substitutes, which may not be as effective.[21] The key factor may not be the actual quality of legal decision making as much as the reputation of the judiciary. A judiciary with real skill but a bad reputation will not produce the important developmental benefits that conventional theories expect.

Reputation also plays an important role in the recruitment of judges. A more reputable judicial system attracts candidates with higher levels of human capital. Judiciaries with low reputations or reputations for corruption will attract the ill qualified and greedy. A lazy judiciary will attract lazy individuals. Even if a system has overcome these problems, it is still the case that different reputation mechanisms might attract different types of people.[22] Selection processes tend to reinforce the status quo, since the new judges are interested in reinforcing the reputation that attracted them to the profession in the first place (or the easy working conditions that might lead to a bad collective reputation).[23]

In short, we believe that reputation is a central quality of judiciaries. Virtually every function for which societies rely on the judiciary depends on the production of a reputation for high-quality, impartial, and independent decision making. Without a good reputation, judiciaries are doomed to irrelevance. As such, reputation building and its strategic components are important factors to contemplate when analyzing judicial behavior. As we will emphasize, while the determinants of reputation are necessarily contextual, reflecting local social preferences, we can provide a framework for analyzing the dynamics of reputation over time.

A Theory of Reputation

As we have suggested, reputation can be divided into two components: individual and collective. Individual reputation is related to the name recognition of each judge.[24] Collective reputation is linked to the perceived role of the judiciary in any given society.[25] Each and every judge is affected by both individual and collective reputation and consequently cares about both. Nevertheless, depending on incentives and the institutional framework, judges might be more concerned with one or the other in different societies.

Individual reputation building is fundamentally an activity that each judge must accomplish on his own, while collective reputation building is the product of teamwork. Furthermore, it is not always the case that efforts allocated to individual reputation building enhance collective reputation and vice versa. In fact, in some circumstances these two goals may conflict. For example, the goal of establishing individual reputation might encourage each judge to differentiate herself from other judges, but excessive differentiation across the bench might seriously undermine collective reputation. High variance in the performance of individual judges can hurt the reputation of the judiciary as a whole.

In our view, judges allocate their efforts to build individual or collective reputations in response to the institutional environment. This means that a judge might have to decide between advancing her own preferences (hence building individual reputation) or conforming with the general preferences of her colleagues (hence promoting a collective reputation for consensus). In many circumstances, a particular action can enhance both individual and collective reputation at the same time. But in other circumstances, by investing more in building individual reputation, a judge contributes less to building collective reputation. This presents each judge with a choice as to which type of reputation to invest in. Choices are influenced by incentives, which in turn are established by different actors. These actors can be considered principals on whose behalf the judiciary works.

Collective reputation is essentially determined by external audiences. It reflects the views of society or public opinion in general toward the judiciary but also the interests of the relevant particular constituencies with special power over the courts. These constituencies might include the bar, other branches of government, political parties, and others, depending on the institutional environment of courts. Collective reputation shapes the social and political influence of the judiciary as a whole and consequently has monetary and nonmonetary implications for the welfare of the judges. For example, collective reputation may impact the overall judicial budget, salaries, pensions, and other perks available to the judiciary, as well the level of social prestige and overall working conditions in the courts. In other words, collective reputation determines the size of the pie to be divided among individual judges.

Individual reputation is established by external audiences (such as academic commentators, the bar, and political actors) but also by internal audiences (such as other judges engaged in peer evaluation). Individual reputation, as established by these internal audiences, determines the share each judge gets of the pie, while the outside appraisal by relevant external constituencies determines potential supplementary payoffs obtained individually. The balance between external and internal audiences shapes individual reputation building.[26]

In our analysis, we assume that reputation is a noiseless signal of judicial quality, however defined. (In information theory, noise refers to distortion in the accuracy of the received signal, so that a noiseless signal is one that provides accurate information about judicial quality.) Reputation provides information about individual and collective performance. Although in the real world reputations are noisy, we make the simplifying assumption that reputation maps accurately onto judicial quality. This assumption is not necessary, strictly speaking, for our analysis—all we need to assume is that noise does not vary systematically across the institutional structures that we analyze. Nevertheless, we set aside noise in the present discussion. This means we need not consider how reputation dissipates after it is acquired. In the real world, the fact that reputation is noisy means that relevant constituencies may continue to accord the judiciary with status, even after behavior changes. Reputations in the real world are sticky, a feature that heightens the importance of investing in reputation and makes the problems we discuss even more salient.

Judicial Reputation as a Problem of Team Production

The legal system and courts are complex, and the role of judges is multifaceted. In theory, one might be able to produce a measure or a set of appropriate measures of performance to evaluate the contribution of an individual judge to each case or decision. However, when we look at the quality of the legal system as a whole, in terms of uniform application and enforcement of the law, conflict resolution, and norm articulation, the marginal contribution of each judge cannot be perfectly determined. In other words, measuring individual judicial performance might be possible in individual cases, but from an aggregate perspective, it is quite difficult due to significant interdependencies in production.

We can see that the output produced by each judge has an individual component reflected in each case decided and a nonseparable component that contributes to the overall quality of the judicial system.[27] This is neatly captured by Ronald Dworkin in his description of judicial production as coauthorship in a chain novel.[28] The nonseparable nature of judicial output is aggravated by the specific human capital required to perform judicial work.[29] The characteristics of the job require specific knowledge and training in order to achieve a sophisticated understanding of the law. Therefore any assessment concerning individual output requires identifying an identical or similar stock of specific human capital. The most important beneficiaries of a high-quality legal system, the general public, lack the knowledge and sophistication to make such an assessment at the individual level. Generally speaking, the public is more likely to have an overall perception of the judicial system than a precise assessment of each member of the judiciary.

Given the nonseparable nature of the output coupled with the need for specific human capital, the judiciary operates as a team, and therefore every member of the judiciary benefits from a collective reputation. Individual reputation matters to the extent that different constituencies look at the individual component of the output. Nevertheless, since each judge operates within a judicial system with a given quality, collective reputation necessarily matters as well. The balance between these two depends on institutional attributes and incentives. Significantly, as in any team, coordination issues and collective action problems arise. The ways in which these problems are addressed by a given legal system generate its specific configuration and the balance between individual and collective reputation.

The standard economic theory of teams considers two solutions to problems of team production, known as ex ante and ex post sharing rules (both in reference to output production by the team). Ex ante sharing means that each member of the team is assigned a certain component of the output before engaging in the effort. Ex post sharing means that the shares are assigned after the results of the effort are revealed. One can think of a system of salary bonuses, as is frequently found on Wall Street, as an ex post sharing rule. As we explain below, ex ante sharing rules correspond to our collective reputation model and ex post sharing rules correspond to our individual reputation model.

Ex Ante Sharing Rules: Collective Reputation Only

One solution to the problems of team production is to rely on ex ante sharing rules, which in our context would mean that each judge of the same rank would earn an equal share of reputation. This implies a judiciary that is reliant solely on collective reputation. Given the nonseparable nature of output and the need for specific human capital, collective reputation is necessarily part of the payoff function. However, an overemphasis on collective reputation naturally raises concerns with shirking, in which individual agents exert low levels of effort; this is the most common problem with ex ante sharing rules. Knowing that everyone will get an equal share regardless of effort, judges may be driven to reduce their own effort in reputation building by free riding on their peers. The argument cuts two ways: First, lazy judges will benefit from collective reputation and may therefore appropriate surplus reputation for which they did not contribute. Second, the costs of reduced reputation are disseminated across the judiciary.

Another important aspect of ex ante sharing is that it also generates a collective action problem of monitoring free riders. In the absence of specialized actors (or an intermediate hierarchy such as a judicial council), individual judges have no incentive to unilaterally invest time and resources in detecting lazy judges. Hence not only does shirking take place, but detection and punishment of shirking are very infrequent.

A legal system that relies exclusively on collective judicial reputation will produce "low-powered" incentives for individual judges. The idea of low-powered incentives in the literature on transaction cost economics refers to systems of compensation in which individuals do not share in the gains from particular transactions, while high-powered incentives allow individuals to benefit from their marginal contribution.[30] In judiciaries without information about individual judicial performance, judges can free ride and shirk. Pure ex ante sharing rules alone are thus an insufficient solution to the problem.

Ex Post Sharing Rules: Individual Reputation Only

Implementing an institutional design that relies on ex post sharing rules would involve, in this context, a judiciary totally reliant on individual reputation. An ex post allocation of rewards will likely induce opportunistic rent seeking, as judges will invest time and effort to grab a larger share of resources available to the judiciary and enhance their individual reputations. This waste of time and effort is particularly damaging, given the partially nonseparable nature of judicial output. That is, relying only on ex post rewards will induce judges to expend more effort on the separable component of output and less effort on the nonseparable components. It seems clear that a judicial system solely based on individual reputation could reduce shirking but would become dysfunctional in other ways.

This framework may suggest why no judiciary of which we are aware seeks to pay judges exclusively at a rate equivalent to their marginal output. Salaries tend to be identical at each level of the judicial hierarchy in all legal systems, regardless of a judge's productivity or quality. This is not simply a matter of administrative convenience but an implicit recognition that differentiated salaries may discourage investment in those activities that tend to contribute to collective reputation.[31]

To provide a concrete illustration, suppose managers of the judicial system attempted to improve efficiency by paying judges on the basis of the number of cases they decide. This could lead judges to seek out the easiest cases or to spend less time deciding any individual case. While many individual judges would improve their reputations for efficiency, the difficult cases would not be handled well, and overall quality could decline. This in turn would affect the reputation of the judiciary as a whole.

A legal system that only relies on individual reputation promotes information about individual judges but treats collective reputation as a mere aggregation of individual reputations. This is a legal system that operates with high-powered incentives.[32] However, due to the nature of team production, high-powered incentives might be inefficient and reduce appropriate investment in the nonseparable component of judicial production. Consider seriatim opinions, used in the British House of Lords before the creation of the UK Supreme Court and also used on the US Supreme Court before Chief Justice John Marshall. Each judge would speak in sequence, and observers would have to pay close attention to figure out the outcome of the case. The collective jurisprudence suffered, even if each judge was able to cultivate her individual reputation freely. (British judges report greater collective effort after the recent establishment of the UK Supreme Court.[33])

The Need for Accountability

Either pure mechanism using only ex ante or ex post sharing rules creates serious problems. Therefore, a superior approach is to utilize a combination of both ex ante and ex post sharing rules, so as to induce production of both collective and individual reputation. However, the coexistence of both modes might not be enough to curtail the problems of shirking and rent seeking that we have identified, given the nonseparable nature of output and the specific human capital inherent to the judiciary. Furthermore, external constraints (such as future job opportunities or political interference) might shape incentives one way or the other.

Some palliatives might be necessary to mitigate these problems. In many situations, ex ante and ex post sharing rules could conflict in serious ways. Suppose an elected judge is faced with a case in which the rule of law requires something very unpopular with the judge's political allies—say failing to implement the death penalty in a conservative American state. The judge might be able to maximize his own reputation (and thus his likelihood of remaining on the bench) by upholding a death sentence, but if this conflicts with the relevant rules of law, the reputation of the judiciary as a whole might be harmed.

One controversial issue is the proper relationship between the judiciary and other branches of government. In recent years, there has been an increase in what is known as the judicialization of public policies, in which courts are responsible for more and more decisions that traditionally were associated with other branches of government. Judicialization may serve to enhance both collective reputation and individual reputation, but it may unleash countervailing forces that harm the collective reputation of the judiciary through politicization. A serious political problem may occur when one branch of government (the judiciary or the executive) seeks to raise its relative status in the public eye by lowering the relative status of the other branches, generating institutional conflicts.

At the same time, the linkage between reputational incentives and accountability may depend on the interaction with other institutional features. For example, when the control mechanisms exercised by senior judges weaken, junior judges may shift their investment in collective reputation to individual reputation, and this can serve as a powerful mechanism to enhance accountability. In other cases, where the judiciary is subject to external influence from multiple sources, conflicting goals could in fact impede the development of an effective mediating hierarchy. Much of our analysis concerns these kinds of institutional variations and their effect on reputation.

Comparative Institutional Analysis

In every legal system, both individual and collective judicial reputation is important. However, the relative degree of importance varies not only across legal families but even within the same legal family. If we look at the US federal judiciary, for example, individual reputation seems to matter a great deal. The Supreme Court is identified by the name of the chief justice (such as Warren, Rehnquist, or Roberts), and the great judges of the past are heroes. Newspapers frequently discuss how individual justices vote in particular cases and quote from dissents. Federal judges give talks to the public and write books advancing their views on important issues, and the appointment mechanism includes Senate confirmation hearings in which individual candidates to the federal courts have to expose their views. Academics study the judicial contribution of individual justices in detail,[34] and they are the subjects of popular biographies.[35] This pattern of serious assessment of individual performance is not found in the United Kingdom. Most judges of the UK Supreme Court are not well known and tend only to appear in the public discussion when they engage in extrajudicial tasks such as leading commissions of inquiry.

In this sense, the United Kingdom judiciary is more akin to those of France, Japan, and Germany, where most people do not even know the identity of the chief justice, much less the other justices of the Supreme Court.[36] Newspapers in these countries very rarely report on dissenting views; justices usually avoid exposure to and contact with public opinion in general, and very few judges become known by the public in general.[37] If justice is blind, then judges are anonymous. In these legal systems, information about individual performance seems to be intentionally underplayed, if not systematically hidden from the general public.[38]

In short, in some legal systems, collective reputation prevails over individual reputation, whereas in other legal systems, the reverse occurs: some legal systems pursue individual performance, whereas others prefer to limit information about individual performance and rely more on collective assessment.[39] This section discusses some of the different institutional structures that condition the development of judicial reputation. We do not provide a theory of why these institutional structures exist but rather focus on the contribution of institutional structure to disclosure of information and reputation building. For example, we do not discuss the rationale for the existence of an appeal system but rather examine how the different designs of an appeal system generate information on individual or collective performance, contributing to the different forms of reputation.

Career versus Recognition Judiciary

One way of contrasting different types of judicial structures is to distinguish the "career" from "recognition" judiciaries.[40] The career system involves judges entering a judicial bureaucracy at a young age and spending an entire career as a judge.[41] The recognition system appoints judges later in life, usually after candidates have established themselves as highly qualified. It involves fewer opportunities for promotion. The appointment is based on the individual reputation of the candidate, as assessed by the relevant constituency, by some mechanism external to the judiciary. For example, in the United States, the president appoints federal judges, with the advice and consent of the Senate, after the candidates have developed a stellar reputation in other spheres. In some American states and in the Supreme Court of Bolivia, judges run in judicial elections in which each candidate has to present a distinctive platform.[42] The external appointment process involving ex ante screening helps compensate for the absence of a vertical hierarchy in the judiciary, which decreases the incentives to comply with rigid professional norms. The appointment system by external principals dilutes the collective identity of the judiciary but enhances the individual reputation of the judge who has been screened. Thus, in recognition judiciaries, individual reputation as perceived by external audiences is the dominant factor in judicial appointments.

In contrast, a career judiciary is selected and promoted based on internal judicial assessments of individual merit. Relatively little information is available to the public about judges; the judiciary itself develops and uses internal performance measures to make promotion decisions. Compliance with internal mechanisms makes collective reputation much more important. The credibility of a given judge does not depend on her individual merits but on the reputation of the entire judiciary. Any concerns about judicial appointment or promotion do not tend to be directed at any particular judge but at the entire profession. Consequently, collective reputation building is very important for career judges.[43] Such systems tend to emphasize the anonymity of the law and the myth that there is a single correct answer for legal questions that in principle is invariant to the individual judge making the decision.

Yet external audiences have gained importance in many civil law countries in recent decades. Some of this development is due to exogenous factors that have changed the general public perception of the judiciary and have provided for new kinds of incentives. Greater media accessibility is a global phenomenon that has effects on many institutions. External audiences may also become more important because of factors endogenous to the legal system, such as the introduction of new constitutional courts, which are very different in function and nature from the traditional judiciary. The interaction between new constitutional courts and the traditional judiciary and other branches of government has dramatically changed the balance between internal and external audiences in many countries, and we wrestle with this in chapter 5.

Individual Opinions, Dissents, and Votes

When the Supreme Court of Mexico held a public session announcing its 2008 decision upholding Mexico City's statute legalizing abortion, it attracted significant attention both inside the country and abroad. The court's fifteen justices justified their decision in a complicated set of orally delivered opinions, with the final vote to uphold decided by a single vote. When the final written decision was released some months later in February 2009, the eight justices in the majority issued a majority decision along with seven concurrences; there were also three dissents. Two years later, the court returned to the abortion issue to consider two new state statutes criminalizing abortion (passed in a backlash to the earlier ruling). The divided court could not come to a majority opinion and so the challenge to the statutes failed, leaving abortion illegal in some states, but a flurry of separate opinions accompanied the short procedural notice announcing the failure. Commentators have criticized the divided jurisprudence as incoherent.[44]

The availability of information on the particular judges—whether in the form of individual opinions, the possibility of dissent by judges, or the availability of judicial votes in a transparent and verifiable way that is visible to laymen—has two important consequences. First, it helps each judge to establish an individual reputation.[45] As Justice Ginsburg wrote in 1990, putting a name on an opinion "serves to hold the individual judge accountable" by putting the judge's reputation on the line.[46] Some judges relish in this opportunity: Justice William Rehnquist was known as the "Lone Ranger" during the period in which he was the most conservative member of the Burger Court because he wrote so many dissenting opinions.[47] Eventually judges may come to create informal coalitions with like-minded judges, allowing outsiders to assign labels to specific judges as liberal, conservative, originalist, or activist. The second consequence of individual opinions and dissent is that they help undercut the idea of a homogeneous, uniform, bureaucratic judiciary. Both aspects favor individual over collective reputation building.[48] This is enhanced when the judiciary is faced with big public policy decisions that are controversial or at the center of intense debate across a society, such as those involving abortion, gay marriage, segregation, or the welfare state.[49] Dissents in such cases may play the special function of allowing the judiciary to signal to the losers that there is hope for the future.

When individual opinions cannot be recorded and dissent is not allowed, the judiciary is seen as a homogeneous body, faceless and bureaucratic, in which discussion and diversity are replaced with compromise and uniformity.[50] The content of decisions hurts or enhances the reputation of the judiciary as a whole and not that of a particular judge. Peer pressure may be more important, since decisions must be reached by consensus, resulting eventually in complex language to disguise divergences on the bench and further reducing the ability of the public to scrutinize opinions. Perhaps the paradigm of this approach is that of France, in which public judicial opinions are formulaic and sparse.[51]

Beyond individual opinions, oral proceedings also offer opportunities for the cultivation of individual reputation. Oral proceedings allow judges to reveal not only their legal skills but also their individual positions and make specific contributions to the decision taken by the court. They can also communicate to the specialist audience of lawyers, distinguishing themselves from their colleagues. And for both written and oral proceedings, judges' use of language and tone may be important. An authoritative tone signals that the law is determinant. But recent psychological research has shown that a more exploratory tone is likely to be more persuasive to laypeople who disagree with the outcome of a given decision.[52]

Besides tone, complexity is another dimension on which opinions can vary and might affect judicial reputation. Opinions that are too technical will not be intelligible to ordinary citizens, who will instead have to rely on experts or the media to digest them. One might expect that judges too focused on impressing other judges would write in overly complex language and thus hurt their reputation with outsiders. But the so-called plain language movement, which seeks to enhance ease of communication, has some advocates in law.[53] For example, in the 1990s, the Supreme Court of Canada tried to write in less technical terms to be understood by the "educated public."[54]

These aspects of institutional design do not map neatly onto the civil–common law distinction. Many constitutional courts in civil law jurisdictions now allow for separate opinions. The Constitutional Court under the 1997 Constitution of Thailand *required* each justice to issue a separate opinion—a practice that no doubt contributed to a nontransparent and sometimes confused jurisprudence. Similarly, the Supreme Court of Mexico has moved toward oral and public proceedings in recent years.

Our theory of dissent complements at least one account of the practice. In tracing the history of opinion practices in common law jurisdictions, Professor Todd Henderson argues that opinion practices reflect the desire of courts to expand their role in a competitive milieu of norm articulation.[55] He further argues that those encouraging dissent have sometimes wanted to use the presence of multiple opinions as a way of constraining the courts, while others have sought to use the practice of dissent to advance judicial power.

In our view, changes in the overall reputation of the judiciary are the driving force for changes in common law opinion practice, rather than political views about the relative power of the judiciary per se. Thus particular problems with individual or collective reputation will trigger pressures to move in one direction or the other. For example, Chief Justice Marshall shifted toward unanimous opinions at a time when the status of the judiciary was low, in part because seriatim opinions (in which each judge announces his own opinion) were difficult to understand.[56] Centralizing opinion practice enhanced collective reputation, and deviation was explicitly discouraged.[57] Canon 19 of the American

Bar Association's 1924 Canons of Judicial Ethics called on judges not to "yield to pride of opinion or value more highly his individual reputation than that of the court to which he should be loyal. Except in cases of conscientious difference of opinion on fundamental principle, dissenting opinions should be discouraged in courts of last resort."[58]

Beginning around 1941, Chief Justice Harlan Fiske Stone presided over a rapid increase in individual opinions—a practice that continues to this day.[59] The percentage of decisions with one or more separate opinions jumped from around 20 percent to more than 50 percent within a period of just three years.[60] Professor Henderson ties this latter shift to the need to maintain power for the court in an era of legal realism, when formalist claims to "truth" would not be convincing to relevant audiences.[61] Professor Cass Sunstein attributes the shift in part to the leadership of Chief Justice Stone, who wrote unambiguously that "I do not think it is the appropriate function of a Chief Justice to attempt to dissuade members of the Court from dissenting in individual cases."[62]

We can characterize Stone's encouragement of individual opinions as facilitating investment in individual reputation at a time when the court contained a diverse set of personalities and had just avoided collective disaster from Roosevelt's court-packing plan. That plan involved a threat to appoint additional justices to the court in the face of judicial resistance to the New Deal; the plan was never implemented because of the famous "switch in time that saved nine" by Justice Owen Roberts.[63] Those justices who fought Roosevelt had put the collective reputation of the entire judiciary at risk; one can imagine that afterward there would have been internal pressures from the judges not associated with the risky strategy to allow segmenting of reputations to individual authors. This was desirable for both the new minority, which could continue to fight and risk only their individual reputations, and the new majority supportive of Roosevelt, which could avoid negative reputational consequences of the minority position.[64]

In short, we see the practice of dissent as reflecting alternative institutional designs to enhance reputation. Individual opinions are associated with a relatively flat organizational structure, in which superior judges have little control over inferiors. Collective opinions are associated with the suppression of individual reputation and the institution of hierarchical controls to overcome collective action problems in the production of collective reputation.[65] Small wonder, then, that judges who support the institution of dissent have criticized the alternative model as suppressing individual conscience. Justice William Brennan, for example, critiqued Chief Justice Marshall (who strongly pushed for unanimous judicial opinions of the court as a whole) as trying to "shut down the marketplace of ideas."[66]

Of course, even within systems that encourage individual opinions, they may not actually be required. Under Chief Justice John Roberts, the US Supreme Court has issued an increasing number of per curiam opinions that do not identify the individual author. Indeed, by one account, almost 9 percent of opinions were issued in this way during the first six years of Roberts's tenure, a substantial increase from earlier periods.[67] This may reflect Roberts's oft-stated desire to enhance consensus on the court, though some such opinions actually include dissents. Roberts himself is rarely in dissent and has argued that it is important to advance "the notion that we are a Court—not simply an assemblage of individual justices."[68]

Like other chief justices, Roberts has also been known to use the power of assigning a majority opinion to himself in important cases, and the assignment power can be an important tool in constructing both individual reputation and the collective reputation of the court.[69] Justice John Paul Stevens thought that Chief Justice Warren Burger would assign First Amendment cases to Justice Byron White when the opinion was likely to be criticized in the press but keep the case for himself when the opinion was likely to be praised. "That practice," he notes, "contributed to Byron's reputation in the press as an enemy of the First Amendment."[70]

Beyond the possibility of individual opinions, the legal impact of decisions is also relevant. Dicta—language not directly related to the holding—can allow the court to signal to particular external audiences and so may be helpful in some circumstances, and there is some evidence that judges use references to classic texts and famous individuals in a strategic way.[71]

In the United States, precedent from a higher court generally controls lower courts, and this provides an incentive for higher court judges to issue clear, well-reasoned decisions that induce lower courts to comply. Across lower courts, however, precedents do not have the same power. For example, in the United States, federal district court opinions do not count as precedent within the same district. An individual federal district court judge need not follow the legal holding of a prior decision in the same district. This device seems to encourage experimentation in lower courts and to reward investment in individual reputation at the expense of collective reputation at the lower court level. At the same time, the requirement of following superior court precedents means that the costs to the collective reputation of the judiciary as a whole can be contained. The US system thus favors individual reputation, with some offsetting devices to ensure some collective consistency. But there are continuing concerns that the emphasis on the individual judge has costs for the system as a whole, particularly at the Supreme Court level, where opinions are increasingly complex and long and involve multiple different views on many issues.

Publicity

Publicity is another important element of the institutional structure that can facilitate—or retard—the development of reputation. The Supreme Court of Mexico made a decision to open up its proceedings to the public, and as Professor Jeffrey Staton has shown, this decision served as part of a strategy to cultivate reputation in a new, democratic era.[72] Indeed, the court launched its own television station in 2006. The court also has a somewhat unusual practice of announcing its decision orally at a public hearing but not releasing the written decision for many months thereafter. In the abortion case mentioned earlier, the written decision was not issued for six months. This has led to significant problems as justices try to reconstruct their reasoning, and it has hindered the development of a coherent jurisprudence.[73]

Publicity is helpful for the cultivation of reputation and can be used strategically by courts. But if the courts do not communicate clearly in an increasingly dense media environment, they will find that publicity may actually harm the reputation of the court as a whole. Furthermore, appearances on television may encourage individual justices to seek to distinguish themselves, leading to a more incoherent jurisprudence and harming collective reputation.

Access to the public comes in many forms. The Supreme Court of Mexico has a long tradition of informal meetings with litigants and other interested parties *in camera*, even concerning pending cases. These sessions allow the judges to hear privately about aspects of the cases considered to be important but also communicate the image of a court that values private access. While other courts might view this practice as highly problematic and compromising the appearance of propriety, in this particular case, it seems to be viewed as a necessary way of transmitting information to the litigants and thus as helpful for establishing the legitimacy of the court.

More conventionally, courts may give public tours of the courtroom, allow some cases to be broadcast,[74] and can craft their media image through press releases. Judicial websites and Twitter accounts are increasingly common and used for various purposes. Courts also produce a wide variety of publications, about either themselves or the law.[75] All these media allow courts to try to shape their reputation.

Sentencing and Procedural Discretion

Discretion in criminal sentencing and in procedural rulings favors individual reputation over collective reputation by providing yet another way for judges to distinguish themselves from each other.[76] Reduced discretion in sentencing and in procedure favors homogeneity across the bench. There are two relevant consequences of this observation: First, differences in sentencing or in procedure could be exacerbated by judges who are purely interested in building individual reputation. In other words, the variance in sentencing or in applying procedural rules could increase significantly if judges focus on individual rather than collective reputation. Second, strict sentencing rules could have very different consequences in a system in which collective reputation prevails, where such rules would enhance uniformity and hence reinforce collective reputation, as opposed to a system where individual reputation is important. In the latter, strict sentencing guidelines might have perverse consequences. If the degree of judicial discretion is higher with regard to procedure than in sentencing, judges might be tempted to use procedure to undermine sentencing rules as a way of maintaining individual reputation.

This account sheds some light on judicial resistance to sentencing guidelines in the United States. In the 1980s, following a wave of sentencing guideline projects at the state level, the US Sentencing Commission issued federal guidelines to reduce sentencing variance. The guidelines sought to limit sentencing determination to two main factors, the severity of the crime and the criminal history of the defendant, and provide a set range within which sentences should fall. This limited the discretion of individual judges significantly. When the US Supreme Court struck down the guidelines as a violation of the Sixth Amendment in *United States v. Booker*,[77] it restored at least some power of the judges, even though the decision focused on the jury fact-finding requirement. We thus see some pressures on occasion toward collective external reputation, even in the most individuated judicial system. But judges embedded in a set of structures that encourage investment in individual reputation may resist such attempts.

In some sense, this discussion raises broader themes in legal scholarship about the distinction between rules and standards.[78] Rules, it is often argued, are useful for constraining the discretion of individual judges but are expensive to produce at a sufficient level of detail. In addition, rules can be over- and underinclusive, subsuming within their ambit behavior not intended to be covered by the norm. Standards, on the other hand, empower the individual judicial decision maker at the expense of uniformity. Ceteris paribus, we should expect that the institutional structure of the judiciary will tend to favor rules when collective reputation is valuable and standards when individual reputation is valuable.

Appeals

The appeal system and the nature of the relationship between superior and inferior courts play an important role in shaping incentives to invest in individual versus collective reputation building. A generous appeal system that essentially allows superior courts to review and evaluate the decisions made by inferior courts induces compliance by junior judges and favors homogeneity and uniformity in decision making.[79] An appeal system that imposes few constraints on junior judges gives them more discretion and naturally generates more heterogeneity in decision making, which favors individual reputation. At the same time, an appeal system that permits conflicts of jurisdiction and law across courts—such as the American system, which allows for the possibility of circuit splits—disfavors collective reputation and pushes toward investment in individual reputation. An appeal system that effectively internalizes potential conflicts and therefore reduces discrepancies in courts' decisions contributes decisively to collective reputation.

A crucial dimension on which appeals systems differ is the question of de novo review. In common law jurisdictions, appeals courts generally only hear questions of law, leaving the factual record to be developed at the trial level. This is often explained as originating in the institution of the jury, which finds facts and would have to be reconvened or reproduced to have de novo review. In contrast, civil law jurisdictions have de novo review of facts at the higher levels. This involves replication but also allows fuller monitoring of junior instances to ensure quality. Our interpretation is that de novo review is a device to ensure collective reputation, while the lack of such review encourages individual judges to develop novel interpretations of law and to use their fact-finding power for reputational development.

Citations

The use of citations in decisions reflects the importance of individual opinions and hence generally contributes to enhancing individual reputation.[80] Citations presuppose that some cases and court decisions are path breaking, not just because the object of the action is extremely relevant, but because the doctrine and legal interpretation offered by a given judge is worthy of consideration. Controversial decisions attract attention and generate debate even when they do not reflect what experts would deem good law. Obviously, this may allow individual judges to become associated with a famous case or notorious decision. The widespread use of citations in Anglo-American jurisprudence clearly favors individual reputation building, particularly when combined with the institution of individually signed opinions. But many systems do not cite extensively to other cases. These systems treat the law as a collective, uniformly determined product.

Case Selection

The degree to which the judiciary controls the dockets of courts plays an important role in the process of establishing reputation.[81] The control of dockets can operate at what we might call the retail level, in choosing particular cases, and at the wholesale level, through standing and justiciability doctrines that narrow or expand the scope of judicial review. When judges cannot, in most cases, effectively control the cases they hear, collective reputation operates as a type of insurance, since some judges will randomly be assigned cases that are more suited for enhancing individual reputation than others through a mechanism that does not take into account different skill levels across the bench.[82] In other words, collective reputation reduces the potential reputational damage a judge could incur by being assigned cases that are not suited to her particular preferences or skills. The doctrine of a right to a "lawful judge," originating in the German legal tradition, essentially requires random assignment of cases and so achieves this function.

When dockets are effectively controlled by the judiciary itself or a senior judge, case assignment is no longer truly random. Individual reputation becomes an asset in such a system in two complementary ways: First, reputation allows individual judges to become favored (or disfavored) relative to other colleagues in the distribution of cases to be reviewed by the courts. Second, reputation allows further enhancement of individual reputation by allowing judges to pick cases that are more appropriate for the relevant constituencies. Case selection is a strategic variable in preparing the setting for reputation building.

We note that some courts, especially in South Asia, have occasionally taken cases without even having a formal claim filed before them. The Supreme Court of Pakistan, for example, is allowed to take action under its own initiative to protect fundamental rights under Article 184(3) of the country's constitution. In recent years, it has used the so-called *suo moto* power to demand that the government deal with the high murder rate in Karachi, deaths in Lahore caused by substandard medicine, and many other issues. These cases allow the court to interact directly with the public and be seen as a responsive actor in a country that is sorely lacking them.

One interesting example of docket control in the civil law tradition is the institution of the so-called investigating judge. These are career judges who, in some countries, are not involved in deciding or deliberating on cases but instead supervise the investigation and gathering of evidence. In some countries, individual investigating judges have become very prominent. The Spanish judge Baltasar Garzón, for example, became a kind of international superstar for his indictment of Chilean general Augusto Pinochet in 1999, leading to a very important decision by the British House of Lords on the international immunity of ex-presidents. Garzón had done a stint in electoral politics and was an example of what Professor David Kosar has called a "superjudge"— someone who has moved from the judiciary to politics and then back.[83] After the Pinochet indictment, Garzón opened cases against the Argentine junta, sought to interview Henry Kissinger in relation to a case, and considered whether to open up a case against George W. Bush and several members of his administration. Garzón's cultivation of his individual reputation ultimately led to his suspension from the judiciary in 2012, after he opened an inquiry into crimes against humanity during the Spanish Civil War that had been explicitly subject to an amnesty in 1977. He was ultimately put on trial for violating Spanish law by using an illegal wiretap in an overly vigorous corruption investigation and suspended for eleven years.

Branding

A legal system that allows judges to attach their names to opinions, doctrines, extrajudicial inquiries, and law reform projects obviously places great value on individual reputation. For example, as we will discuss in chapter 3, in the United Kingdom, judges are frequently called upon to lead inquiries into government behavior.[84] A legal system in which law reforms are conducted by bureaucrats and law professors, quasijudicial inquiries are led by government officials, and doctrines are developed by law professors does not provide significant incentives for judges to invest in their individual reputation.

Branding also extends to private sector opportunities after retirement, including corporate advisory positions, participation in politics, opportunities in higher education, and presentations at prestigious conferences. Clearly individual reputation is more important than collective reputation for private sector opportunities after retirement, although a collective reputation for honesty and transparency could be beneficial from this point of view.

Another important component of branding is a legacy, broadly defined. For example, judges may be concerned with how they will be cited and discussed in casebooks and how their decisions will be vindicated by future generations of judges. Concern for legacy motivates judges to invest more in their individual reputation and less in the collective reputation of the entire judiciary.

Of course, collective bodies can engage in branding as well. As described further in chapter 6, the South Korean Constitutional Court has invested a good deal of energy in promoting itself both abroad and within South Korean society. It has produced comic books to explain its role to children; translated selected opinions into English and made them available on the web; and successfully encouraged its government to join the Venice Commission, a European organization devoted to constitutional law.[85] The South Korean court is developing a global "brand" as a leading exponent of constitutionalism, showing that collective reputation can also be promoted.

Size

The size of the judiciary is important in structuring incentives to invest in reputation. A larger judiciary raises the cost for each judge to engage in individual reputation building, because there is more competition, and decreases the cost for each judge to engage in collective reputation building, since the investment required of any individual judge will be smaller. In a supreme court with nine justices, the actions of a single individual are easily monitored and assessed by the media and the public. In a supreme court of seventy-five justices, as is not uncommon in the world of civil law, only experts can assess the actions of individual judges and effective monitoring is limited to other judges or the members of the high judicial council. Even this monitoring may be difficult: the absolute cost of monitoring other judges on the same court increases with size. A small judiciary generates investment in individual reputation and recognition; larger numbers induce uniformity and investment in collective reputation, as well as opportunities for horizontal "internal" monitoring by other judges.

Larger judiciaries also affect incentives in another way: they provide opportunities for advancement and promotion. If there are relatively few opportunities for promotion, judges will be less sensitive to pressures from higher levels of the hierarchy. They may therefore be less willing to sacrifice elements of individual reputation for the collective reputation. In contrast, in a large bureaucratic judiciary, there are significant opportunities for advancement, and judges will be sensitive to the concerns of their superiors.[86] This design tends to suppress individual variance and lead to greater investments in collective reputation.

Discipline

The collective reputation of judges everywhere suffers when any one of them engages in inappropriate behavior. To protect the collective reputation against harms caused by judicial malfeasance, all judicial systems contain mechanisms for judicial discipline. These are obviously implicated when a judge breaks the law or acts corruptly but can also involve interventions into less significant wrongs. For example, in 2012, Peter Hiett, a British magistrate, lost his job after a disciplinary panel found that "his behavior and appearance while shopping fell below the standards expected."[87]

There is a wide range of different systems of judicial discipline, some of which are implemented by the judicial councils discussed in chapter 4.[88] From our perspective, one can evaluate judicial systems depending on how much they constrain individual judges. Key variables are the set of actions that constitute the basis for potential discipline, the processes used, and the potential sanctions. If judges can be subjected to discipline for minor actions or on the basis of broad standards, they will be more considerate of the views of their superiors in the judiciary. For example, the French system defines a disciplinary fault as any breach "committed by a judge in the discharge of his function, against honor, scrupulousness, or dignity."[89] This relatively vague standard has demanded interpretation over the years and has included breaches of professional norms, political activity, and notorious private behavior.

Judges have been removed for activities like passing bad checks, entering into personal relationships with parties before the court, and even making outrageous statements criticizing the judiciary.[90] This regulation of many aspects of a judge's life obviously favors a certain esprit de corps among judges by reinforcing ethical norms.

If the process is relatively quick and informal, judges will have less protection for idiosyncratic views. But many systems have moved toward full hearings, in secret, to protect both the individual rights of judges and also the collective reputation of the judiciary. This is a point on which the disciplinary process differs from ordinary criminal trials. While a norm of public trials is seen as an essential element of the rule of law, the internal process of disciplining judges is often carried out behind closed doors, preventing the proverbial dirty laundry from being aired. In the United States, however, federal judges may be subjected to full impeachment hearings in the legislature, so the judiciary does not have complete control over the removal process and there is no secrecy. Impeachment is difficult; indeed, in some instances, disgraced federal judges have continued to receive their salaries while in prison for crimes, without being impeached.[91]

Sanctions typically range from a reprimand to a loss of seniority, an involuntary transfer, and even removal and dismissal. But if the penalties are relatively light, the managers of the collective reputation may be unable to deter bad behavior. Furthermore, considerations of judicial independence may come into play. In many systems, judges have immunity for their decisions, meaning that they cannot be subjected to civil or criminal liability for actions taken in the course of their courtroom duties.

To illustrate some of the tensions in disciplinary systems, consider the recent case of a German judge named Thomas Schulte-Kellinghaus, who was subjected to discipline for failing to decide enough cases.[92] The context was a retrenchment of the German judiciary in the face of the financial crisis that forced significant budget cuts. The judge brought a legal case, defending himself under the principle that discipline interfered with judicial independence. (He also asserted that the fact that he had published a number of articles critical of the court administration was part of the motive for the disciplinary action.) The court administration responded that they needed to manage a large caseload and allowing judges to slack would ultimately hurt the judiciary as a whole. This case illustrates the core tension at play in team production. The judiciary as a whole would suffer if case delays were too significant; but since all cases are not alike, we would not generally expect each judge to decide cases equally quickly. Mass justice might not be of the same quality as in-dividuated justice, but given budget constraints, trade-offs are inevitable.

Budget and Allocation of Resources

In most countries, judges are also managers of the judicial system, re-quiring them to negotiate with the government for resources. While courts may generate their own resources from fees, these do not typi-cally account for a significant portion of the revenues for the judicial system. The dependence on the government for resources creates a need for bargaining with the government, as well as bargaining within the court system for shares of overall resources.

If resources were allocated to judges as individuals, then individual reputation would become a major asset in bargaining over resources within the judicial system. However, if resources are allocated in a man-ner that is administratively independent of the individual judge, collec-tive reputation becomes crucial, since only through collective reputation can the judiciary obtain more resources from the government. As men-tioned previously, the practice of identical pay for judges of a similar rank can be viewed as a device to encourage investment in collective over individual reputation. Another possible implication is that judges in systems that rely heavily on individual reputation may be unable to overcome the collective action problems necessary to obtain sufficient budgetary resources from politicians. The oft-noted failure of the US government to raise judicial salaries in real terms provides support for this conjecture.[93]

The Interdependence of Institutional Choices

Each of the institutions discussed so far in this chapter is conceptually distinct from the others. Crucially, however, they are reinforcing in terms of reputation and provision of information about performance. The common law tendency toward a "recognition" judiciary relies on judges who are selected because their earlier investments in reputation allow ex ante screening for quality and effort. Such judges can be trusted to write high-quality individual opinions. In contrast, the "career" sys-tem associated with the civil law hires judges at a young age and there-fore cannot ensure they will adequately invest in individual reputation without extensive monitoring. Hence there is an implicit logic to anon-ymous, collective opinions; it is not a culture of citation. Branding is frowned upon.

The career system also requires many more judges, because monitoring output at the lowest level requires an intermediate supervisory level (itself an autonomous body or a different layer of a more hierarchical judicial system). Appeal is essential to maintain quality and discourage shirking. Appeals are de novo, in order to ensure that individual judges do not harm the collective reputation of the judiciary. We thus observe much larger judiciaries to accomplish de novo review. This reinforces the notion of team rather than individual production and reduces the amount of effort required by any single judge to produce reputation.

We also see differences in the discretion over dockets in the two systems. The judges in recognition systems have a variety of devices to exercise docket control, particularly at the senior levels. This allows the judiciary to control its policy-making role. In contrast, career judges are viewed as relatively low-level functionaries without individual discretion.

It is interesting to think about the ideology of the common law and civil law as reinforcing these institutional features. It is generally understood that the civil law tradition conceives of "the law" as a unified coherent whole, with preexisting answers to legal questions that are identifiable through the exercise of legal science.[94] This idea deemphasizes the role of the individual judge in crafting the law, and in principle, different judges are not thought to be able to arrive at different answers to legal questions. In contrast, common law judiciaries tend to see law as more akin to policy. Policy matters are those on which, in principle, reasonable minds can disagree. This is not to suggest that law is infinitely plastic, but rather that for hard legal questions (of the type most likely to be litigated), different judges may come up with different answers. Seeing law as policy means that we need to identify the particular reasoning and to associate it with an individual judge. These different conceptions of the law obviously track the distinction between collective and individual reputation.

An Initial Illustration: The United States and Japan

By way of illustration, contrast the US federal judiciary with that of Japan. We consider these two countries as representative of ideal-typical poles in the organization of judiciaries and hence use them to illustrate the argument.[95] The United States is a classic example of a "recognition" judiciary, in which judges are appointed to the bench at a relatively late age in large part because of individual accomplishments in other spheres. They are known as superior individuals who have already

developed a certain amount of reputation; indeed, the collective reputation of the judiciary may in part derive from achievements in other
spheres. An extreme case was former president Taft, who subsequently
became chief justice. Individual judges in the United States sit alone at
the trial level and do not move courts unless they are lucky enough to
be appointed to a higher level. At the appellate level, judges frequently
write their own dissenting and concurring opinions. A vigorous citation
practice encourages this individuation of opinions.

Individual judges have a good deal of discretion. At the trial level,
notwithstanding efforts to develop sentencing guidelines, judges retain
a good deal of control over procedure. The appellate system is limited to
questions of law, meaning that the system tolerates a good deal of diversity both across first-instance courts and across regions of the country.
Lawyers, of course, know this and so sometimes seek to forum shop to
obtain a favorable venue; less formally, most lawyers will have strong
views about the character of individual justices at the appellate level.

The limited appellate system means that a relatively small judiciary
is tolerable. The United States has one of the lowest ratios of judges
to lawyers in the world.[96] This in turn enhances the prestige of those
lawyers who actually do make it onto the bench. Judges are generalist
wise men and women, and many of them develop a reputation as judicial statesmen or public intellectuals. Supreme Court cases are routinely
front-page news and scrutinized by the chattering classes for their public
policy implications. Many judges become heroes, and their names live
on in history. This is a system that greatly values individual reputation.

The United States has some other features that heighten pressures to
invest in individual and external reputation. Many states continue to
elect judges, sometimes on a partisan basis. Without entering the normative debate on the practice, we note that it should enhance investment in individual reputation, as judges seek to signal their views both
in the campaign process and while serving as incumbents. Judges try to
distinguish themselves and emphasize their relatively unique suitability
for their positions vis-à-vis competitors.

Contrast all this with the Japanese judiciary. Japanese judges enter
the judiciary at a young age and spend their careers in a hierarchical
structure. They spend their career in a series of two- and three-year rota-
tions, moving around the country and so unable to be identified with
any particular court location.[97] Opinions are unsigned at all levels, save
the Supreme Court, and dissenting opinions have traditionally been
rare. Japanese Supreme Court decisions are rarely front-page news, and
even many lawyers cannot name the justices of the court. Decisions

at the lower level are unsigned, and so the judge is essentially faceless, reflecting the civil law ideology that the decision reflects the law rather than views of any particular judge. The judiciary as a whole has a reputation for quality and predictability, but individual judges have no reputation at all outside the courts.[98]

The ideology of judging is such that judges are seen as having no independent influence on case outcomes and there is a theoretical correct answer for every case. Indeed, in any given case, the judge may be replaced because of the rotation system, with no concern for problems that may result.[99] There are also internal systems for uniformity, including tables of formulae for damage awards, so that like cases will be treated similarly, regardless of the judge hearing the case. The rotation system also provides for suppression of discretion: judges who are outliers can and will suffer in terms of being assigned to undesirable locations.[100] This can be seen as a device for ensuring that individuals contribute to collective reputation and that an overall reputation for uniformity is maintained.

A major scholarly debate concerns whether or not the Japanese judiciary is independent.[101] Professor Mark Ramseyer and collaborators have emphasized the ability of the Supreme Court Secretariat to discipline judges at lower levels. Because the Secretariat is appointed by the Supreme Court itself, the Supreme Court is appointed by the Diet, and the Diet has been controlled by a single political party for most of the last six decades, Professor Ramseyer argues that judges are ultimately subject to external control.[102] He provides evidence that judges who ruled against the interests of the ruling Liberal Democratic Party suffered career sanctions. This account emphasizes the ruling party as an important external audience for the courts, affecting incentives at the individual level.

Professor John Haley, by contrast, emphasizes the internal audience and the collective quality of the judiciary.[103] Japanese judges work in a hierarchy that is similar to that of other large Japanese organizations, in which managers typically join at a young age and remain in the same institution for their entire career. For all large organizations, internal controls help socialize staff. The emphasis is on mechanisms of collective reputation, in which Japanese judges are evaluated by society only on a collective basis. Haley points to the relative rarity of sanctions, the complete absence of reported instances of judicial corruption, and the strong corporate identity of the judiciary to argue that the Japanese judiciary is indeed quite independent.

Our concern is not with independence per se. Much of the debate between Haley and Ramseyer turns on one's conception of judicial independence and whether it inheres in the individual judge or the judiciary as a whole. From our perspective, the key question is what audience the judiciary is addressing in its decision making. Even if Ramseyer is correct (and we find his evidence convincing), it does not explain judicial decision making in the vast majority of cases with low political salience. For these cases, internal audiences are indeed the most important. Certainly, when compared with a judiciary such as that of the United States, Japan's institutional structures lean heavily toward collective reputation.

This situation has begun to change slightly. In the late 1990s, after several years of economic malaise, Japan's elites initiated a major program of legal reform, culminating in the creation of a Justice System Reform Council in 1999. The council issued its report two years later and was quite critical of the judiciary for maintaining a detached stance toward society and being insufficiently transparent.[104] It called for increasing the number of appointments from the ranks of practicing lawyers. Though the number of such appointees remains low so far, this has the potential to introduce new incentives for judges to focus on the legal profession as a relevant audience. Another recommendation focused on allowing citizens some role in the reappointment of judges. This is required for Supreme Court justices every ten years under Japan's constitution, though in practice was never utilized because judges are traditionally appointed to the Supreme Court relatively close to the retirement age.[105] In 2003, an eleven-member Advisory Committee for the Nomination of Judges was established, with five "insider" members (judges, prosecutors, or lawyers) and the remaining six from academia and the general public. The committee has already rejected some proposed candidates for judgeships on the basis of its own investigations.[106] This shifts the screening process away from judges themselves, and so we expect to see more investment in individual reputation from candidates before their selection to the judiciary.

We are indeed starting to observe a gradual shift toward more individual opinions in the judiciary. Changho Kim, a Japanese lawyer, notes that the percentage of Supreme Court cases in which individual opinions are filed has increased dramatically in the late 2000s after more than three decades of stability.[107] This seems to be driven by former lawyers and scholars who have been appointed to the bench, rather than by the justices who spent their prior career inside the judiciary. Justice Tokiyasu Fujita, a former professor who retired in 2010, made a public call for more individual opinions as a means of enhancing public accountability.[108] Fujita noted that "majority opinions are by nature products of compromise and as a result inevitably ambiguous. However, ordinary people cannot grasp what the Court means in such ambiguous judgments, and justices should provide information about what majority opinions mean by writing individual opinions."[109]

Perhaps even more radically, the Justice System Reform Council recommended the introduction of a quasi–jury system, in which citizens sit in a mixed panel with judges in serious criminal cases. This reform, while not demanded by the public, was seen as an important step toward improving the transparency and legitimacy of the justice system as a whole. As a result, from August of 2009, ordinary citizens began to sit as *saiban-in*, lay decision makers, deciding serious criminal cases.[110] One can view this development as seeking to force the judiciary to make its decisions more transparent to the ordinary citizen, reflecting a shift from internal toward external audiences for judges. One also observes increased coverage of legal cases in newspapers and even criticism of some decisions in public. These reforms show that experimentation is occurring in Japan in ways that do not align with the conventional distinction between common law and civil law. Still, the core institutions of the career judiciary have remained in place, and the shift is only a matter of degree.

Conclusion

Judicial reputation matters. It provides information about performance and indirectly affects judicial resources and power. As of yet, however, we do not have a complete understanding of the determinants of reputation. This chapter has used law and economics tools to understand investment in reputation as a problem of team production. Judiciaries require individual effort by judges, but it is difficult to observe any particular judge's contribution to overall performance. Furthermore, judges who are concerned only with their own reputations might undermine collective judicial reputation. On the other hand, too much emphasis on collective reputation might lead judges to shirk, producing lower quality justice.

This framework helps us understand the inner workings of judicial systems. We have identified a set of particular institutional choices, roughly but not perfectly corresponding to the distinction between the common law and civil law systems that provide the incentive structure for judges. We believe that these institutional choices are linked and, in the aggregate, determine the particular texture of judicial reputation. Crucially, legal systems can experience pathologies when institutional reforms skew investment incentives in one direction or another. As a normative matter, designers of judicial systems need to think about incentives for reputation building, so as to maximize production of the various outputs expected from the judiciary.

We believe that there have been secular pressures on all countries that are forcing judiciaries to place greater weight on external audiences. No doubt the increasing importance of the media forces all government agencies to consider the public relations aspects of their work. Beyond this general trend, there has been an increasing "judicialization of politics" in many countries.[111] If judges are having a greater impact on matters of political and social importance, it is only natural that there will be greater interest in the operation of the judiciary and demands for greater judicial accountability. This creates both a demand for judicial reputation and incentives to supply it. This is also likely to be accompanied by significant institutional reforms, which we begin to consider in later chapters.

TWO

Pockets of Exception

The traditional approach to understanding judicial organization considers legal tradition to be the primary source of differences across countries. One of the problems with this view is that it does not grapple with the complex internal variations in each of the paradigmatic legal families, nor can it help to explain reforms over time. After all, if legal institutions adopted centuries ago continue to drive decision making about judicial organization, why are so many countries, from both the civil and common law traditions, continuing to tinker with judicial reforms?

Chapter 1 explained how the nature of judicial reputation is directly linked to judicial structure. Career judiciaries tend to create and reinforce collective reputation; recognition judiciaries tend to emphasize individual reputation. This chapter discusses why and how some systems use hybrid structures in which some parts of the judiciary are career-based and others are recognition-based. Our approach to the problem is functional, rather than historical. Function, not tradition, is a better tool for understanding the particular balance between the career and recognition models exhibited in any given system.

In chapter 1, we noted that there are several different functions played by courts. Courts are an instrument of social control, but they also play a role in resolving disputes and in making law. These functions have different institutional consequences, and the balance among these functions differs across countries. Accordingly, pockets of the career model have developed in legal systems dominated by recognition judiciaries (and vice versa), and we argue that these pockets appear in precisely those areas that are better served by a different institutional arrangement. For example, in constitutional law, in which judges wrestle with the grand principles of democratic governance in high-stakes issues, lawmaking is the dominant function. Unsurprisingly, most common and civil law jurisdictions use recognition judiciaries. On the other hand, in many areas of administrative law, where social control of lower officials is the more relevant consideration, both common and civil law jurisdictions have shown a strong preference for career judiciaries. Administrative law involves the control and monitoring of technical decisions by experts, frequently involving relatively low stakes; constitutional law involves higher stakes because it helps establish the general principles regulating the role of government.

Our theory explains the relevant differences between career and recognition judiciaries from a novel perspective. It also helps explain why legal systems favor a mix of the two, rather than a pure institutional design. From this starting point, we argue that all systems are institutionally hybrid, and there are good reasons to be so.

Legal scholars tend to argue about the merits of career and recognition judiciaries as pure types. For example, career judiciaries resemble a bureaucracy and so raise issues of shirking and sabotage of the agency's mission that are familiar to organizational theorists.[1] Not surprisingly, we observe a formal reliance on codes and significant procedural limitations to constrain judges, limit their ability to sabotage the law, and decrease the costs of monitoring their performance.[2] As a result, a career judiciary is methodologically conservative and systematically unadventurous—unwilling to acknowledge its role in lawmaking.[3] Strict rules predominate, especially at the level of ideology. Recognition judiciaries are different. They are dominated by lateral entry, and promotion is of little significance to the individual judge. Since ex ante quality is easier to observe, judges are less constrained and tend to apply more flexible standards as opposed to clear rules.[4] There are two possible behavioral consequences for the recognition model. First, the judiciary may be more politicized (but not necessarily more democratic, since it might not follow the legislature). Second, recognition judiciaries may be more creative in establishing and developing precedents (presumably inducing higher rates of reversal).[5]

Our point is that precisely because each type of judiciary has different institutional implications, legal systems tend to blend both models. We do not observe career and recognition judiciaries in their pure forms but instead see the types interact in a given legal system within a particular historical context. In short, we observe hybrid arrangements. Obviously the particular mix of career and recognition varies across countries. We recognize that, notwithstanding the hybrids, one type of judiciary tends to dominate in any given legal system. This might in fact be an artifact of historical factors: particular institutional patterns may become established through contingent factors and remain relatively stable thereafter.[6] However, by neglecting the presence and persistence of hybrid systems, the existing literature has failed to truly analyze the coexistence of both ideal types and its implications. We offer an institutional account of the emergence of hybrids using the principal-agent model, while recognizing that the dominant structure in each system might still be explained as a result of historical contingency and limited convergence.[7] Another way to express our idea is that legal systems develop a default institutional arrangement due to historical and contextual factors. However, the default arrangement can be modified, depending on institutional needs and responding to significant contextual changes, leading to the existence of pockets. For example, as we will elaborate in some detail later on, higher courts in civil law jurisdictions were traditionally made up of exclusively career judges, following the classic French model. However, these courts have evolved to partially accommodate a recognition structure.

We should distinguish our account of hybrid systems from the standard comparative law literature. Comparativists describe Louisiana, Scotland, and South Africa as hybrid or mixed legal systems, focusing on the coexistence of code law and case law (or, more mundanely, the application of both common and civil law in those particular jurisdictions).[8] We are less concerned with the formal sources of law than the institutional structures of judicial organization. Therefore, we argue that most, if not all, legal systems are institutional hybrids. In a sense, our understanding of hybrid legal systems is narrower, since we are only looking at institutional structures and not substantive or procedural law. However, as a consequence of our approach, the pool of hybrid legal systems is much broader than the one usually considered by comparativists, since it is difficult to find a pure-type legal institutional arrangement that pervades an entire system.

The simple observation that legal systems frequently combine career and recognition judiciaries (although in different ways and degrees) indicates that pure solutions are unlikely to be optimal in institutional terms. Our theory explains positively and normatively why hybrids are the norm and seem to be more functional than pure types. In mathematical language, if jurisdictions maximize the net benefit from their institutional arrangements, a combination of career and recognition judiciaries is generally optimal, whereas corner solutions are suboptimal.

Pockets: Some Examples

In this section, we consider several prominent examples of pockets: recognition judiciaries in the traditionally "careerist" civil law jurisdictions and career judiciaries in common law jurisdictions usually considered to be "recognition" systems.

Recognition Systems in Civil Law Countries

Constitutional Judges

The design of most constitutional courts in the Western world has been influenced by the original ideas and legal theories of Hans Kelsen.[9] Kelsen emphasized a normative hierarchy of law. Under his legal theory, ordinary (career) judges are mandated to apply law as legislated or decided by the parliament (the legislative branch of government). Consequently, there is subordination of the ordinary (career) judges to the legislature, and judicial review of legislation would be incompatible with the work of an ordinary court. Hence only an extrajudicial organ can effectively restrain the legislature and act as the guarantor of the will of the constitutional legislator. The Kelsenian model proposes a centralized body outside the structure of the conventional judiciary to exercise constitutional review—namely, a constitutional court.[10]

From its origins in interwar Austria, this model has spread around the world and is now a conventional choice for constitutional designers. The application of the Kelsenian model in each country has conformed to local conditions, so there are a variety of institutional designs with different judicial competences, access, composition, and appointment mechanisms. Kelsenian-type courts for constitutional review exist now in most European countries of the civil law tradition, with the Netherlands and the Scandinavian countries being the most striking exceptions. Also, most former communist central and eastern European countries have now developed a similar institutional structure. South Korea, Thailand, Taiwan, Colombia, and Chile, among others, also follow this model.

Table 2.1 Selected European constitutional courts

	Germany	France	Italy	Spain	Portugal
Year of creation	1951	1958	1955	1979	1982
Number of judges	16	9	15	12	13
Appointers	8 by Bundestag and 8 by Bundesrat	3 each by president, senate, and national assembly	5 each by president, parliament, and judiciary	4 by congress, 4 by senate, 2 by government, and 2 by judiciary	10 by parliament and 3 by constitutional court
Term duration (in years)	12	9	9	9	9
Renewable term	No	No	No	Once if the previous term was less than 3 years	Once (before 1997), No (after 1997)
Minimum number of career judges	6	0	5	2	6

The centralization of constitutional review in a body outside the conventional career judiciary has been attractive during periods of democratization after authoritarian rule in many countries in Europe, Asia, and Latin America. The career judiciary is usually suspected of allegiance to the former regime, and hence, a new court is expected to be more responsive to the democratic ideals contemplated in the new constitution.

The particular composition of constitutional courts differs across the world, but the appointment mechanisms tend to be political in nature. Unlike the traditional career judiciary, which is politically insulated and generally subject to some form of judicial council, constitutional judges are selected in a manner closer to the recognition model. They are usually chosen by a combination of the other branches of government, such as the executive and legislative and, in some cases, third parties such as a judicial council. Table 2.1 provides some examples from Europe. In practice, in most countries, a large fraction of constitutional judges is originally from the career judiciary; in some countries, as noted on the table, there is even a mandatory minimum quota for career judges in the constitutional court, though these never reach a required majority. However, the politicization of the appointment mechanism is inevitable, thus making it significantly different from the standard career judiciary.

In some instances, there is a de facto quota system. Each political party has a number of slots on the court, and new appointments are the product of party negotiations with little resemblance to judicial appointments in other courts.[11] The main consequence is the alignment of the preferences of the constitutional judges with those of the political parties, which is not surprising, given that political interests tend to prevail in the selection of candidates.[12] In turn, the perception of a politicized constitutional court (mostly because of the selection and appointment mechanisms) generates conflicts with the career judiciary that populates the ordinary courts, which we describe in chapter 5.[13] Significant fluctuations in the political composition of the constitutional court tend to exacerbate these conflicts.[14]

Commercial Courts in France

The French commercial courts (*Tribunaux de commerce*) are not populated by career judges.[15] It is a system of courts that can be traced back to 1563 and survived the important reforms that occurred during the professionalization of the French court system. The enforcement of the 1807 *Code du commerce* is entrusted to these courts, staffed only by businessmen that deal with litigation concerning commercial matters (such as company law, bankruptcy, and business contracts, including unfair competition and patent litigation). These lay judges are elected for terms of four years by the members of the local chamber of commerce after practicing as businessmen for at least five years.[16] In the court, they sit in panels of at least three for complex cases.[17] Commercial litigation is dominated by oral proceedings, unlike the general arrangements in the civil law tradition. They are considered to be reasonably fast in comparison to the regular courts. There are few appeals to the Cour d'Appeal and even fewer reversals.[18] The extensive use of judicial elections in France—with, by some accounts, over twenty-five thousand commercial and labor court judges elected—implies cultivation of individual reputation.

Recognition Judiciaries in Higher Courts

Many civil law countries reserve some places at the higher courts for noncareer judges, usually introduced as lawyers, prosecutors, or law professors recognized by the appropriate committee as of high merit. For example, in Spain, under some conditions established by law, lawyers and law professors can become judges at the higher courts without previous experience serving as lower court judges. (They are called the *cuarto turno* in reference to the fact that it used to be the case that the three previous hiring seasons had to be completed with career judges.) The process of appointment is administrative in nature (involving an examination plus assessment of merits) but conceptually closer to that of recognition judiciaries. A similar example is found in Brazil, where the president can appoint up to one-fifth of the federal appellate judiciary from among lawyers and prosecutors. Such judges are called the *quinto constitucional* by virtue of the fact that they constitute one-fifth of the judiciary in the higher courts. The remaining seats are taken by career judges. The *quinto constitucional* candidates are suggested by the law society and the federal prosecution body, respectively. The president picks only one name out of every three suggested.[19] Bolivia's Supreme Court has been directly elected by the public since 2009, even though it is categorized as a civil law jurisdiction.

Another example can be found in Japan. While the lower courts are populated with career judges, the Supreme Court is different. The justices are appointed by the prime minister and include a mix of career judges from lower courts, law professors, prosecutors, bureaucrats, and lawyers. The appointment mechanism is potentially politicized, and many believe that the Supreme Court appointees tend to be aligned with the preferences of the ruling party, as mentioned previously.[20] In France, the Conseil d'État is the supreme administrative court. Serving in the judiciary in the regular courts is an entirely different career path than serving in the Conseil d'État. However, appointment to the highest rank in the Conseil d'État is open to highly prestigious bureaucrats and lawyers (called the *tour éxterieur*, as they are supposed to constitute a third of the new *conselleirs d'état* appointed every year).[21] In the Netherlands, entrance to the judiciary is open to lawyers, law professors, and civil servants with a law degree. Candidates' merits are evaluated by a committee that usually proposes a training period before making a final recommendation to appointment. These outsiders now account for 70 percent or more of all judges in the Netherlands.[22]

Other Specialized Courts

Many civil law countries have specialized courts for electoral matters, military courts, or courts for certain specific business matters (such as antitrust law, intellectual property, or bankruptcy). Usually these courts are composed not of career judges but of individuals who are subject to a special selection and appointment process. Generally, entry into these judiciaries requires specialization in the particular relevant area of the law. The special selection and appointment process is frequently more administrative and less political in nature, but nevertheless different from the standard career judiciary, and the judges usually have an ambiguous relationship with the ordinary judiciary. While these special-ized judges are part of the judiciary, they are not always perceived as such by the ordinary (career) judiciary.

Career Systems in Common Law Countries

Despite the general view that the United States and United Kingdom have recognition judiciaries, this imagery is drawn from higher judicia-ries in both countries: the federal judiciary in the United States and the group nominally identified as "judges" in the United Kingdom. But the fact is that most judges in the both systems operate in structures that look more like career judiciaries than recognition ones. This is especially apparent in administrative law, in which judges are utilized as monitors of government agencies.

Administrative Law Judges in the United States

Administrative law judges (ALJs) in the United States appear to be a hy-brid institution. They are established by the Administrative Procedures Act (APA) to act and are considered "Article I judges," meaning they are part of the executive rather than the judicial branch (which is set up by Article III of the US Constitution).[23] They sit within particular agen-cies, and in many cases, their decisions are considered subject to being overturned by the head of the agency. These decisions can be appealed to the federal courts under the APA, and the ALJ decision is part of the record to be taken into account when reviewing agency action.[24] Never-theless, they are guaranteed independence and insulated from the line staff of agencies.[25] ALJs are appointed on the basis of a comprehensive written and oral test,[26] and so entry to the profession looks much more like the merit-based "career" approach than the political process used for the federal judiciary. They can be fired only for good cause, based on a decision by a Merit Systems Protections Board that sits outside the agency.

American states also have systems of administrative law judges, though there is a good deal of variation in the structure of the systems. Several states have central panel systems for administrative law judges, so that all agencies share a pool of ALJs.[27] In other states, administra-tive law judges sit within each agency, paralleling the federal system. In either case, they serve in a hierarchical bureaucratic career model char-acterized by merit selection and long careers.

There are thousands of administrative law judges in the United States, in both the state and federal systems. They are the primary decision makers for hundreds of thousands of decisions and hence ought to be considered part of the overall judicial apparatus in the country. Clearly this pocket is a significant and important one, in terms of the number of cases it encompasses and its impact on ordinary people's lives.

Tribunals in the United Kingdom

While it is true that the senior judiciary in the United Kingdom is appointed nearly exclusively from the ranks of practicing barristers, there are other systems within the British judiciary that look more like career systems. The British system of tribunals is established to hear cases against the administration.[28] There has historically been great diversity within the tribunal system, and many cases, especially those involving specialized areas, are decided by panels in which only the chairman is legally qualified. But recent years have seen efforts to standardize the tribunals system, ensuring that the judges who sit in it are qualified and independent. They are now subject to appointment from the Judicial Appointments Commission, and some five hundred of them sit full time.

Military Judiciaries

Military judiciaries are another career system within the common law tradition. In the United States Armed Forces, judge advocate generals (JAGs) join the military soon out of law school and typically spend their whole careers within the military service. They undergo special training soon after joining to qualify. In some branches, they form a separate corps, while in others, they are line officers who can be pulled into active duty. JAGs serve as military prosecutors and defense counsel in trials and also provide legal advice to the command. Some JAGs will serve as military judges in court-martial cases. Cases can be appealed to the Court of Criminal Appeals, staffed by appellate military judges. The apex of the system is a Court of Appeals for the Armed Forces, which is similar to the federal judiciary in that its appointees are nominated by the president and approved by the Senate. The basic military judge is appointed by the senior JAG in each sector of the service. The judges form a standing judiciary that is independent of the parties to the case, and military judges cannot be removed or unseated without following a specific protocol.[29]

Theory of Judicial Pockets

We have demonstrated that the traditional distinction between the common law operating a recognition judiciary and civil law operating a careerist one is not fully accurate. What might explain the hybrids we observe? The traditional account of the choice between career and recognition judiciaries relies on legal culture and tradition. The common law system developed a prestigious judiciary because of its evolution from a group of the monarch's officers over many centuries. In turn, the US federal institutional design was a strategic response to the perceived shortcomings of the British model. The civil law system fostered career judiciaries as a mechanism to comply with the predominant ideology of state positivism and to ensure legal certainty, particularly in an atmosphere of distrust of judges in the early nineteenth century. Prior to that time, France had a form of recognition judiciary, but after the codification of the civil law, judges were viewed as subservient to the will of the legislature. The choice of career or recognition judiciaries was therefore historically determined by different local concerns and ideologies, and according to many, these initial choices persisted so as to have long-run effects on legal institutions.

However, these historical and cultural explanations leave little space for understanding the current trends within both types of judiciary, unless pure path dependence persists. They also fail to grasp the hybridization of legal systems in terms of institutional settings that seems to be a feature of the contemporary world.

Another set of accounts focuses on the development of institutional structures as a solution to commitment problems on the part of rulers. According to this literature, the historical development of constitutional structures, including an independent judiciary, arose out of a need for monarchs to tie their hands and make promises credible.[30] This literature has focused on contingent factors that led to divergent historical experiences, as well as the consequences of institutional choices. We view the precommitment framework as complementary to the agency framework that we develop below, but we do not take a stance on which particular form of judicial organization is superior in terms of commitment.

We provide an alternative account of variation in institutional structures. Our departing point is the principal-agent model of the judiciary, which we briefly outlined in the introduction and has been applied with some success in particular national contexts in recent years.[31] In the model, each society has a sovereign, modeled as a unitary actor—that is, the principal. The principal might be the people in a democracy, the government, or an individual in a monarchy. The principal hires judges as agents to accomplish a certain set of tasks, including social control, dispute resolution, and a certain amount of lawmaking. The precise balance among these three functions is fixed for our purposes. The principal's task is to hire, within a budget constraint, a group of agents with a mix of high skills (for lawmaking) and lower level skills (for applying preexisting rules to factual situations). The high-skill agents have more human capital and hence are more expensive, though they may also find it easier to shirk (since they are better at deceiving the principal because they have an informational advantage). Low-skill agents are cheaper and less able to shirk, but they are also less valuable. Due to these differences in quality of potential agents, there are trade-offs between hiring large numbers of low-skill agents and a smaller number of high-skill agents.

Judges are like any other agents in that there are agency costs involved in hiring them. Judges may wish to pursue their own vision of justice or may exert insufficient effort. Loosely speaking, there are two potential problems that are fundamental sources of agency costs in this context: The first potential problem is the preferences of the judiciary may be isolated from those of society. In other words, the judiciary attracts the wrong kind of individuals from the perspective of the principal. This is a standard adverse selection issue. The other potential problem is that the judiciary is not sufficiently incentivized to perform well and therefore prefers to expropriate from the principal some of the benefits of its performance. Shirking is the classical example, but this category could also include judicial development of doctrines that benefit the judiciary directly rather than society, such as procedural rules that empower judges or force society to allocate more resources to the judiciary. The most extreme example of judicial expropriation is corruption. These kinds of moves can be seen as raising a moral hazard problem.

Adverse selection and moral hazard generate significant agency costs in every legal system. However, the balance between them varies, and this may lead to different institutional solutions. The institutional designer has a variety of mechanisms to control agency costs. These are familiar. One can "screen" by requiring that agents engage in costly signaling before hiring, through investment in activities that indicate fitness for the job.[32] One can shape the composition of the bench in terms of which agents serve on it. One can encourage or constrain agents to be loyal to the principal by virtue of institutional devices, such as those that require agents to follow legal precedent and those that control dockets and jurisdiction. One can hire superior agents to supervise the lower level agents in a hierarchical structure, and one can set up external monitors to watch what judges are doing. The first three solutions deal with the adverse selection problem, while the latter two focus on the moral hazard problem.

Adverse Selection

Addressing adverse selection frequently requires more screening on the principal's side and more signaling on the agent's side. The creation and disclosure of information concerning the preferences of potential judges is necessary to minimize the misalignment of the goals of the principal and the goals of the agent. The recognition judiciary seems to be a better option to address these issues. Reputation and prestige with external audiences provide more disclosure of information, and previous experience in a legal profession can be used as a proxy to identify judicial preferences. The more intense politicization of judicial appointments associated with the recognition judiciary merely reflects the importance of scrutinizing preferences and avoiding a bench that does not mirror society. By more strongly addressing the adverse selection problem, a system with a recognition judiciary can more easily rely on the judges to engage in the high-skill activity of lawmaking, since they tend to more accurately reproduce the options favored by society. On the other hand, the costliness of the screening process raises the costs of hiring, and so we would expect fewer judges to be hired.

It is also possible that, once hired, judges will be more susceptible to moral hazard. This might be particularly true if one thinks of the principal as a political party that initially supports the judiciary but loses power.[33] However, if the principal is society, alternation in power may enhance the alignment of preferences between principal and agent.[34] Political and procedural checks and balances have to be used to avoid excessive agency costs due to moral hazard. Developments in many common law jurisdictions seem to be largely responding to these issues (for example, attempts to curb excessive judicialization of public policy, the growing importance of statute law, and the use of sentencing and procedural guidelines to minimize judicial discretion).

There are institutional factors that are relevant to understanding the impact of adverse selection. Binding precedents, docket control, and judicially created doctrines on justiciability (including the political questions doctrine) are associated with recognition judiciaries but are hardly observable in legal environments with career judiciaries. If the screening mechanism is effective and the misalignment of prefer-ences between agent and principal is minimized, the legal system can develop institutional practices that make lawmaking by courts more ef-fective. Not surprisingly, courts with recognition judiciaries tend to issue binding or absolute precedents, exert some form of docket control (not necessarily as generous as the *writ of certiorari*), and address justiciabil-ity questions and conflicts of jurisdiction. If the screening mechanism does not provide for a judiciary with aligned preferences, we tend to observe institutional features that heavily constrain judicial lawmaking. Opinions are explanatory or clarify legal rules (but are not precedential), there is little to no docket control, and justiciability questions and ju-risdictional conflicts cannot be addressed by the court. This description applies to courts dominated by career judiciaries. In fact, in civil law countries, precedent *erga omnes*, docket control (by some form of proce-dural rules of access), and jurisdiction over justiciability questions and jurisdictional conflicts are common features of the constitutional court (recognition judiciary) and not of the supreme court (career judiciary), consistent with our theory.

Moral Hazard

Directly addressing moral hazard usually requires control of agents through monitoring and ongoing evaluation based on output. In the context of separation of powers, the principal cannot do this directly, and so a career judiciary might develop as an appropriate mechanism to reduce moral hazard. Hierarchical control, systematic monitoring by a specialized agency composed of judges, and periodic rotation to avoid too much local control of expertise and knowledge are consistent with the idea of reducing moral hazard. The shortcoming with this solution is that the principal has little *direct* control over judicial selection, thus enhancing a potential adverse selection problem. Codification and strict limitations on case law are useful for effectively constraining the ju-diciary and forcing conformity with the preferences of the principal.[35] Codes that enhance clarity and minimize interstitial lawmaking provide a cost-effective technology for reducing preference asymmetry.[36] While codification in the common law world is regarded as a mere instrument of organizing legislation in a more systematic and coherent way than dispersed statute law, even this may be effective in restraining the judi-ciary because it imposes internal consistency and significantly reduces the need for judicial interpretation and creativity. Specialized training encourages the so-called esprit de corps (which we could translate as strong professional norms) that induce adherence to legalism and its emphasis on the illegitimacy of judicial lawmaking, thus minimizing agency slack.[37]

We have explained how the choice between career and recognition judiciaries can be understood in the context of identifying and reducing agency costs in the form of adverse selection and moral hazard. The career model emphasizes hierarchical supervision and internalized norms to deal with both moral hazard and adverse selection. The recognition model emphasizes ex ante screening to deal with adverse selection and external monitoring (through transparent opinions and the existence of monitors of the courts) to deal with moral hazard. This suggests that the career systems are more focused on moral hazard, whereas the recognition systems emphasize adverse selection as the primary problem to be addressed.

Corruption can be seen as evidence of a severe moral hazard problem. According to our model, if a particular jurisdiction has a significant concern about judicial corruption, it should favor a career judiciary, because the mechanisms of monitoring are more appropriate. Some countries, such as India, seem to have shifted away from a traditional recognition judiciary into a more career judiciary because appointments by elected politicians are seen as inducing or supporting corruption in the bench. Although this would raise natural questions about democratic legitimacy and the role of the principal, in the context of our model, the argument would be that the traditional institutional design fostered, rather than reduced, adverse selection (from the viewpoint of the corrupt preferences of the politicians).

It is likely that the balance of these agency costs change over time with political, economic, and cultural factors. However, it is also the case that within any given legal system, it is likely that some areas of law raise more adverse selection concerns and other areas of the law raise more moral hazard concerns. In particular, the high-skill areas of law, where judicial lawmaking is needed, rely on selecting agents to exercise discretion responsibly, and hence the adverse selection mechanisms are predominant. Lower-skill areas, in which judges are simply applying preexisting rules, require less expertise but raise moral hazard problems of shirking.

For example, consider constitutional law or electoral law. It is likely that the principal is more concerned about the preferences of the judiciary being aligned rather than shirking or expropriation. Lawmaking in these two areas is of central political importance. Therefore, recognition judiciaries should tend to prevail in constitutional adjudication or electoral disputes. At the same time, higher courts are more likely to address socially and economically relevant principles of law than lower courts, which deal more systematically with facts. Adverse selection concerns are likely to predominate in higher courts, whereas moral hazard is the greater concern in lower courts. This could explain why civil law jurisdictions develop some pockets of recognition judiciaries in higher courts.

The opposite is true in areas such as administrative law or military law, in which the job of the judiciary is essentially to serve as a monitor of lower level government agents.[38] These tasks are more routine, and hence less likely to involve high-skill recognition judiciaries. In this context, social control is a major goal and cannot easily be subverted by the judiciary. Not surprisingly, career judiciaries tend to predominate in these areas of the law.[39]

Our quantitative exploration in a later section seems to largely confirm these observations. We find a strong correlation between the use of recognition judiciaries and constitutional adjudication. At the same time, we find little to no correlation between the use of recognition judiciaries and administrative adjudication. Further confirming this evidence, we find that in many countries a court invested with powers to exert constitutional review is not invested with identical powers to exercise administrative review.

Of course, many (if not all) areas of the law involve some degree of social control and also require judges to develop the law. We have provided two extreme examples—constitutional law and administrative adjudication. What about areas of private law, such as contracts, torts, or property or criminal law? Since they involve both judicial roles, the principal has to supplement the selection mechanism with an institutional design that minimizes agency costs. Recognition judiciaries address adverse selection problems; hence, in such systems, we should expect moral hazard to be the dominant concern when it comes to private law and criminal law. Not surprisingly, we observe the expansion of statutory law and judicial guidelines in such systems as means to effectively monitor the judiciary. Career judiciaries address moral hazard problems; therefore, adverse selection could be a significant concern in private law and criminal law. As described above, we have observed an expansion in the use of lawyers, prosecutors, or law professors recognized by the appropriate committee as being of high merit in traditional career judiciaries, along with the development of specialized courts.

Institutional logic provides a better general explanation of variation than mere cultural and historical path dependency, which cannot easily explain changes over time and are not always falsifiable. First, the balance of agency costs derived from adverse selection and moral hazard varies and therefore explains the diversity of institutional arrangements when it comes to selection and appointment of judges. Second, unlike standard accounts, institutional logic provides a rational explanation for the existence and persistence of pockets in certain areas of the law. Furthermore, it also suggests that judicial reforms can move in one or the other direction, depending on the particular type of agency problem to be corrected. Adverse selection problems are likely to be addressed with recognition judiciaries (reconfiguring the judiciary to reflect social preferences), whereas moral hazard shortcomings imply a more structured career judiciary (developing judicial councils or establishing stricter mechanisms of promotion). The diversity of judicial reforms in the last couple of decades attests to a variety of local conditions that reflect one or the other type of agency problem.

To be sure, we recognize that agency problems may not differ that systematically across contexts. It may be that some of the continued divergence among systems is indeed attributable to path dependencies from initial conditions. Our argument, though, is that the partial convergence on hybrid models calls into question "purist" descriptions now dominant in the literature.[40]

Implications

There is an institutional logic to the combination of career and recognition judiciaries, in which many countries use a dominant institutional design with pockets of the other available alternatives. The advantage of combining recognition and career judiciaries is that it can tailor institutions to address either adverse selection or moral hazard, depending on which is the main concern. It tends to a more structured hierarchy with more rigid codification when moral hazard needs to be minimized, using pockets of a recognition judiciary in areas of the law that raise concerns about judicial preferences. It favors a more politicized selection mechanism and a more diffused organization when adverse selection is the main source of concern, introducing pockets of a career judiciary where shirking or expropriation is socially more costly.

The hybrid system combines the benefits of both institutional solutions. It implicates both internal (judicial) and external (mainly political) audiences. Hence it provides a more appropriate balance of incentives, rather than a focus on a particular one. Internal audiences enhance collective reputation. External audiences provide opportunities to engage in individual reputation building. The combination of both presumably reduces potential conflicts between collective and individual reputation building that we would observe in a world of pure types. Career judiciaries tend to sacrifice individual reputation. Recognition judiciaries put less weight on collective reputation. The existence of pockets counterbalances the standard trends. Simultaneously, the hybrid model permits different social and professional backgrounds and diverse degrees of judicial training to coexist in the judiciary, therefore responding in a more specific way to particular needs.

As a consequence, a hybrid system is also more accountable than each of the pure solutions. As we have seen, it combines the accountability standards and practices of both systems. At the same time, the coexistence of both models permits comparisons. From this point of view, even conflicts such as those that we discuss in chapter 5 between constitutional (recognition) judges and supreme court (career) judges are welcome because they are informative and reduce the costs of enforcing accountability. Each type of judiciary monitors the other one, thus further reducing agency costs and exposing the shortcoming of each pure solution. In this light, conflicts of jurisdiction or skirmishes over procedural rules are productive and help the principal detect adverse selection and moral hazard.

Clearly, a hybrid system is not entirely advantageous. Otherwise legal systems would expand their pockets of institutional design infinitely and eventually all converge to a similar institutional arrangement. There are significant costs with allowing and promoting pockets that need to be accounted for when thinking about these institutions. For example, internal rivalries and conflicts of jurisdiction provide information but also waste resources. They can hurt the normal functioning of the courts. A conflict-ridden hybrid system could be highly dysfunctional, therefore undermining appropriate lawmaking and hurting social control.

More realistically, consistency and institutional compatibilities could be a serious concern. Take codification, for example. Enacting codes is more important when we have career judges and less so when we have recognition judges. Once both coexist, it might be difficult to manage the appropriate degree of codification, which should be high in certain areas of the law and low in others. Another example is procedural independence. As we explained above, it should be the case that we need more independence for recognition judges and less for career judges. When both coexist, either different procedural rules are developed, thus creating the usual problems known in the specialized courts literature,[41] or procedural rules are uniform across courts, hence significantly reducing the benefits of having pockets.

Our account has a number of empirical implications for comparative law, which are consistent with general observation. We will never see a pure recognition judiciary do primary administrative or criminal adjudication or mere law-applying tasks; we will never see a pure career judiciary doing policy making. In other words, administrative courts are unlikely to be staffed through recognition mechanisms. And constitutional adjudication is almost always left only to the highest courts, formed through a recognition model.

It is also the case that if our theory is correct—that is, a recognition system is more appropriate for lawmaking (which mainly takes place in higher level courts) while a career system is better for social control functions (at lower level courts)—then we would never observe a hybrid using a recognition system for lower level courts and a career system for higher level courts. In theory, some might believe this inversion of the current practice would be a good idea because career judges are more insulated from politics. But this type of hybrid does not address the problem of agency costs and hence has not been tried.

Empirical Analysis

We have constructed an original data set to provide for a crude empirical test of our theory. The dataset includes 134 higher courts from 73 different countries (and although technically the selection of countries is not random, it is in no way related to our main predictor variables). The full list of courts included in the sample is available in appendix A (and includes fifty-one civil law countries and twenty-two common law countries, which roughly reflects the proportion around the world).[42] Generally speaking, for common law jurisdictions, we include the highest court of the jurisdiction, while for the civil law jurisdictions, we include the various high courts, since they tend to have specialized jurisdictions and multiple high courts. For example, France has three highest courts: the Conseil d'État for administrative law, the Conseil Constitutionnel for constitutional cases, and the Cour de Cassation for ordinary appeals.

For each of these 134 higher courts, we collected the following information:

1. Whether it has competence over constitutional review, indicated by a dummy variable (seventy-one courts have competence over constitutional review while sixty-three courts do not)
2. Whether it has competence over judicial review of administrative acts, indicated by a dummy variable (seventy-three courts have competence over judicial review of administrative acts while sixty-one courts do not)
3. Whether the appointment mechanism to the court is mainly based on recognition or career, as operationalized by whether the appointments are professionalized or political (112 courts are mainly staffed with a recognition judiciary and 22 courts are mainly composed of career judges)[43]
4. The size of the court: when the number of justices is specified by the constitution, we use that figure; for other courts, we have counted the current number of active judges (while recognizing that actual size may vary slightly at any particular point in time)

We also include control variables such as the legal family (common law or civil law), the rule of law and control of corruption indicators of the World Bank,[44] federalism,[45] gross domestic product (GDP) per capita,[46] population estimates,[47] and the Doing Business rankings for contractual enforcement (quality of courts) and overall ease of doing business.[48] Due to missing data for some of these courts, we only have information about all the variables for a smaller sample. The descriptive statistics are summarized in table 2.2; country-level data are reported by country rather than court.

Table 2.3 summarizes the basic correlations. All correlations are generally consistent with our model. (Lawmaking courts should be more likely

Table 2.2 Descriptive statistics (2012 data)

Variable	Observations	Mean	Standard deviation	Minimum	Maximum
Number of judges	119	26.75	33.43	3	250
Constitutional powers	134	0.53	0.50	0	1
Administrative powers	134	0.55	0.50	0	1
Recognition	134	0.84	0.37	0	1
Common law	134	0.19	0.39	0	1
Federalism	134	0.26	0.44	0	1
Population (in millions)	73	52.27	145.82	0.033	1188.69
GDP per capita (in US$1000)	73	25.82	31.57	0.322	186.175
World Bank rule of law	73	0.56	0.94	−1.69	1.95
World Bank control of corruption	73	0.48	1.02	−1.27	2.39
Doing Business contract	71	63.18	50.28	1	184
Doing Business overall	71	60.18	46.97	1	180

Table 2.3 Correlation matrix

	Size	Constitutional powers	Administrative powers	Recognition	Common law	Federal	Population	GDP per capita	World Bank rule of law	World Bank control corruption	Doing Business contracts	Doing Business overall
Size	1											
Constitutional powers	-0.51	1										
Administrative powers	0.17	-0.11	1									
Recognition	-0.68	0.43	0.02	1								
Common law	-0.37	0.24	0.47	0.25	1							
Federal	-0.03	0.08	0.03	0.14	0.23	1						
Population	0.03	0.12	0.04	0.05	0.26	0.33	1					
GDP per capita	0.02	-0.03	-0.03	-0.00	-0.06	-0.04	-0.16	1				
World Bank rule of law	0.04	-0.05	-0.05	-0.03	-0.01	-0.06	-0.16	0.80	1			
World Bank control corruption	-0.05	-0.05	-0.15	0.04	-0.01	-0.03	-0.20	0.84	0.96	1		
Doing Business overall	0.06	0.12	0.03	-0.02	0.05	0.11	0.26	-0.58	-0.82	-0.80		1
Doing Business contracts	0.19	0.06	0.24	0.05	0.27	0.02	0.36	-0.56	-0.66	-0.66	0.65	1

related to recognition judiciaries rather than career systems, while the opposite should take place with courts more prone to social control.) Constitutional review is positively correlated with recognition mechanisms, while administrative review is not. (Administrative review seems to be correlated with common law, which is not surprising, given that it generally has no specialized jurisdictions at the apex level.) Size is heavily reduced when we have recognition judiciaries and when courts exercise constitutional review. Although there is a positive correlation between recognition judiciaries and common law legal origin, the relationship is weaker than that between recognition and constitutional review, as our theory suggests. This correlation alone suggests a modification of the legal origin story as the explanation for judicial structure.

To fully understand the relationships, a multivariate model is necessary. Our primary dependent variable of interest is whether the appointment to the court utilizes a predominately career or recognition model. The independent variables in this model include the powers of the court in administrative and in constitutional law and the control variables. In terms of institutional design, the appointment mechanism and the scope of constitutional law (in particular, the choice of which court performs constitutional review) are likely to be decided simultaneously, during the moment of constitutional adoption. As a consequence, there might be an endogeneity problem in thinking about the relationships between appointments and the powers of the court in constitutional law.[49] This means that there may be a missing variable that explains both the choice of appointment mechanisms and whether to give the court constitutional jurisdiction.

Table 2.4 reports four regression models. We start by estimating the probit regression with clustering of standard errors by country (since some countries have multiple high courts). We first look at the type of appointment mechanism as the dependent variable (column 1). We then look at whether the court has constitutional review powers (column 2). Due to the potential endogeneity problem with regard to constitutional jurisdiction, we also estimate a bivariate probit regression for both appointment and constitutional powers (columns 3 and 4). The models show the expected signs of the coefficients according to our theory, with recognition mechanisms being associated with constitutional jurisdiction. Notice that there is only a limited effect for administrative jurisdiction on recognition mechanisms (while it has a negative impact on constitutional jurisdiction). This result may be a product of the fact that we are looking at apex courts; lower level administrative adjudication is everywhere careerist, but some systems with a unified apex court

Table 2.4 Probit model of recognition appointment mechanisms

Dependent variable	Recognition appointments	Constitutional jurisdiction	Recognition appointments	Constitutional jurisdiction
Model	Probit	Probit	Bivariate probit	Bivariate probit
Constitutional jurisdiction	2.29***			
	(0.48)			
Recognition		2.49***		
		(0.63)		
Administrative powers	0.59*	−1.21***	0.03	−1.1***
	(0.35)	(0.24)	(0.23)	(0.25)
GDP per capita	0.01	0.01	0.01	−0.05
	(0.01)	(0.01)	(0.01)	(0.009)
Population (in millions)	−0.002*	0.005*	−0.0005	0.004*
	(0.001)	(0.002)	(0.0009)	(0.002)
World Bank rule of law	1.58*	−1.34**	0.85	−1.18***
measure	(0.95)	(0.52)	(0.62)	(0.045)
World Bank corruption	−0.36	1.31***	0.2	1.22***
measure	(0.7)	(0.45)	(0.53)	(0.43)
World Bank voice measure	−2.13**	0.42	−1.68***	0.07
	(0.89)	(0.37)	(0.57)	(0.35)
Federalism	0.35	−0.16	0.28	−0.13
	(0.52)	(0.32)	(0.45)	(0.30)
Doing Business contracts	0.006	0.003	0.007	0.004
	(0.005)	(0.004)	(0.004)	(0.003)
Doing Business overall	−0.002	−0.001	−0.001	0.0003
	(0.006)	(0.005)	(0.005)	(0.004)
Rho			1***	1***
			(0.000)	(0.000)
Constant	0.09	−1.73**	0.80	0.44*
	(0.72)	(0.77)	(0.50)	(0.36)
Observations	129	129	129	129
Clusters	71	71	71	71
Pseudo R²	0.354	0.304		
Prob > Chi²	0.0004	0.0000	0.0000	0.0000

Standard errors appear in parentheses.
*** p<0.01, ** p<0.05, * p<0.1

might assign administrative judicial review powers to the top court constituted by recognition mechanisms.

We also observe a negative effect for the World Bank's rule of law scores on recognition mechanisms and constitutional powers. This result could be driven by some of the jurisdictions with recognition judiciaries that perform quite badly on rule of law indices, such as India, Kenya, Mexico, Uganda, Venezuela, Zambia, and Zimbabwe. Many of these poorly performing judiciaries are plagued with corruption, realizing the moral hazard risk associated with the recognition model.[50]

Notice that for this specific dependent variable (recognition appointment mechanisms), we have not included the common law variable in

Table 2.5 OLS Model of court size

	OLS
Recognition	−55.11***
	(12.32)
Constitutional powers	−10.69***
	(3.58)
Administrative powers	2.38
	(5.24)
Common law	−13.78***
	(4.77)
Federalism	3.22
	(4.34)
GDP per capita	−0.07
	(0.15)
Population	0.02
	(0.01)
World Bank rule of law	13.00*
	(7.07)
World Bank corruption	−6.93
	(7.34)
World Bank voice	−8.68
	(10.58)
Doing Business contracts	0.06
	(0.04)
Doing Business overall	0.02
	(0.05)
Constant	73.62***
	(15.57)
Observations	114
Clusters	69
R^2	0.54

Robust standard errors are in parentheses.
*** $p<0.01$, ** $p<0.05$, * $p<0.1$

the regressions presented in table 2.4. The reason is that, in our sample of high courts, all common law courts have recognition judiciaries, while career systems only exist in (some) civil law courts.

The second dependent variable we analyze is the size of the court, to test our conjecture that recognition judiciaries are smaller. The independent variable is whether the appointment to the court is career or recognition, and we include the same control variables as in the previous analysis. We estimate the regression with ordinary least squares with clustering of standard errors by country.[51] We believe that the endogeneity problem in this context is less severe since, for most countries, court size is determined either independent of constitutional design or set after the initial constitutional design by later constitutional amendment or ordinary statute. However, in unreported robustness analysis, we also estimated a 3SLS regression, with results fairly similar to the reported OLS regression.[52] Table 2.5 presents the results, which indicate a strong negative relationship between recognition systems of appointment and court size, even controlling for common law tradition. Courts with constitutional jurisdiction tend to be significantly smaller than those exercising administrative jurisdiction. The evidence suggests that judicial structure is explained by more than legal tradition, as argued by our theory, and that institutional factors are important in understanding the design of courts.

Conclusion

This chapter examines the distinction between the career and recognition judiciaries from a new perspective. We suggest that the design of judicial institutions responds to particular agency problems—namely, adverse selection (the misalignment of preferences between the judiciary and society) and moral hazard (shirking and expropriation by the judiciary of the benefits created by social control).

We argue and provide evidence that certain areas of the law are better served by career judiciaries while others are better served by recognition judiciaries. Hybrid systems try to supplement the choice of a particular pure arrangement with some pockets of a different nature that can benefit certain areas of the law. Constitutional law and administrative law provide two good examples. In systems dominated by career judiciaries, constitutional adjudication tends to be assigned to recognition judges. In systems that are primarily based on recognition, administrative adjudication tends to be decided by career judges. Consistent with the theory, we find that constitutional courts are smaller and more likely to be composed through a recognition mechanism; we find no statistically significant effect for administrative courts.

A mix of a dominant system with pockets of the other pure solution seems to be an appropriate technique to address agency problems. However, we have recognized that there are inevitable costs, including institutional inconsistencies and incompatibilities. Conflicts between coexisting models may be informative and productive (in terms of helping institutional monitoring) but can also waste resources and be dysfunctional. Pockets therefore tend to be self-contained and are usually not generalized to the entire court system. Rather, they are tailored to particular functions of the legal system and special areas of the law. Because we see hybrids as responding to institutional needs, we suspect that there will continue to be evolution in observed patterns. For example, we might imagine that all systems will eventually shift toward appointment after at least a medium-length career (as in the recognition model), followed by possibilities of promotion, transfer, and so on (as in the career model). This might solve adverse selection problems on the front end while addressing moral hazard on the back end, though it could also exacerbate other problems: late appointment with subsequent promotion might lead to pressures to politicize the promotion process to an even greater degree than is currently found in recognition judiciaries.

There are two important implications of our analysis for legal reform. First, we provide a useful taxonomy to identify areas of the law that could benefit from different institutional arrangements. Second, in contrast with the influential literature on legal origins, our agency-cost approach is one in which judicial reform can potentially overcome historical and cultural path dependence. If the nature of agency costs changes in a certain jurisdiction, we suggest that policy makers ought to, and frequently do, respond by considering institutional reforms to the judiciary to address the new conditions. Obviously there are short-run costs to institutional change, including sunk costs of human capital and institution-specific assets. However, at minimum, our approach shifts the explanatory focus away from institutions predetermined by fate or history to a more productive incentive analysis with greater capacity to explain variation across time and space and to inform institutional design.

In our view, the structure of judicial institutions is not predetermined by history, although the historical context is obviously important. Instead we see institutional structure as responding to broader incentives within any particular jurisdiction. From a positive perspective, hybrid judiciaries have emerged in many jurisdictions because the default regime (career or recognition) was not the most appropriate in certain areas of the law. From a normative perspective, we suggest that hybrid judiciaries are attractive because variation in agency costs across different areas of the law and different political environments shapes optimal institutional design in a variety of ways. Our approach thus provides a theoretical basis for comparative law beyond categorization by legal origin.

THREE

Wearing Two Hats: Judges and Nonjudicial Functions

Introduction

We all know that the job of judges is to decide cases. Yet in many jurisdictions, judges also engage in multiple nonjudicial functions, ranging from serving on law commissions, to playing management roles, to serving as public intellectuals, to serving as chief executives. In a notable recent example, the Egyptian military named the chief judge of the country's Constitutional Court as the interim president after deposing elected President Mohamed Morsi in 2013. The previous year, in the midst of a serious political and economic turmoil, the president of the Greek Supreme Administrative Court was appointed to be the interim prime minister.[1] Justices have also served as acting presidents in Bolivia,[2] Bangladesh,[3] Nepal, and Pakistan.[4] One of the most significant constitutional crises in Brazilian history, in October 1945, was resolved when the incumbent president was forced to resign and the chief justice was appointed as acting president.[5]

In the late 2000s, Chief Justice Reynato Puno of the Philippines Supreme Court began to be solicited by many to run for president in 2010. He started to appear at crime scenes and prisons, and he made other high-profile public appearances. A lay Methodist preacher, he also appeared at televangelist performances, courted news organizations, and appeared on magazine covers as well as national television. He called and hosted a national summit on extrajudicial killings, which made recommendations about resolving the long-standing conflict in Mindanao.[6] In 2009, he met with government officials to discuss his leading a "transition council," a proposal to ease embattled President Gloria Macapagal-Arroyo out of power. This proposed body would amend the constitution to fix various problems in the political and electoral systems.[7] When exposed, this proposal led to significant controversy, pressures to resign, and accusations that the chief had badly overstepped the proper role of a judge. But Puno's activities illustrate both the demand for broad judicial engagement in political functions as well as the risks of backlash.

Are there any limits to judicial engagement in nonjudicial functions? Evidently, the distinction between a judicial and a nonjudicial function is itself complicated and convoluted.[8] Case law has not been particularly clear in providing a concise definition of the judicial function.[9] One might start with the idea of impartial, nonpartisan adjudication of legal cases, which seems to be the essential job of judges.[10] However, this conceptualization leaves an enormous grey area, as many of the activities that judges engage in inside the courtroom, such as deciding on applications for naturalization or conducting administrative proceedings in bankruptcy jurisdiction, might be argued to be more administrative than judicial in nature.[11] Furthermore, there are many tasks outside the formal legal system that are fundamentally adjudicative in nature, in which judges are welcome due to their perceived independence and impartiality. For example, when judges are involved in private arbitration, is this a judicial function or not? The answer to this question is all but clear.[12]

The involvement of judges in nonjudicial functions also raises significant questions concerning the separation of powers doctrine.[13] When judges take on important roles outside the judicial branch of government, they might be seen as interfering with other branches as well as undermining the independence of the judiciary. Furthermore, too much involvement in nonjudicial functions could seriously compromise the impartiality of the judges in question. Another issue raised by judicial participation in extrajudicial roles is how far privileges of judicial immunity, which are usually seen as necessary for judicial independence, should be extended to nonjudicial functions.[14]

Not surprisingly, most jurisdictions regulate judicial involvement in nonjudicial functions. In the United States, the Federal Code of Judicial Conduct allows judges to participate in some activities, mostly related to academic, educational, and charitable work, while prohibiting the practice of law, among other things. The general standard is that judges must avoid anything that would "detract from the dignity of the judge's office, interfere with the performance of the judge's official duties, reflect adversely on the judge's impartiality, [or] lead to frequent disqualification."[15] Other jurisdictions, such as South Africa, have developed a specific incompatibility test to apply when judges are engaged in nonjudicial functions.[16] Yet there are also jurisdictions that place very few formal restrictions on judges.[17] Most jurisdictions distinguish between nonjudicial functions during the judge's tenure and those undertaken post-tenure, with the latter subject to less intensive restrictions. In the words of the US Supreme Court in *Mistretta v. United States,* "The ultimate inquiry remains whether a particular extrajudicial assignment undermines the integrity of the Judicial Branch."[18]

Without significant statutory limitations, Canada and Australia have seen the development of the *persona designata* doctrine to regulate judicial participation in activities outside the judicial branch of government. This doctrine treats powers as conferred personally on an individual specifically designated for a given task, rather than on the person in their capacity as a judge or as a member of a court. An individual can exercise individually conferred powers as long as they do not conflict with those enjoyed in her role as a judge.[19] Perceived to be based on the doctrine of separation of powers, the goal of this doctrine is to assuage, through the use of a legal fiction, possible concerns about judicial involvement in nonjudicial functions.

For the purpose of our analysis, we consider a judicial function any official activity exercised by a judge inside the courtroom, whereas we consider a nonjudicial role any activity exercised by a judge outside the courtroom.[20] To illustrate, a judge serving on an advisory board for a charity is engaged in a nonjudicial function, while a judge sentencing a defendant is exercising a judicial function. Importantly, the phenomenon recently characterized as the judicialization of public policy is usually achieved through formal court decisions and hence is considered to be within the judicial function in our framework.[21] We recognize that there is some relationship between judicialization and the expansion of judicial involvement to nonjudicial roles in the sense that more "political" decisions in the courtroom might encourage (or discourage) nonjudicial roles in the sense we understand them. We do not make a strong prediction about the trade-offs and dynamics here: one can imagine that judges whose decisions increasingly shape public policy will become more prominent and trustworthy, but they may also become more controversial and provoke a backlash against extending their roles outside the court. Our modest goal in this chapter is to distinguish non-judicial functions from other phenomena, so as to provide a better understanding of the full scope of judicial behavior and to explain why judges might become involved in nonjudicial functions, using our theory of judicial reputation.

Judicial involvement in nonjudicial functions requires two things—supply and demand. First, judges have to be willing to perform such functions voluntarily, which means they must enjoy some benefits from nonjudicial tasks. This is the supply side. Second, other political and social relevant actors must desire and benefit from judicial participation. This is the demand side. We contend that both parties are motivated, in part, by concerns about reputation—the judges wish to enhance their reputations, while other actors seek to draw on the reputation of the judiciary for impartiality and integrity. However, given that nonjudicial functions may impose some costs in terms of the collective reputation on the judiciary, some limitations are likely appropriate. In fact, we contend that potential market failures justify some form of regulation in this context.

Nonjudicial Functions

We can consider a continuum of nonjudicial functions by gauging degrees of similarity to or difference from judicial functions. At one end of the spectrum, there are nonjudicial functions that can be seen as essentially judicial or quasijudicial in nature. Next we move to nonjudicial functions that benefit from judicial expertise or are related to the legal system more generally. We also have nonjudicial functions that simply reflect community engagement. Finally, we have nonjudicial functions that involve the other two branches of government: legislative and executive. We also add business activities at the end of the list, since they are not even governmental in character (table 3.1).

These nonjudicial functions are not equivalent in nature. Arguments that certain activities benefit from judicial skills and independence might apply to the top of the list, but they become less convincing when we move toward the bottom of the list. Similarly, arguments against judicial involvement in nonjudicial functions are apparently stronger for those at the bottom than at the top of the list. Not surprisingly, most jurisdictions are permissive with seemingly or quasijudicial functions but regulate

Table 3.1 Continuum of nonjudicial functions

	Category	Examples
More judicial	Seemingly judicial functions	Private arbitration; serving in tribunals as a mediator or in ad hoc tribunals on restorative justice
	Quasijudicial functions	Auxiliary functions such as serving on electoral courts or evaluating the programs of political parties for purposes of assessing unconstitutionality
	Nonjudicial governance functions related to judicial functions	Management of courts; serving on a judicial council or other commissions related to the court system or to judicial selection, retention, promotion, or discipline
	Nonjudicial functions that are adjudicative in nature	Chairing inquiries, such as royal commissions in the United Kingdom or in Australia or public hearings in the United States; serving as special prosecutors; undertaking specialized investigations on corruption or terrorism; adjudicating impeachment of political actors
	Nonjudicial functions that promote the law	Teaching and writing; working in judicial associations
	Social and community activities	Involvement with nonprofit activities; participation in nonjudicial associations
	Seemingly legislative functions	Participation in lawmaking commissions or working groups; serving on electoral boundary commissions; supervising constitutional amendments
	Seemingly executive functions	Chairing administrative agencies (often related to crime prevention); making appointments; serving as ambassadors or executive officers
	Fully legislative functions	Serving as a legislator
	Fully executive functions	Serving as a member of the administration or ambassador
Less judicial	Business activities	Involvement in for-profit activities, including lawyering and serving on corporate boards or directorships

more extensively any judicial involvement in legislative and executive functions.

Business activities, in particular if they are law related, might benefit from judicial knowledge and human capital, but they expropriate from the entire judiciary its collective investment in reputation and prestige. Unlike the other activities, which arguably benefit the state or society as a whole, the beneficiaries of judges' time and effort in business are entirely private. These activities also undermine judicial impartiality and raise considerable concerns with regard to professional conflicts of interest. It is not surprising that most jurisdictions prohibit such activities.

Some nonjudicial functions are exercised by individual judges, while others involve collective action. Many countries allow their supreme court or constitutional court to exercise ancillary powers beyond their main judicial functions, and these might also be considered nonjudicial functions. Some recent constitutions, for example, allow the constitutional court to propose constitutional amendments[22] or propose appointments to certain offices.[23] The constitutional traditions of many Latin American countries have allowed the supreme court to propose legislation that is related to judicial matters,[24] and a similar pattern has emerged in post-Soviet countries and socialist Southeast Asia.[25] Similarly, some countries require the constitutional court's involvement in the declaration of states of emergency. This is a feature of the French Fifth Republic, adopted in a number of other countries as well.[26] These collective tasks also can be analyzed using the framework we set out below.

A Theory of Judicial Roles in Nonjudicial Functions

Supply Side

Judges may perform some nonjudicial functions because they want to, but it is unclear why they should. Multiple reasons might explain judicial willingness to accept additional workload over and beyond their basic duties, and these are the determinants of the supply side. It might be a question of remuneration, either because the nonjudicial functions pay more or because they generate rents to be recouped in the future. Monetary payoffs, immediate or deferred, frequently motivate human behaviors, even for judges. A second possible set of reasons is related to enhancing individual prestige or reputation. Nonjudicial functions could provide better or new opportunities for individual judges to become more popular with relevant audiences. Nonjudicial functions could also reduce an individual's workload if they are less demanding than judging in terms of hours or intensity of work. Finally, a third possible factor is that nonjudicial roles enhance political and social influence. An individual judge with a particular ideological or social agenda could view nonjudicial functions as instrumental to promoting her views.

Let us begin with our theory of reputation. We argued in chapter 1 that judges need a good reputation in order to accomplish their tasks. Furthermore, reputation requires team production; it has both an individual and a collective component. A judge's reputation contributes to that of the judiciary as a whole but also depends on that collective reputation.

A judge taking on nonjudicial functions has to compare the benefits with the potential costs. Nonjudicial functions might generate two significant costs. First, the judicial aura of impartiality and independence could be compromised by a nonjudicial function. As the US Supreme Court said in *Mistretta v. United States*, "The legitimacy of the Judicial Branch ultimately depends upon its reputation for impartiality and non-partisanship. That reputation may not be borrowed by the political branches to cloak their work in the neutral colours of judicial action."[27] An erosion of judicial prestige and reputation in the future might be a significant risk in terms of both future monetary and future nonmonetary payoffs. Second, nonjudicial functions could undermine a particular judge's reputation, limiting promotion to higher courts, depending on the response of others to the judge's actions.

At the same time, judges may benefit from engaging in nonjudicial functions. One benefit is the diversification of markets in which reputation is built. A judge who works exclusively within the judiciary may be less well known outside of it and may want to diversify sources of reputation building. This strategy may only make sense once a certain amount of internal reputational capital has been built. Furthermore, some judges may have particular skills such as a talent for writing books and magazine articles. These judges may receive more marginal payoff to reputation building by engaging in extrajudicial activities, at least up to a certain point. The existence of multiple markets for reputation building may enhance the overall prestige of the judiciary, given a range of judicial skills and personalities.

The balance between anticipated benefits and expected costs will determine the extent to which an individual judge might accept an offer to engage in a nonjudicial function. It is likely that the profile of costs and benefits for any particular nonjudicial function varies for individual judges. The possibility of nonjudicial functions induces a selection effect. Certain types of individuals will be more prone to seek nonjudicial appointments than others, and some people may be more willing to become judges if they know they can also engage in other activities. For example, consider the standard distinction between career and recognition judiciaries as discussed in chapter 3. Nonjudicial functions are likely to appeal more to recognition judiciaries, for whom external audiences are more important, than to career judges, who are usually more focused on internal incentives. It is also plausible that the potential costs of nonjudicial functions will be more significant when judicial selection and promotion is totally depoliticized and there is a well-structured career. Engagement in nonjudicial issues may be more costly in a career judiciary than in a recognition judiciary given the institutional design, as it invites external interference. We would expect that the roles of nonjudicial functions are more visible in recognition judiciaries than in career judiciaries—an observation that seems fairly consistent with the evidence presented below.

There are also significant moral hazard implications. The existence of nonjudicial functions is likely to distort or influence the incentives for judicial performance. To the extent that nonjudicial roles for judges are created by external audiences, individual judges might be more willing to appeal to such audiences. In some ways, judges might seek to enhance judicial independence if a reputation for independence is instrumental to benefit from these outside opportunities. But if partiality or partisanship is important to obtain the nonjudicial payoffs, this dynamic could undermine judicial independence.

Another plausible effect of nonjudicial payoffs is adverse selection at the entry level. Certain individuals might be more interested in a judicial career or appointment if nonjudicial functions are available. This could be problematic if it induces individuals to perceive a judgeship as merely instrumental to acquiring a nonjudicial function. If the skills and attributes of judicial and nonjudicial functions are aligned, this effect is not so relevant. However, if the skills and attributes of a nonjudicial function conflict with those of the judicial function, the "wrong" kind of individuals might seek judicial appointments.

Shifts in the supply function for nonjudicial functions will respond to changes in the balance of costs and benefits. For example, a continuous erosion of monetary payoffs from judicial work (for example, because salaries are not increased) might lead to an increased desire for judges to exercise nonjudicial functions. Fewer opportunities to get promotions in the judicial career could also expand the supply curve. At the same time, excessive political polarization in nonjudicial roles is likely to diminish the supply curve, as judges may become more cautious about risking their prestige. The perception that nonjudicial functions might increase the likelihood of being expelled from the judiciary could have a significant chilling effect.[28]

Demand Side

We turn now for explanations as to why certain groups or other branches of government might want judges to perform nonjudicial functions. The most obvious explanation is that judicial skills and human capital are well suited for particular nonjudicial tasks. Unsurprisingly, this may lead audiences to recruit judges to perform such nonjudicial functions. Tasks related to law, adjudication, interpretation, review, or fact finding all draw on judicial skills.

If in some cases there is a genuine demand for judicial independence and impartiality, then in other cases, political actors may seek to recruit judges to free ride on judicial prestige. One example involves using judges to lead politically sensitive inquiries or involving them in consultations over new legislation. Judicial participation in these nonjudicial functions might be beneficial given judicial human capital, but it also gives credibility or legitimizes a particular outcome that might be potentially politicized. Some tasks will be viewed in a better light when performed by judges rather than politicians.

There are collective costs of using judges to perform nonjudicial functions. The most serious one is eroding judicial prestige, which could undermine judicial independence and the separation of powers in the future.[29] Another potential cost is the creation of alternative methods of problem solving, such as arbitration, that will inevitably compete and possibly undermine the public system of adjudication.

The general quality of institutions might help determine shifts in the demand curve. In a system of generally poor institutions with a good judiciary, we expect demand to be high and will likely observe judicial involvement with nonjudicial functions more frequently. Where the judiciary is poor but other institutions are high in quality, demand will likely be low. This might explain why some countries turn to judges to lead the nation as interim executives during times of crisis: when other institutions are discredited, there is a greater demand for judicial leadership to "restore integrity to the system." On the other hand, excessively controversial judicial decisions could reduce demand in later periods.

Potential Market Failures

Having explained the demand and supply curves for judicial involvement in nonjudicial functions, we can easily derive an equilibrium in
which judges will serve in nonjudicial functions in response to demand
and supply determinants. There are good reasons to suspect that said
equilibrium is not efficient because there are potential market failures.
The most immediate is that the demand-side costs might be externalized
and therefore not actually borne by those who want judges to exercise
nonjudicial functions.

For the society as a whole, judicial involvement with nonjudicial
functions would be appropriate when the benefits outweigh the costs.
The critical issue is that such benefits and costs may not be symmetri-
cally distributed across the population of interested parties. In some instances, the benefits are given to the particular political or social actor
who has the power to appoint a judge to a nonjudicial function. Yet the
costs may be borne by the judiciary at large. Those who bear these costs
might not be in a position to effectively oppose judicial involvement in
nonjudicial functions.

An unbalanced distribution of costs and benefits might justify external regulation of judicial involvement in nonjudicial functions. Judges
might value such regulation as a precommitment mechanism to avoid
opportunism by those who benefit. Inevitably this regulation has to be
effective and sufficiently clear to avoid conflicts of interpretation, which
might require the courts to adjudicate on cases where they have a direct interest. Another possible solution is self-regulation by the judiciary
itself. However, it is unclear if the interests of the judiciary are always
aligned with those of the community at large.

Not all nonjudicial functions will generate the same balance of potential costs and benefits. Those that are more judicial in nature are
likely to maximize the net benefit for both judges and their audiences.
It is not surprising that most legal systems are more permissive in allowing such functions, even if there may be some particular constraints,
such as requiring that a judge take a leave of absence without remuneration. As we go down in the list toward functions that are less judicial
in character, not only is it less likely that there will be an aggregate net
benefit, but conflicts of interest across actors are expected to emerge.
As expected, most legal systems prohibit judges from engaging in truly
nonjudicial functions. They might even limit judges after they retire by

imposing some time lag between leaving the bench and engaging in nonjudicial functions.

A different way to approach this problem is to consider judicial independence, reputation, and prestige as public goods. Judges contribute to creating the public good, which forms a collective stock of reputational capital. But once built, there is a danger that it will be overused and dissipated in the pursuit of nonjudicial functions that may benefit only a particular group of political actors. If judicial reputation is a public good, then some form of regulatory intervention may be required to avoid excessive dissipation.

Another potential market failure can occur when there is supply-induced demand. The judiciary could engage in strategic development of a reputation for independence and impartiality to induce additional demand for nonjudicial functions. This is a risky strategy since judicial decisions would be merely instrumental in order to achieve a longer-term goal, unrelated to judicial functions. Furthermore, this strategy could be perceived as a kind of expropriation. The external benefits created by an independent judiciary may be appropriated by individual judges pursuing nonjudicial roles. While it seems appropriate to limit opportunities for supply-induced demand, self-regulation by the judiciary itself is unlikely to be an efficient mechanism, since it could easily be captured to promote supply-induced demand. Regulation by an external body or by statutory intervention seems advisable.

Another related concern is the different market structure for judicial and nonjudicial functions. Judges enjoy a monopoly over judicial functions and have the exclusive ability to engage in them. However, when it comes to nonjudicial functions, judges inevitably compete with other groups or professions. One possible consequence is that judges could use their monopoly rents obtained in the course of judicial functions to promote their involvement in nonjudicial functions. One might think of this, in economic terms, as exercising a form of dumping against competing groups—expanding market share using subsidized production. Judges might shape adjudication and judge-made law to promote their reputation with relevant audiences and undermine possible competition for nonjudicial functions. For example, imagine a judicial decision *requiring* certain forms of investigative commission to have judicial membership. Regulation might be necessary to prevent judicial attempts to exploit these monopoly rents. In this context, it is also unlikely that self-regulation by the judiciary would be enough since, precisely due to monopoly power, there is little pressure within the judiciary to curtail their monopoly rents. However, regulation by a third party should also be carefully designed because competing groups might lobby for excessive limitations, so to avoid the competition of judges for nonjudicial functions.

Comparative Examples

United States

Judges in the United States, at both federal and state levels, engage in a range of nonjudicial functions, and this has been the topic of public debate, academic commentary, and official hearings.[30] The very first chief justice, John Jay, was given ex officio roles serving on a debt commission and inspecting the mint.[31] He later ran for governor of New York and eventually resigned from the court to take the position. Chief Justice Jay was also appointed ambassador to England, in which capacity he negotiated a major trade treaty that is widely credited with averting war. Although there has been less explicit involvement in public offices in more recent times, particular justices may have political ambitions or otherwise be thinking about postjudicial jobs.[32] And there has, by some accounts, been an increase in judicial authorship of commentaries and public speaking.

Nonjudicial functions are regulated by judicial codes of conduct, found in virtually every state. The American Bar Association Model Code of Judicial Conduct includes, as Canon 3, a requirement that "a judge shall conduct the judge's personal and extrajudicial activities to minimize the risk of conflict with the obligations of judicial office."[33] The rules include relatively strict prohibitions against judicial engagement in nonjudicial functions.[34] For example, Rule 3.4 requires that "a judge shall not accept appointment to a governmental committee, board, commission, or other governmental position, unless it is one that concerns the law, the legal system, or the administration of justice."[35] Typically, judges may speak, write, lecture, teach, and participate in other professional activities on legal and nonlegal subject matters.[36] Judges may sit on professional and nonprofit boards but are to limit their involvement in organizations that might be engaged in judicial proceedings.[37] On occasion, states discipline judges for such involvement.[38]

The issue has raised particular attention with regard to the US Supreme Court, whose justices have spoken publically on various topics of public import.[39] The extent of this activity has on some accounts increased since the days in which Justice Frankfurter referred to the need for judicial self-restraint as a case of "judicial lockjaw."[40] The standard analysis cautions about how judicial speech giving, authorship, and public appearances affect judicial independence.[41] The same issues arise with regard to other nonjudicial functions, such as serving on commissions or government bodies. The US Supreme Court itself considered the issue in *Mistretta v. United States*, already discussed above, which considered the constitutionality of a judge serving on the US Sentencing Commission.[42] It was alleged that, as a rule-making body, the Sentencing Commission involved administrative rather than judicial power. The court found that the activity did not violate the separation of powers but clearly identified the risks of other political actors seeking to utilize judicial reputation to legitimate their projects. In short, the US approach tends to limit judicial involvement through codes of ethics and has over the years shifted in the direction of limited judicial involvement, relative to some other jurisdictions.

United Kingdom

Judges in the United Kingdom have a long tradition of leading commissions of inquiry in matters of public importance, including the 2014 inquiry into the role of the press and police in the Rupert Murdoch phone-hacking scandal.[43] The role of judges in extrajudicial roles garnered a good deal of public attention in the case of *Ex Parte Pinochet*, when it was learned that one of the judges in the case, Lord Hoffman, had been a director of Amnesty International while hearing the case.[44] This was seen as problematic because Amnesty had intervened in the case. Another notable recent case involved an inquiry into the death of David Butler, a former UN weapons inspector.[45] Along with other prominent cases, the Butler inquiry led to a debate about the use of judges to chair public investigations into matters of political controversy.[46] The Government Department of Constitutional Affairs subsequently produced a consultation paper on "Effective Inquiries," reporting that there had been thirty major inquiries since 1990, costing an estimated £300 million.[47] The report concluded that it can be appropriate for judges to chair inquiries, "because the judiciary has a great deal of experience in analyzing evidence, determining facts and reaching conclusions, albeit in an adversarial rather than inquisitorial context. The judiciary also has a long tradition of independence from politics, and judges are widely accepted to be free from any party political bias."[48] The report seems to double down on judicial leadership in nonjudicial functions, as it recommends the expansion of statutory powers for inquiries to include powers to compel attendance of witnesses and production of documents, as well as other quasijudicial processes.[49] Other cases of judges becoming involved in nonjudicial functions include a recent case in which a private company appointed a sitting judge to inquire into its own financial malpractice.[50] And there has been a significant increase in judicial testimony before Parliament, much of which concerns legislative projects.[51]

France

In France, nonjudicial functions by judges are regulated by statutory law, mainly the *Code de l'organisation judiciaire* and the *Ordonnance n° 58-1270 portant loi organique relative au statut de la magistrature*.[52] Enforcement of the rules is mainly left to the Judicial Council, which will be described extensively in chapter 4. According to French law, the exercise of judicial functions is incompatible with the exercise of all public functions and any other occupation or employment. Individual exemptions may, however, be granted to the judges by decision of the president of the court in which they work. These exemptions cover teaching and other functions or activities that do not harm independence. Even without prior authorization, judges may engage in scientific, literary, or artistic work. However, arbitration activities are not allowed, nor is anything political.[53]

French judges traditionally are not known for becoming involved in nonjudicial roles, which is consistent with the local legal culture that has historically been based on a general distrust of the *"noblesse de robe."* Since the French Revolution, the dominant idea of separation of powers has effectively kept judges from overstepping their bounds, so as to protect the core of the judicial function.[54]

Germany

In Germany, there is a long tradition of judges serving high-profile nonjudicial functions. For example, Roman Herzog held the office of president of Germany (a largely ceremonial role) from 1994 to 1999 as a member of the center-right Christian Democratic Union (CDU). Prior to this political office, Herzog served as a judge of the German Constitutional Court (*Bundesverfassungsgericht*). He was appointed to the federal court in 1983 and, from 1987 to 1994, served as the president of the Constitutional Court. He went straight from this post to the presidency of the country.

Nonjudicial functions are generally regulated by statute. For example, a judge may act as chairman in conciliation agencies and in independent agencies pursuant to the Federal Personnel Representation Act (*Bundespesonalvertretungsgesetz*).[55] Additionally, a judge can act as a conciliator in disputes between associations or between the latter and third parties.[56] A judge may only be granted permission to act additionally as an arbitrator or to give an expert opinion in arbitration proceedings when the parties in the arbitration agreement jointly designate her or when she is appointed by an agency that is not a party to the proceeding. Such permission must be refused if at the time of the decision, the judge is seized of the case.[57] Furthermore, "a professor of law or of political science who has civil servant status and who is also a judge may draw up expert legal opinions and give legal advice with the permission of the highest public authority administering the courts." This permission may only be granted where there is no fear that official interests may be impaired.[58] A judge may "undertake research and give lessons at a scientific institution of higher education, at a public teaching institution, or at an official teaching institution and perform duties in matters concerned with examination."[59] Finally, statutory provision can be made to the effect that, where the situation in the labor market is such that there is an exceptional shortage of applicants and consequently an urgent public interest in employing larger numbers of candidates for the public service, a judge may, on application, be granted unpaid leave for a duration of one to six years. During the period for which permission has been granted, she must refrain from engaging in additional paid activities and only engage in paid activities pursuant the law without infringing her official duties.[60] Extrajudicial professional commitments are limited by the Federal Personnel Representation Act, read in conjunction with the Federal Civil Service Act.[61] Clearly German judges face significant limitations on nonjudicial activity, but these are largely comparable to other civil servants.

Other Examples

Israel

As in other common law jurisdictions, judges in Israel routinely lead commissions of inquiry. High-profile examples include the Kahan Commission, which investigated the conduct of troops in the 1982 Lebanon war; a commission to inquire into the Gaza flotilla incident, in which the armed forces killed several Turkish activists; and the Agranat

Commission, which investigated the Yom Kippur War.[62] The latter commission in particular delved deeply into issues of military tactics and operations, far afield from the normal expertise of judges.

Canada

Canada also regularly relies on judges to participate in commissions of inquiry.[63] On occasion, such activities have led to controversy. In 2003, retired Supreme Court Justice John Gomery was named to lead an inquiry into allegations of corruption and mismanagement in a federal sponsorship program and to formulate positive recommendations. The ultimate report, which implicated Prime Minister Jean Chretien, led to significant controversy and was characterized as overly partisan activity. When Chretien engaged in legal action to clear his name, the Federal Court ultimately quashed the finding of the inquiry.[64] In another case, controversy erupted over the chief justice's involvement in the award of the Order of Canada to a doctor who performed abortions.[65]

Yet such controversies have not reduced the practice of judicial service in commissions. It is particularly common for retired judges to play this role, as illustrated by a recent appointment to head an inquiry into so-called queue-jumping in the public health system in Alberta.[66]

Australia

Judges in Australia have a long tradition of engaging in a number of nonjudicial functions, including sitting on the Law Reform Commission,[67] presiding over the Australian Competition Tribunal,[68] and taking on various executive tasks. At least three members of the senior judiciary have served as ambassadors, including Owen Dixon, who served as ambassador to the United States during the crucial years of World War II before returning to the bench and becoming one of the great chief justices in Australian history.[69] Judges regularly serve as leaders of the Administrative Appeals Tribunal, which is an administrative body. And recently the chief justice of the New South Wales Supreme Court was named as appointed chairman of Australian Broadcasting Corporation.[70]

This practice has prompted a nuanced jurisprudence and some good academic commentary, including a recent contribution from Chief Justice R. S. French.[71] The courts in at least one state have taken the position that sitting judges should not be able to sit on extrajudicial government bodies, as it might undermine public confidence in the judiciary.[72] There has also been discussion over whether the proper role of judges might vary depending on circumstances, with a potentially greater role in wartime or emergency.[73]

Australian law defines judicial power as involving a dispute to be resolved by a binding decision applying specified legal criteria to ascertained facts.[74] In cases refining this test, Australian courts have found that judicial engagement in some inquiry-type functions is incompatible with the judicial role.[75] One distinction in Australian law is between nonjudicial tasks conferred upon the office of the judge and those conferred upon an individual judge in her personal capacity—the so-called *persona designata* exception. Courts tend to ask whether the conferral of the function in a personal capacity will undermine the performance of judicial functions or the appearance of independence.[76]

For example, in the case of *Wilson v. Minister for Aboriginal and Torres Strait Islander Affairs* (1997), the court considered whether a sitting federal judge could be nominated, in his personal capacity, to provide a report to the government as part of a scheme of external evaluation of Aboriginal claims for preservation of particular lands. The court found the scheme to violate the separation of powers, as it involved the judge in a function that was essentially political in character.[77]

South Africa

South African judges sometimes lead commission of inquiry.[78] In one notable case, the South African Special Investigating Units and Special Tribunals Act (SIU Act) empowered the president to set up special units, which included judges, to investigate corruption.[79] In *South African Association of Personal Injury Lawyers v. Heath*, the Constitutional Court found that the functions conferred on a judge by the SIU Act compromised the separation of the courts from other branches of government.[80] Citing several Australian cases, the court argued that the scheme undermined the independence of the judiciary.

Other Common Law Jurisdictions

Judges in South Asia are among the most respected figures in government, and hence they are sometimes called upon to take on very high-profile nonjudicial tasks.[81] As mentioned above, judges have served as heads of state in Pakistan, Nepal, and Bangladesh, and a judge in Sri Lanka was recently appointed to a cabinet post.[82] Judges in India have headed the Press Council, a body that serves as a press watchdog; the Human Rights Panel of West Bengal;[83] and the Competition Tribunal.[84]

The activity of these tribunals has generated some tensions with the judiciary. Because judges in India must retire at age sixty-five but can serve thereafter on specialized tribunals until at least age sixty-seven, some judges have started to develop substantive expertise in particular areas of law, so as to seem well qualified for tribunal work. This is a classic example of the tension between investment in individual reputation building and collective reputation building: the cherry-picking of cases in some fields naturally means that other types of cases get less attention.

Indian judges also routinely serve as heads of commissions of inquiry, including cases involving foreign policy, such as when a former chief justice was sent to the investigate the change of power in the Maldives in 2012.[85] That same year, a retired justice of the Supreme Court aroused controversy by engaging in an extensive debate in print over the merits of a decision in which he had been involved.[86]

Pakistan's judiciary has likewise been involved in commissions investigating such matters as the causes and circumstances of the 1971 civil war,[87] the sheltering and killing of Osama bin Laden in Abbotabad,[88] and the murder of a journalist that had reported on Al-Qaeda.[89] In one notable case, a two-judge panel of the Pakistani Supreme Court heard corruption allegations against the court itself, gave a verdict, and found the court and its judges not guilty![90]

In the Gambia, a Court of Appeal judge was recently appointed as attorney general and minister of justice.[91] And other countries use judges regularly for commissions of inquiry.[92]

Other Civil Law Jurisdictions in Europe

In Italy, nonjudicial functions are regulated by statute—in particular, the law of judicial organization (*ordinamento giudiziario*). Most enforcement, however, is left to the Italian Judicial Council. For example, a judge may only be granted permission to act as an arbitrator or give an expert opinion in arbitration proceedings by the Judicial Council (Consiglio Superiore della Magistratura). Furthermore, a judge may participate in the management of a public charity institution but is not allowed to receive any fees or remuneration.[93] A judge may undertake research and give instruction at a scientific institution of higher education, at a public teaching institution, or at an official teaching institution and perform duties in matters concerned with examination. Some political functions are also expressly allowed: judges can serve in the Judicial Council or as senators.[94]

The Italian judiciary has become involved in some nonjudicial roles. To a large extent, the nominally strict rules provided in the statute law are diluted by the practices of the Italian Judicial Council, which routinely grants permission to judges who wish to engage in extrajudicial activities. Italian judges and prosecutors have been active in party politics and have served in both the executive and legislative branches. This may be an example of the dynamic we identify above, in which the regulators are captured by judges who wish to enhance their reputations with external audiences.

A similar observation can be made for Spain and Portugal. In both countries, nonjudicial functions are regulated by law (the Estatuto dos Magistrados Judiciais in Portugal and Ley Orgánica del Poder Judicial in Spain). These statutes broadly impede judges' ability to serve in nonjudicial functions but also allow the local judicial council to make exceptions.[95] The practice of these councils, which are dominated by judges, shapes the involvement of judges in nonjudicial roles.

In Spain and Portugal, several judges have served in the executive branch, usually as minister of justice, as heads of agencies within the ministry of justice or ministry of interior, or on committees of experts for legislative reforms. These situations typically require exceptions granted by the local judicial council. Judicial involvement in the legislative branch, as congresspersons or senators, is less common. But the overall pattern seems to be one in which the formal restrictions are undermined through capture of the nominal regulator—the judicial council.

Other Civil Law Jurisdictions in Latin America

In Latin America, judicial activities are defined by organic statutes on judicial power.[96] These laws tend to be strict, but the practice varies with the political context and the role played by judicial councils. For example, in Mexico, judges are only allowed to engage in nonjudicial functions if not remunerated.[97] But involvement in political or quasi-political activities is managed by the Federal Judicial Council (Consejo de la Judicatura Federal). In particular, the role of the Electoral Court, in which judges can challenge the results of federal elections of legislators and the president, has been controversial.[98]

An identical situation is found in Argentina. The role of both the Judicial Council (Consejo de la Magistratura) and the Supreme Court has been significant in expanding nonjudicial functions in an environment with nominally strict statutory rules. Some judges have become famous for performing seemingly executive functions: an example is Judge

Norberto Oyarbide, who has served in prominent investigative roles.[99] At the same time, judges investigating political figures have sometimes been removed by the judicial councils in a politicized environment.[100]

Brazil is no different. The judicial council (Conselho Nacional de Justiça) has struggled to effectively limit nonjudicial functions, with corruption and nepotism being a serious concern. Although judges cannot legally participate in politics,[101] they play an important role in practice. Judicial associations are very active and shape relevant areas of public policy; judges can be involved with outside organizations but cannot be remunerated.[102]

In short, Latin American jurisdictions are similar to European civil law countries in their treatment of nonjudicial functions. Strict statutory prohibitions are softened by a more flexible practice under local judicial councils or supreme courts. Corruption seems to be more of an issue in this context than in Europe.

A special note should be made of the Bolivian case. In 2005, the president and vice president of Bolivia were forced to resign because of mass protests; and the chief justice became the interim president. He presided over elections, leading to the historic election of President Evo Morales. Yet, shortly afterward, Congress attempted to impeach the chief justice because of clashes with President Morales. There is, it seems, a real risk of politicization that comes from nonjudicial functions of a certain type.

China

Nonjudicial functions in the People's Republic of China (PRC) are regulated by statute—in particular, the Law on Judges of PRC. Article 15 provides that "judges cannot serve concurrently as members of the Standing Committee of China's National People's Congress; or serve concurrently in agencies, the procuracy, enterprises and institutions, or serve concurrently as lawyers." Article 17 adds that "judges cannot act as lawyers, as agents *ad litem* or defense counsel within two years after their departure from the court." Clearly PRC judges are quite limited in their ability to pursue nonjudicial functions. In fact, in 2004, the PRC Supreme Court published a notice prohibiting in-service judges from acting as arbitrators.

There are, however, a few exceptions that reflect some of the possibilities we have discussed. The Code of Judicial Ethics, promulgated by the Supreme Court, provides that judges may engage in writing and teaching in their spare time and receive legitimate compensation for such activities. However, the Code also states that judges should not engage in activities that may conflict with judicial impartiality and the judicial function. Recent revisions to this Code are quite specific: judges may not engage in media interviews without prior approval from judicial superiors, cannot join for-profit organizations, and must decline meals or gifts that will violate requirements of honesty and integrity.

Finally, the involvement of the Chinese judiciary in the administration of the courts is regulated by the Law on Judges of PRC, Rule 6. This rule states that "besides judicial functions, the president, justice clerk, members of judicial committees, chief judges, and associate chief judges of divisions, shall, in addition to the judicial functions and duties, perform other functions and duties commensurate with their posts." In practice, the judicial leadership of Chinese courts will typically play roles in the Communist Party.

It is apparent that nonjudicial functions in the PRC are quite restricted by governmental regulations. One possible explanation is that the Chinese judiciary does not have the political influence and prestige to relax these regulations. Supply and demand of nonjudicial functions are weak in an environment where the judiciary faces other significant challenges, not least of which is corruption. As institutional reform takes place in the PRC and the courts become more independent and less corrupt, we might see growing demand for nonjudicial functions that might challenge the current strict regulations. But such a shift seems a long way off at the moment.

The Philippines

Nonjudicial functions have been at the center of a major controversy regarding the judiciary in the Philippines. In 1984, Ferdinand Marcos created a Judiciary Development Fund (JDF), funded with court fees and bar exam fees, to supplement the budget of the judiciary. The JDF was administered by the Supreme Court and was to contribute 80 percent of its distributions to employee salaries, with the rest going to facilities. While this enhanced the fiscal autonomy of the judiciary, the JDF involved the judiciary directly in procurement and management, with associated opportunities for favoritism and even corruption. There was, historically, relatively little outside scrutiny of the fund.

In the early 2000s, a group of disgruntled court staff complained that their salaries were too low and managed to get a congressman interested in their case.[103] After the court refused to provide him with information, the congressman accused the chief justice of illegal use of public funds. The court reacted quite defensively. An independent investigation found very lax oversight of the use of JDF funds. The congressman then responded with an impeachment complaint against Chief Justice Hilario Davide that resulted in several months of hearings. Before the complaint could be transmitted to the Senate, the court stepped in, declaring the impeachment complaint unconstitutional and enjoining the House and Senate from acting on it.[104] The court relied on a constitutional provision stating that no impeachment proceeding could be initiated twice within one year against the same official. Another complaint against the chief had just been dismissed.

The administrative responsibilities of managing budgets and personnel are clearly nonjudicial in nature. Yet proponents of judicial independence often argue that they must be placed with the courts themselves. The Philippine example illustrates some of the dangers of this approach: by burdening courts with tasks in which they have no comparative advantage, there is a risk that courts will perform their job poorly, exposing them to criticism and controversy. The JDF continues to be a source of controversy in the Philippines; while the court has become much more transparent about the expenditures, Congress has continued to scrutinize the fund, and accusations of pork-barrel spending continue to arise on occasion. At the same time, internal control of budgets and resources provides senior judges, especially the chief justice, with a set of powerful tools to manage the collective reputation of the judiciary.

Conclusion

If judges are doing their jobs well, they will be confronted with opportunities to become involved in functions outside the courtroom. We have articulated a positive theory of such judicial involvement in nonjudicial functions, emphasizing the interaction of demand (why judges want to perform such roles) and supply (why political and social actors want judges to perform nonjudicial functions). In this context, the interaction of supply and demand may create a potential market failure due to external costs and the possibility of demand-induced supply. As a consequence, some regulation is appropriate. Self-regulation seems ineffective given the likelihood of capture, and we have shown how, in several cases, judicial councils were able to undermine strict regulation. (We will provide a deeper analysis of judicial councils in chapter 4.) Most legal systems seem to take an approach consistent with our theory, limiting judicial involvement in some way. All else equal, recognition judiciaries, which tend to enjoy greater reputation with external audiences, may play a more visible role in nonjudicial functions. But the range of regulatory approaches is fairly broad, suggesting there is no universal optimum.

The possibility of judicial involvement in nonjudicial functions creates an interesting set of challenges for courts, since it can induce serious contradictions between incentives for individual reputation building and incentives for collective reputation building. Managing these tensions requires some regulatory intervention, and as we show in chapter 4, judicial councils are frequently called on to play a role in this regard. We do not, in this analysis, wrestle with normative questions about the ideal level of judicial involvement in nonjudicial functions, in part because we do not start with an essentialist view of the judicial role. We recognize that such roles have evolved over time and are likely to continue to evolve. Conceptions about the role of judges differ dramatically across countries as well. Our empirical survey has shown, though, that there has been a trend toward expansion of the ambit of judicial decision making and roles in many different traditions. This is perhaps unsurprising in an era of growing judicialization of public policy.

FOUR

The Selection and Monitoring of Judges: The Spread of Judicial Councils

Judges everywhere strive to have a reputation for judicial independence, and the selection of judges is a central consideration in most theories of ensuring independence as well as accountability.[1] Judges who are dependent in some way upon the person who appoints them cannot be relied upon to deliver neutral, legitimate, high-quality decisions. But there are a great variety of ways to appoint judges around the world: some are selected based on exams; others through political processes; and some, particularly in the United States, are even elected.[2] The diversity of systems of judicial selection suggests that there is no consensus on the best means to guarantee independence or quality.[3]

At the same time, there is a trend toward insulating judicial selection from partisan politics. In the United States, this is reflected in the growing scholarly consensus in favor of "merit selection."[4] In other countries, it is reflected in the adoption of judicial councils, an international "best practice" designed to help ensure judicial independence and external accountability. Judicial councils are institutions in which multiple stakeholders come together to govern the judiciary, taking on various tasks that might include selecting judges, disciplining them, managing them, and promoting them. Proponents of judicial councils argue that they are better able to pick judges on the basis of merit rather than politics. We thus see the emergence of a new orthodoxy in many different jurisdictions and legal traditions: merit selection of judges is good and other methods are retrograde. Because there are few common metrics to evaluate the comparative independence or quality of judiciaries, the new scholarly consensus is largely theoretical, built on anecdotal rather than systematic evidence.[5]

It is worth emphasizing that, along with our account of hybrid systems in chapter 2, the spread of judicial councils undermines the classic distinction between civil and common law systems, embodied in career and recognition models of appointment systems. As we discussed in chapter 1, these two structures are based on very different logics and produce different reputational incentives for the courts. But the ubiquity of institutional reforms of judicial appointment processes should help us dismiss the idea that legal traditions represent unchanging institutional configurations. And the fact that systems as diverse as those in the United Kingdom and Mongolia have adopted judicial councils suggests that something is going on that defies traditional categorizations of legal systems. There seem to be forces far greater than tradition at work.

We have already argued that the distinction between career judiciaries and recognition judiciaries is sometimes misleading, and this is apparent when one looks at the selection and appointment of judges. In Britain, judges traditionally tended to be selected from among those who served as barristers and later as Queen's Counsel (or King's Counsel). All current justices of the UK Supreme Court (but one[6]) were recruited from the English, Scottish, and Northern Ireland appellate courts (the High Court of Justice, Court of Appeal, and Court of Session, respectively). Some scholars have seen this as a version of the career model.[7] In Israel, most appointments to the Supreme Court are individuals who have served previously as clerks. Although India's constitution provides that the composition of the Supreme Court can include lawyers of high recognition, it is overwhelmingly dominated by the senior judges from the states' high courts.[8] In the United States, all but one member of the current Supreme Court served previously in appellate courts, confirming a trend established long ago.[9] These recognition judiciaries have some careerist elements.

To be sure, these "career" models are distinct from the classical bureaucratic model in many ways, as noted in chapters 2 and 3. First, career judiciaries are fundamentally dominated by a bureaucratic approach to the career, in which apolitical seniority considerations are central, encouraging the development of collective reputation. Recognition judiciaries, on the other hand, have an informal or unstructured "career" mingled with a selection mechanism that is more politicized in nature and hence amenable to the cultivation of individual reputation. Second, judges in career judiciaries have a judicial position as the formal first step in the career, while judges in recognition systems start with a non-judicial position. This allows for different levels of screening. Finally, transfers to courts of equal seniority are generally part of the career path in career judiciaries but not in recognition judiciaries.

If we look at the supreme courts of US states, we see a wide range of different selection mechanisms, all within the broad category of recognition judiciaries. Table 4.1 presents the data and shows that merit selection is the most popular mechanism. (Note, though, the size of these courts is fairly stable across states and across selection mechanisms; we also find that there is little variation in the average age of the current justices across US states.)

Table 4.1 American states' supreme courts

State	Court size	Mechanism of appointment
Alabama	9	Election
Alaska	5	Merit selection
Arizona	5	Merit selection
Arkansas	7	Election
California	7	Appointment
Colorado	7	Merit selection
Connecticut	7	Merit selection
Delaware	5	Merit selection
Florida	7	Merit selection
Georgia	7	Election
Hawaii	5	Merit selection
Idaho	5	Election
Illinois	7	Election
Indiana	5	Merit selection
Iowa	9	Merit selection
Kansas	7	Merit selection
Kentucky	7	Election
Louisiana	8	Election
Maine	7	Appointment
Maryland	7	Merit selection
Massachusetts	7	Appointment
Michigan	7	Election
Minnesota	7	Election
Mississippi	9	Election
Missouri	7	Merit selection
Montana	7	Election
Nebraska	7	Merit selection
Nevada	5	Election

Table 4.1 (*continued*)

State	Court size	Mechanism of appointment
New Hampshire	5	Appointment
New Jersey	7	Appointment
New Mexico	5	Merit selection
New York	7	Merit selection
North Carolina	7	Election
North Dakota	5	Election
Ohio	7	Election
Oklahoma (civil)	9	Merit selection
Oklahoma (criminal)	5	Merit selection
Oregon	7	Election
Pennsylvania	7	Election
Rhode Island	5	Appointment
South Carolina	5	Appointment
South Dakota	5	Merit selection
Tennessee	5	Election
Texas (civil)	9	Election
Texas (criminal)	9	Election
Utah	5	Merit selection
Vermont	5	Merit selection
Virginia	7	Appointment
Washington	9	Election
West Virginia	5	Election
Wisconsin	7	Election
Wyoming	5	Merit selection

Source: Websites of the American states' supreme courts.

From our comparative perspective, the selection of judges is a crucial mechanism for screening agents and thus indirectly affects the environment for building reputation. People who wish to become judges must invest their time and energy in certain activities to develop their reputations. If selection is dominated by a political process, political investment will be the most important; if it is a bureaucratic process, a different type of effort will be required. Judicial councils, by nature, are usually mixed bodies involving different types of audiences. They prevent any one audience from dominating, while also providing close monitoring of the judiciary.

This chapter describes the global spread of judicial councils and provides a theory of their formation and features. By our estimate, over 60 percent of countries have some form of judicial council—up from 10 percent thirty years ago.[10] We also provide some evidence as to whether different designs of judicial council affect the judicial reputation for quality. Although we find that there is little relationship between council adoption and quality, this chapter argues that the eternal struggle for balance between independence and accountability ensures that judicial councils will continue to be a locus of institutional reform. Yet there are limits to the efficacy of institutional solutions to problems of judicial independence. Although councils serve as an arena for contestation for various groups with an interest in judicial performance, they do not by themselves guarantee the substantive outputs of independence and quality.

This chapter is organized as follows. First, we provide an economic theory of the formation of judicial councils and identify some of the dimensions along which they differ. Next, we test the extent to which different designs of judicial council affect judicial quality. We find that there is little relationship between council design and quality. Our theory nevertheless offers a positive explanation for why judicial councils remain attractive institutions. Finally, we discuss the national experience of several legal systems in light of our theory, and we conclude with a discussion about the implications of the analysis for state judicial selection.

The Tension between Accountability and Independence

A long and established literature argues that the ideal of judicial independence is a crucial quality of legal systems and indeed inherent in the notion of judging.[11] Naturally, the ideal is not always met—for it remains the case that in every legal system judges are appointed and employed by the state. It would be unusual indeed if judges did *not* have a role in implementing social policy, broadly conceived.[12] Typically, then, in democracies, the degree of judicial independence actually granted reflects broad choices of the regime. It may make sense, for example, to have relatively greater judicial independence in the economic sphere so as to maintain credible commitments for investment. Alternatively, liberal polities may wish to use judicial power to ensure a zone of autonomy for individuals.

The delegation of power to judges implies some need for judicial accountability. While judicial independence has been widely studied,[13] accountability has been the subject of much less inquiry.[14] Accountability requires that the judiciary as a whole maintain some level of responsiveness to society, as well as a high level of professionalism and quality on the part of its members.

Judicial councils are bodies that are designed to insulate the functions of appointment, promotion, and discipline of judges from the partisan political process, while ensuring some level of accountability. Judicial councils lie somewhere in between the polar extremes of letting judges manage their own affairs and the alternative of complete political control of appointments, promotions, and discipline. The first model of judicial self-management arguably errs too far on the side of independence and typically a collective form of reputation. The alternative of pure political control may make judges *too* accountable in the sense that they will consider the preferences of their political principals and external audiences in the course of deciding specific cases. There is a wide variety of models of councils, in which the composition and competences reflect the concern about the judiciary in a specific context, balancing demands for accountability and independence.

While adequate institutions might enhance judicial independence and minimize the problems of a politicized judiciary, increasing the independence enjoyed by judges risks creating the opposite problem— overjudicializing public policy.[15] There is a risk of judges with a reputation for independence being called on to decide ever more important cases beyond their traditional purview. It is our view that the periodic reforms of judicial appointments and management that we observe within and across countries reflect a dialectic tension between the need to depoliticize the judiciary and the trend toward judicializing politics. Independence is needed to provide the benefits of judicial decision making; once given independence, judges are useful for resolving a wider range of more important disputes. As the judiciary begins to take over functions from democratic processes, however, the pressure for greater accountability mounts.

Figure 4.1 presents a stylized summary of the recurrent calibration between independence and external accountability, synthesizing the different experiences discussed above. Beginning in the upper right corner, a judiciary has little independence or influence. When judges carry little weight over public policy and politics, concerns over independence tend to dominate and reformers may push for a move from a politically dependent weak judiciary to a strong, self-regulated judiciary. This shift gives rise to a judiciary that has some control over its own affairs though is not politicized. Frequently, though not inevitably, judges use this independence to increase their influence over public policy, perhaps as a result of exogenous events. This is represented by a shift to the lower left corner of the figure. However, once politics is judicialized in a significant way, pressures arise for greater political accountability, represented by a shift to the lower right. The judiciary remains strong but is more subject

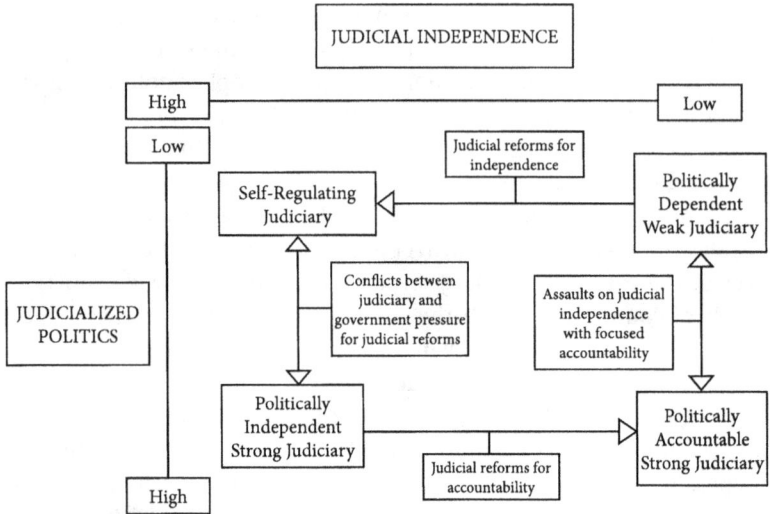

4.1 Controlling the judiciary

to oversight and control. As accountability becomes focused only toward a small group of principals and as assaults on judicial independence become more successful, we may in some circumstances observe a move from a politically accountable strong judiciary back to politically dependent weak judiciary, as in a rising authoritarian regime. The right side of the figure thus represents a politicized judiciary and the lower half a judicialized politics. This dynamic framework provides a tool for understanding the various institutional adjustments observed in different countries, which we will develop in case studies later in this chapter.

Note that we are not asserting that movement across the various zones of the figure is inevitable. Institutional configurations can be stable for long periods of time, and there is no necessary condition that judiciaries must shift their location in the figure. What we believe the figure does capture, however, is the potential for cycling among different models of judicial governance and the nature of the pressures that judiciaries will face in particular configurations. Judicial independence and accountability may tend toward instability.

When problems of cycling occur in governance, institutions tend to be unstable. The cycling problem was, in some sense, first identified by Aristotle in the context of his classic analysis of types of government. He thought dictatorships would generate resistance from powerful groups that would form an oligarchy, which in turn would be replaced by a democracy. But democracy too would lead to chaos and calls for a new dictatorship. Aristotle's solution to this problem was to create a mixed government that would allow representatives of various social forces in different institutional capacities. Similarly, a multipartite governance body may provide an attractive solution to problems of judicial governance under situations in which calibration is constantly needed when new problems arise.

An Agency Theory of Judicial Councils

Judicial Councils as Intermediaries between Principal and Agent

In this section, we use the principal-agent model laid out in the introduction to develop a theory of judicial councils. If judges are the agents and society is the principal, on whose behalf the judges exercise power, we are faced with the standard problem of information asymmetry: as a judge's expertise increases, her potential effectiveness increases as well, but her accountability decreases.

A judicial council is an intermediate body between the society and judges. It might be seen as analogous to a board of directors in a corporation.[16] Just as shareholders utilize a board as a system to monitor the managers of a corporation, the public may wish to set up (and pay for) a judicial council to manage judicial agents. Regardless of whether collective or individual reputation predominates, the principal will benefit from having a specialized monitor. Like a board, the judicial council might have a representative appointment system, in which different stakeholders have agents who then negotiate over governance, in order to minimize possible rents created by asymmetric information. The council thus serves as an intermediary trustee whose role is both to exercise expert oversight and to filter out political influence.[17]

Analogous to a corporate setting, one can think of two different types of "shareholders" within the principal: an uninformed and uninterested majority made up of members of the general public, for whom the opportunity costs of inquiring about judges are high, and very well-informed minorities with leverage to influence agents. The well-informed minority might include politicians, interest groups that would like favorable decisions by courts, and lawyers. The principle of judicial independence aims to avoid possible capture by the minority and also to align the interests of the judges with those of the majority, the general public. But given the asymmetry of information between the vast majority on one hand and the minority (as well as the judges) on the other hand, an intermediate body might be necessary to limit opportunism and minimize agency costs. The judicial council serves as just such a body. Its role is to limit agency costs and reduce the likelihood that any particular minority will use the court system to its advantage vis-à-vis the vast majority of the population.

A multimember judicial council can be considered a kind of governance technology. Before it was invented, appointments of judges were usually handled by politicians (such as a president or minister of justice) or else by judges themselves. Each of these options has its own problems. By including appointees from multiple constituencies, in theory, the judicial council helps prevent domination by any one of them.

At the same time, the nature of specialization creates a new problem—namely, the capture of the judicial council by the judiciary itself or by an external body that wishes to manipulate the judiciary. This is the classic question of "who guards the guardians?"[18] The demand for limiting agency costs, combined with the possibility of capture, suggests that judicial councils might be unstable bodies. Periodic reforms may be required to correct deviations when a judiciary becomes either too accountable or too independent. We imagine that judicial governance requires, to some degree, learning by doing and that as new agency problems materialize, governance structures will be under pressure to change in an attempt to rectify them.[19]

The structure of judicial councils is influenced by the interaction between preferences, incentives, and politicization. When judges are subject to any form of political scrutiny, we should expect to see some alignment between the preferences of judges and politicians. (This might be lagged because of long-term appointments.) This may take the form of what we might call ex ante politicization, in which judges are screened for political criteria, or ex post politicization, through pressure or corruption after the judge is appointed. Our conjecture is that a judicial council is designed to reduce both ex ante and ex post politicization, but councils may have different emphases depending on the institutional problems they face. In stable systems such as the United States, in which ex post interference with judicial independence is rare and frowned upon, the council may play a more important role in screening at the appointment stage. On the other hand, where norms of judicial autonomy are less developed, the council may play a greater role in preventing ex post politicization through control over promotion, management, and discipline.

Judicial Incentives

To understand why councils might be effective, we first need to understand the preferences and incentive structures of the judges as agents. As
the prominent American appeals court judge Richard Posner has argued,
we ought to begin by assuming that judges have the same set of preferences as everybody else.[20] Obviously judges, like others, care about their
income. They may, however, be a bit more risk-averse and care more
about nonmonetary payoffs than the average individual; this would explain why they select a stable, prestigious judicial career instead of the
more lucrative practice of law. This might lead us to expect judges to be
sensitive to changes in prestige or social influence and to shifts in risk.
For example, judges might be worried about threats to "judicial independence" not only for instrumental reasons but because such threats
undermine judicial status and dignity.

To understand why an intermediate body may be a useful mechanism for controlling agents, we need to consider alternatives that might
operate to restrain judicial opportunism. Two standard alternatives in
the literature on institutional design are markets and direct external
control by the principal. Standard market-oriented mechanisms do not
work to constrain judges because judges are state officials operating in
a highly subsidized monopoly (the court system) without market discipline. While individuals can opt out of the state-provided system and
use alternative dispute resolution mechanisms, such behavior is unlikely
to have a significant effect on the welfare of the judiciary (even though
in some jurisdictions, retired judges can serve as "rent-a-judges" dispens-
ing private justice). Another possible mechanism is direct control by
the principals, through the hiring and firing of judges. This is difficult
because of the information asymmetry inherent in judging: external actors typically have trouble verifying whether judges have actually followed the law or not. Furthermore, the threat of external enforcement
potentially reduces judicial independence and therefore is constrained
through structural insulation of the judiciary. For these reasons, we cannot rely on external or market-oriented mechanisms to limit opportunism in the judicial system.

Judicial careers are structured differently in different parts of the
world, as we noted in chapter 1. In some countries, like Japan, judges tend
to operate in bureaucratic hierarchies and spend their entire careers in
the judiciary. Whoever controls advancement in this career hierarchy

is thus very important. For "recognition" judges, such as those in common law systems or those appointed to constitutional courts in civil law countries, prestige among the public or with other branches of government is very important, but once selected into the judiciary, these judges have relatively few opportunities for advancement. For this reason, they may be less sensitive to external pressures and performance evaluations from any source, including judicial councils.[21] We expect that judicial councils in common law countries will be more likely to have power over appointments rather than promotions, which are relatively rare.

Judicial Councils as Monitoring Devices

We view judicial councils as devices to reduce agency costs in the judiciary, although we do not assert that they are necessary or sufficient bodies to accomplish this task. In this section, we describe the membership of a prototypical council and the extent to which powers are shared among the courts and other branches of government.

The council is composed of three possible types: (1) members of the majority (laymen), (2) members of minorities that seek to capture the judicial agents (possibly including lawyers, politicians, and law professors), and (3) judges themselves. Extending the corporate law analogy, we might see judges as analogous to inside directors in a corporation, while the others represent shareholders and perhaps even independent directors. It is important to note that in most situations, distinguishing between laymen and politicians is impossible, since they are all usually appointed by other branches of government.[22] Judges on the council are typically appointed by the supreme court or by other courts, while lawyers are appointed by the law society or bar association.[23] The council is theoretically accountable to the public, but different accountability rules will make the council more or less likely to be captured by the judiciary (which might promote professional interests) or minority shareholders (who might promote lobbying or minority interests).

We expect that the mechanism of appointment of judicial members in the council will matter for outcomes. In some cases, all members of the council are appointed by the same body (for example, the parliament); in other cases, different bodies of government intervene in the appointment process. A more heterogeneous council will result when different bodies are involved in the appointment of the council, either by a sequential process of nomination and confirmation (members of the council must appeal to different constituencies) or by a quota system where different bodies of government appoint a predefined number of members.

The size, appointment, and composition of judicial councils are important design dimensions. It is often argued that judges should constitute the majority of the members of the council to enhance independence. Even when the judges are not a numerical majority in the council, however, they might have a dominant or preponderant role. To start with, most members of a judicial council must rely on information provided by the judiciary itself. In addition, a judicial council does not exert direct control over the judiciary (which would hurt the independence of judiciary) but exercises a configuration of powers that mix authority and accountability. This configuration is usually complex and full of tasks that call for expertise by judges. Furthermore, as between judicial and nonjudicial members of the council, asset specificity is asymmetric, meaning that judges may have particularly strong incentives to represent judicial interests on the council. After their service on the council, judges return to their professional careers inside the judiciary, whereas nonjudges will go back to their careers outside the judiciary, which may or may not have any relationship with judicial management issues. Perhaps this is why we observe very little correlation between the number of judges on the council and the level of independence.

Institutional Environment

The role and importance of the judicial council depend very much on other aspects of the institutional environment. Depending on the power and preferences of the judiciary, the monitoring activity of the council can be more or less extensive. Take performance measurement, for example. Even apart from the technical challenges of devising an adequate metric to evaluate the inherently complex phenomenon of judicial performance, judges might react differently to being measured, depending on how it is likely to affect their careers and role in the community.

In addition, performance measures applied by a judicial council reduce the influence and power of senior judges by limiting their ability and discretion to shape the judiciary for the next generation. Before the creation of a judicial council, the senior judiciary could claim a near monopoly on the expertise required to evaluate judges. After a council is introduced, there might be competition for control among the different actors within the council. For these reasons, transplanting any given model of a judicial council and ignoring the local institutional environment might generate unexpected results.

At the same time, demand for a judicial council is intrinsically linked to the reputation, importance, and functioning of the judicial system as a whole. The more extensive judges' powers, the more important it becomes to address any potential conflict between the common good and judicial incentives. But the less important the judiciary is in a given institutional setup, the less need there is for achieving the appropriate balance between independence and accountability. We expect that judicial councils will have greater competences but fewer judges when judges have a good deal of power. This is because there will be external demand from the public and other constituencies for monitoring of the relatively powerful judiciary. Where judges have less power, outside actors may be more accepting of a council with a majority of judges but seek to assign the council fewer competences. In our analysis that follows, we use the presence or absence of judicial review as a proxy for a more or less important judiciary.[24]

What Do Councils Do?

Competences and Composition

In this section, we categorize the function and structure of judicial councils and note that they operate in very different legal environments.[25] Broadly speaking, judicial councils have three important competences:

1. Housekeeping functions (managing budget, material resources, and operations)
2. Appointment of judges
3. Performance evaluation (promotion, discipline, removal and retention of judges, and judicial salaries)

Applying the agency framework, we note that housekeeping functions seem to be designed to prevent moral hazard: by insulating the judiciary from management of resources, the council prevents corruption or distraction from the core task of judging. Selection processes are designed to deal with problems of adverse selection: we need to screen those who will exercise significant power. Performance evaluation addresses moral hazard in that it prevents judges from shirking, but within our framework, it also contributes to the cultivation of reputation by providing information to particular audiences.

For all these functions, the key factor is effective calibration between judicial independence and external accountability. This calibration can be achieved, for example, by the composition or membership of the council, by the appointment mechanism, or by sharing certain functions with other branches of the government or other bodies (even the public in the case of elected judges). We do not assert that there is a universally optimal balance between independence and accountability but understand that there is a limit to how far one can move in either direction within democracies.[26] Moving too far in either direction may trigger pressures for a shift as idealized in figure 4.1.

Whereas the first competence, housekeeping, is purely managerial, the second and third competences are related to career incentives and more directly contribute to judicial quality. Housekeeping functions deal with practical questions concerning the organization and running of the judiciary.[27] These functions can, of course, potentially affect judicial independence—for example, if material incentives are used to reward certain types of judges. Obviously managerial competences are also important for the efficiency of courts and, in that respect, shape the quality of the legal system. Nevertheless, the other two competences (appointment and performance evaluation) are more directly related to judicial career incentives. If institutions matter for judicial quality, they matter because of their impact on judicial incentives.[28]

The Interaction of Competence and Composition

We are particularly interested in whether composition correlates with competence. One hypothesis is that judges, particularly those in systems that emphasize collective reputation, will resist external regulation and control. Therefore if nonjudges are the majority on the council, we might observe that the council is given less substantive competence, but when judges are the majority, competences are high. A competing hypothesis is that judicial councils (a relatively late historical development) have been set up to control judges and ensure accountability. If this were the case, we should see the percentage of judges on the council *negatively* correlated with the extent of its competence.

We can frame this as the question of whether judicial councils are set up to ensure independence of judges *from* the principals or accountability *to* the principals (see figure 4.1). If judges are a majority on the council, the assumption is that judges utilize the council to exercise self-government and maintain independence. If judges are a minority on the council, the assumption is that the council is a device to constrain the judges and render them more accountable. These two types of councils reflect quite different goals.[29]

To summarize, judicial councils will vary in terms of their competencies and their composition. We view extensive competence of a judicial

Table 4.2 Competence and composition: Typology of judicial councils

Competences	Composition		
	Judges from supreme court dominate	Judges from lower courts dominate	Nonjudges dominate
Extensive (discipline, removal, promotion, appointments)	Strong hierarchical judicial council (Mexico, Thailand)	Strong nonhierarchical judicial council (Italy, France)	Politicized judicial council (Ecuador, Barbados, Singapore)
Intermediate (appointments only)	Hierarchical self-regulating judicial appointments commission (Bangladesh)	Nonhierarchical self-regulating judicial appointments commission (Belgium)	Judicial appointments commission (United States, United Kingdom, Canada, Netherlands, Germany)
Minimal (housekeeping functions)	Weak judicial council (Panama)	Weak judicial council (Brazil, Hungary)	Weak judicial council (Paraguay)

council as enhancing judicial accountability. We also follow the conventional wisdom that assumes that judicial majorities on the judicial council promote independence. Considering competences and composition, we can imagine several different configurations (see table 4.2). A judicial majority with extensive competences indicates a strong council, whereas a judicial minority limited to housekeeping functions is likely to be a weak, and possibly politicized, council. Nevertheless, the performance of the council will depend on whether or not the judges in the council behave as a homogeneous body. This is easily achieved when judges come from superior courts, since these judges tend to reinforce the judicial hierarchy. If the judges come from various different courts, there may be intrajudicial politics that prevent the judiciary from acting in unified fashion: we may sometimes observe the emergence of judicial associations or unions that provide a solution to collective action problems. Table 4.2 displays the various possible models along with some examples of their operation.

This discussion suggests that councils are not at all uniform. Local institutional problems, represented by the location in figure 4.1, will produce pressures for different types of councils in different circumstances. Even within a country, we may see variation over time as different institutional problems arise.

Case Studies

This section describes the operation of judicial councils in a number of different countries to determine whether our argument withstands scrutiny. Judicial councils as such were initially a European phenomenon: building on an earlier model, France established the first High Council of the Judiciary (Conseil Superieur de la Magistrature) in 1946,[30] followed by Italy in 1958.[31] But as we shall see, the American model of merit selection based on proposals by an expert committee is an older analogue. Our focus here is on a range of cases from various legal traditions.

United States

Judicial selection in the United States has gone through several waves.[32] In the early years of the nation, legislative appointment systems dominated. In the mid-nineteenth century, however, partisan elections were introduced in many states in response to concerns that judges were captured by special interest groups. From our perspective, this shift reflected the rise of the uninformed majority within the principal, as citizens responded to concerns of capture by a minority. However, partisan elections led to their own set of problems. Rather than truly arising from the people, judicial candidates came to be controlled by party bosses.[33]

In many American states, concern over traditional methods of judicial selection (either appointment by politicians or direct election by the public) led to the adoption of "merit commissions" to remove partisan politics from judicial appointments and base selection on merit.[34] These emerged as a model in the early twentieth century, reflecting the progressive movement's belief in technocratic government. Merit commissions can be seen as analogous to judicial councils, though their scope of activity may be more limited. Since in common law systems the judiciary is not a "career judiciary" in the civil law sense, there is not as much need for having an independent commission handle discipline, promotions, and reassignments; the more important moment of institutional choice is the initial appointment. Yet the basic institutional design—namely, setting up nonpartisan mixed bodies to screen and select judicial candidates—is identical to the judicial commission.

Sometimes called the "Missouri plan" (although some assert that it was first adopted in California) or "merit plan," this system features a nonpartisan judicial selection commission composed of judges, lawyers, and political appointees. (The percentage of nonlawyers is determined by law and ranges from 18 percent in Tennessee to over 50 percent in Hawaii.) A famous 1906 speech by Roscoe Pound inspired this institution, and it is consistent with early twentieth-century beliefs in the value of technocracy and administrative insulation from politics.[35]

In some states, the merit commission is exclusively responsible for nominating judges, while in other states, it sends a set of candidates from which the governor chooses appointees. Merit plan judges are typically subject to uncontested retention elections, which judges rarely lose.[36] While American states exhibit a variety of approaches, it is clear that the merit plan has become the dominant model within the United States. As Professor F. Andrew Hanssen put it, "There is today a strong consensus that, of all the procedures, the merit plan best insulates the state judiciary from partisan political pressure."[37] As of 1994, twenty-three states used merit plans for initial appointments to the supreme court,[38] with most states adopting these institutions in the 1960s and 1970s.[39]

A general assumption in the literature is that merit plan systems serve to expand judicial independence.[40] For example, Hanssen tests the effect of partisan division on appointment and retention systems, assuming that merit plan implementation correlates with independence.[41] He finds that, broadly speaking, states using merit plans tend to have higher levels of political competition (and hence more presumed demand for judicial independence) than those using partisan elections.[42] Hanssen also finds that states switch to merit plans when they have increased party competition and policy differences between parties. This is consistent with literature that emphasizes the role of partisan competition in incentivizing judicial independence.[43]

Nevertheless, we know of no study that has demonstrated an actual improvement in judicial independence or quality after the adoption of a merit plan, and the actual impact on judicial quality is debatable.[44] In a comprehensive review of the social-scientific literature, Malia Reddick concludes that there is little support for "proponents' claims that merit selection insulates judicial selection from political forces, makes judges accountable to the public, and identifies judges who are substantially different from judges chosen through other systems."[45]

We view the merit plan as a device to mediate between independence and accountability in accordance with our theory. As a common law country with judges who tend to be appointed relatively late in life, the United States has little need for independent bodies to engage in promotion of judges. Thus the commissions play a relatively limited role but one that focuses on the crucial locus of partisan pressure—namely, the appointment process. This illustrates the importance of understanding institutional variation in conditioning demand for the judicial council model.

Brazil

The design of the Brazilian judiciary has traditionally been decentralized, in a model greatly influenced by the United States.[46] Although decentralization has serious administrative and financial advantages, it has also created serious drawbacks in terms of effective disciplinary action against wayward judges and accountability of court administration (including nepotism in court staff appointments).[47]

Brazil's first judicial council was the National Council of the Magistracy (Conselho Nacional da Magistratura, or CNM), which was created through constitutional amendment in 1977[48] and established in 1979. This council had seven judges chosen by the federal Supreme Court out of its members. The primary function of the council was purely disciplinary, and it had no budget or administrative functions. The constitutional amendment was quite limited in empowering the council. At the time, Brazil was under a military dictatorship, and though it gave some formal powers to judges, the council was likely created to assert greater control over the judiciary.[49] The shift toward the CNM meant that judges had some formal control over their affairs, but in law and practice, this was quite limited. Rather, using the Supreme Court as a proxy, the military was able to restrain lower court judges while preserving nominal judicial autonomy.[50] The CNM served as an intermediate body to facilitate control of agents by the principal.

In 1985, the dictatorship fell. With the passage of the Brazilian Constitution of 1988, the CNM was eliminated, leaving judges self-governing and subject to virtually no oversight. Constitutional guarantees of independence were adopted and became effective. In addition, the complexity of the 1988 constitution delegated many types of controversies to the judiciary, including the so-called constitutionalization of private law through recognition of the social functions of property and contracts. While judges had formally enjoyed the power of constitutional review even under the former constitution, the actual exercise of the power was highly constrained. By constitutionalizing many aspects of public life, the 1988 constitution provided an opportunity structure for a major increase in judicial power.[51]

Judges utilized these new opportunities to expand their influence. In time, the combination of little oversight and expanded scope of activity led to increasingly judicialized politics.[52] This naturally produced demands for greater accountability. Many academics and even judges criticized the politicization of the judiciary in Brazil. Although there was agreement on the diagnosis, there was controversy over the best remedy to enhance accountability. Some associated the judicial council with the dictatorship; indeed, this was likely the reason for its abolition in 1988.[53]

A 2004 constitutional amendment introduced a new judicial council (Conselho Nacional de Justiça) with a very different composition than its predecessor: nine judges, two prosecutors, two lawyers, and two laymen appointed by the legislature.[54] The competences of the new council include not only disciplinary action, as with the previous CNM, but also oversight of the budget and administrative matters (for example, providing statistics about the workload and productivity of the judiciary).[55]

The politics of the adoption are telling. It was initially proposed by a member of the then opposition in the year 2000. The proposal did not see the light of day, however, until the election of Lula de Silva to the presidency in 2003. Incoming politicians may feel the need to impose greater discipline on the judiciary, particularly if it is seen as being aligned with their opponents; more generally, changes in power can lead to efforts to institutionalize judicial independence so as to provide insurance for those who are likely to lose in future rounds.[56] One can interpret the creation of the new Brazilian judicial council from either perspective. The new left coalition may have believed that the unconstrained judiciary was more likely to support their political opponents and thus used the council to discipline the judiciary. Alternatively, the coalition may have wanted to institutionalize an *accountable* independent judiciary to make it more viable for the long term, since a system of alternating parties seemed to be developing.

As with so many other judicial councils, there has been some tinkering with the model as Brazil seeks to calibrate judicial accountability and independence. In 2009, a constitutional amendment removed the minimum and maximum age limits for members of the council and clarified that the president of the Supreme Federal Tribunal would head the council.

The Brazilian story illustrates that there is no *necessary* connection between judicial councils and judicial independence. Though formally designed to provide the appearance of independence, the 1977 version of the judicial council did little to constrain potential military interference with the courts. Indeed, judicial independence was in one sense greatest between 1988 and 2004, when judges enjoyed a vastly expanded domain of governance but had little oversight. The 2004 reforms are a promise of a strong but politically accountable judiciary. It remains to be seen, of course, if this will materialize.

Israel

In Israel, judges are appointed by a mixed council established under the Basic Law on the Judiciary, passed in 1984.[57] Under that system, new justices are chosen by a nine-member panel, which includes two government ministers, two members of the Knesset, two bar association representatives, and three sitting justices, including the court president.[58] The judges, although a minority, dominate the process in practice, and a new justice has never been chosen over the objection of sitting justices.[59] This is the paradigm of a self-regulating, strong judiciary, even though judges are not the majority on the council. Professor Ran Hirschl convincingly argues that the creation of the entrenched judiciary, like other steps taken in the 1990s to constitutionalize certain policies, reflected the desire of a powerful but declining "hegemonic" group to ensure that their policies would survive their electoral losses.[60] Essentially, the country's politics were dominated into the 1970s by a set of secular Jews who were of European descent. But from that point, the gradual rise of religious parties, Jews of Middle Eastern descent, and later Russian immigrants threatened the political status quo. Hirschl argues that judicial empowerment and the creation of rights served to preserve the power of the hegemonic group after its electoral defeat. The inclusion in this set of reforms of a judicial council to enhance independence fits our overall story of councils as tools for increased judicial autonomy.

As our framework suggests, the power of the judiciary has led to calls for greater accountability. Observers date the origin of increasing judicialization to the late 1980s.[61] Judicial activism by the Supreme Court under retired president Aharon Barak (who headed the body from 1995 to 2006) has prompted fierce debate over whether the system needs revision.[62] In 2000, Israel created a committee to revisit the system of appointing judges, but it proposed only modest changes, such as making the nominations more transparent.[63] Many believe that the Israeli Supreme Court has been too activist, and we have begun to observe renewed calls for structural reforms to rein in the judiciary.[64] In January 2012, the Knesset passed the so-called Grunis Law, which changed the terms of judicial selection. Before 2007, Israeli law did not limit the term of the president of the court, but in that year, the Courts Act was amended to set a maximum of seven years, with a minimum of three years of eligibility before reaching the mandatory retirement age required for appointment. The latter provision was revoked in the 2012 reforms, thus allowing the Judicial Selection Committee (JSC) to appoint a supreme court chief justice with only two years remaining until retirement.[65] This paved the way for the February 2012 appointment of Justice Asher Grunis, who was seen as conservative and opposed to intervention in Knesset and government affairs.[66]

Another set of proposals has sought to reduce the judicial dominance of the JSC. In October 2013, Prime Minister Benjamin Netanyahu's coalition attempted to pass a series of bills to weaken the JSC. One of the bills proposed the president of the supreme court be elected by the Knesset itself, instead of being determined by seniority among members of the court. Another bill suggested replacing two supreme court members on the JSC with a retired district court judge chosen by the heads of the district courts and an academic chosen by the prime minister, leaving the supreme court with just one vote.[67] In January 2014, the Knesset passed a law ensuring more gender equality on the JSC, reserving four out of nine seats for women.[68] These bills and proposals have sought to rein in what is essentially a self-governing judiciary through changing the composition and accountability of the council.

France

The French approach to the organization of judicial councils has been identified by many as ideal.[69] The French judicial council, the Conseil Superieur de la Magistrature (CSM), was created after World War II in 1946, when the Constitution of the Fourth Republic established a council headed by the president of the republic with the minister of justice as its vice president.[70] The creation of the Fifth Republic in 1958 reinforced the power of the president.[71] The constitution, adopted by referendum, led to some reforms in the judicial council, namely in terms of the composition of its members. The president of the republic and minister of justice remained the president and vice president of the council, respectively, and nine members were to be appointed by the president.[72] Until the 1990s, the powers of the council were basically limited to the nomination of high level magistrates, and the council was influenced by the president of the republic and by senior judges. Senior judges played a very significant role in determining the careers of junior judges. By the early 1990s, the judicial council was facing serious criticism for being dominated by the interests of the executive and for excluding junior judges.[73]

The Constitutional Reform (Loi Constitutionelle) in 1993 and Constitutional Amendment (Loi Organique) in 1994 brought changes in terms of membership, method of appointment, powers, and operating procedures of the council. Among the main changes were the election of magistrate members of the council; the creation of two "formations" or committees, one with jurisdiction over the judges (*siège*)[74] and the other over public prosecutors (*parquet*); the appointment of four members common to both formations by the "high authorities" of the state;[75] the election of the other twelve members (six in each formation) by the judiciary; and the allocation of new competences related to the nomination of presidents of the *Tribunaux de Grande Instance*. Although the French Constitution refers to the existence of a judicial council and its composition, many details of the body are regulated by ordinary legislation.[76]

The reforms in the 1990s were clearly driven by political events that have empowered the judiciary. Generally, the Fifth Republic had maintained the traditional principles of the French judiciary—namely, its subordination to the executive and the legislature, and individual and collective judicial self-restraint (characterized by docile compliance with the doctrines of state supremacy and political sovereignty). However, there were some pressures on the system beginning in the late 1960s and early 1970s.[77] The consolidation of judicial review by the Constitutional Council in the mid-1970s had a major and enduring impact. The sharp increase in litigation, pushed by the criminalization of many activities and the extension of the scope of application of the European Convention of Human Rights, increased the influence of the French judiciary.[78]

Several political scandals gave the judiciary important influence over politics. France, lacking a history of well-known famous judges, was now faced with a new kind of celebrity.[79] Judges who were motivated and willing to investigate corruption scandals and to confront political pressures became heroes of sorts.[80] It is clear, nevertheless, that many of these affairs were pursued by individual judges, while the French judiciary as a whole remained very self-restrained.[81]

It is possible that divided government, known as *cohabitation*,[82] weakened the French executive, as the powers of the minister of justice in relation to the judiciary were reduced and the council's powers have increased.[83] French politicians, however, retain a good deal of influence over the judiciary, especially compared to their counterparts in Spain and Italy.[84] On several occasions, different ministers of justice have come into conflict with the judiciary "when they have tried to hush up 'affairs' linked to their respective parties."[85] As the political system became more competitive in the 1980s and early 1990s, pressure built for judicial reforms that ensured more independence. Nevertheless, the involvement of high-profile politicians in scandals and the increasing prominence of judges and judicial review have initiated a debate about the lack of external accountability of the judiciary. According to Valéry Turcey, a member of the CSM, the increasingly prominent role of the judiciary in French society was reflected in large debates about the role of the CSM in particular.[86]

In 2008, then president Nicolas Sarkozy announced plans to further reform and streamline the French judiciary, which were adopted into law that July.[87] These reforms expanded the nonjudicial members so that judges and prosecutors became a minority. The law also increased the council's power, granting the prosecutors' division the right to give its (advisory) opinion on all appointments, including for general prosecutors with the appellate courts and the Cour de Cassation.[88] Further, any citizen who deems that, in the course of proceedings in which she was involved, a judge has behaved in a way that may require disciplinary sanctions, now has the right to file a complaint with the CSM directly.[89] Further judicial reforms in 2010 prompted new protests from the judiciary.

The long French tradition of hostility to an independent and powerful judicial branch has no doubt played a role in keeping France from shifting to full judicialization of public policies and hence led to increased control over judicial behavior.[90] We observe continued willingness to tinker with the council to ensure accountability to the political system.

Italy

Although it had been approved after World War II and envisaged in the Italian Constitution of 1948,[91] the Consiglio Superiore della Magistratura (CSM) was not officially created until 1958 and fully operational until 1959.[92] The Constitution defines the existence, composition, and tasks of the CSM, but it also states that rules governing the judiciary and the judges are laid out by ordinary law.[93] Two-thirds of the membership of the council were magistrates, elected by their peers at various ranks, with the remaining members being appointed by Parliament.[94] According to the Italian Constitution, the council is in charge of the employment, assignment, transfer, promotion, and disciplining of judges.[95] The Constitution pays special attention to the autonomy and independence of the judiciary, in reaction to executive dominance during the Fascist period. The Italian judicial system is notable for its near absolute independence, in which the CSM controls virtually all aspects of judicial appointment and the conditions of the judicial career.[96] The balance of power within the CSM is clearly in the hands of the judiciary, and as we explain below, because the internal hierarchy of the judiciary has largely been undermined, all decisions on the status of magistrates are made by the CSM.

The Italian story is one in which judges gradually dismantled the classical hierarchical structure of the civil law judiciary. Beginning in the 1960s, judges formed unions, demanding better conditions and freedom from constraints imposed by higher levels of the judiciary. This gradually led to a removal of internal controls. The dismantling of the traditional hierarchy was reinforced by several reforms that took place between 1963 and 1979. Between 1979 and 1992, the role of the CSM was consolidated, with the unions assuming an increasingly important role in determining its members.[97] Although in theory the CSM was set up to ensure a certain level of consistency within the judiciary, the quality of judges varied widely. Judicial unions demanded a new "automatic promotion" doctrine established in the 1970s. The CSM's professional evaluations of the judges were of little significance because they were always positive, and promotion became essentially automatic, even to the highest ranks of the judiciary, with no relationship to actual vacancies.[98] This meant that every judge could gain the benefits of higher office (even if in fact they continued to occupy lower offices) without being assessed for quality. Salaries were high regardless of skill.[99] With no quality control, the incentives for judges to contribute to collective reputation broke down. Rather than invest in quality, judges spent energy cultivating personal ties with those who controlled promotions and, if ambitious, seeking to gain membership to the judicial council. Because these positions are elected by the judges themselves, they result in a good deal of investment in individual reputation by those who seek power within the judiciary. But they have led to an emphasis on connections over quality.

All this resulted in an internal fragmentation of the judiciary that further empowered the associations. The formalist Supreme Court was virtually replaced by the judicial associations in negotiating with politicians, these associations being more activist and less low profile than the traditionalist Supreme Court. With time, the relationship between the judiciary and the politicians changed. The traditional political system where there was a natural friendship between the highest ranks of the judiciary and the executive was progressively replaced by a direct connection between political parties and judicial associations.[100] Judicial investigations into several scandals involving businessmen, politicians, and bureaucrats marked the period from 1992 to 1997, raising questions about the accountability of judicial powers.[101] Several Italian judges fighting corruption and organized crime became well-known public figures, including antimafia judges like Rocco Chinnici, Giovanni Falcone, and Paolo Borsellino, and anticorruption judges like Antonio Di Pietro, Francesco Saverio Borrelli, Ilda Boccassini, Gherardo Colombo, and Piercamillo Davigo.[102] Some judges even launched political careers.

Public debates began to grow, centered on the appointment of judges and the organization of the judiciary, with the aim of preventing runaway judges from conducting overzealous prosecutions. As a result, the composition of the council was altered in 2002. The total number of members was reduced from thirty-three to twenty-four. In addition to sixteen ordinary judges and prosecutors chosen from various levels in the hierarchy, eight university law professors and lawyers with a minimum of fifteen years of experience in the legal profession were appointed by the Italian Parliament.[103] In 2007, the CSM implemented a law passed in 2006 (and amended again by law no. 111/2007), providing for all magistrates to be subjected to an assessment procedure every four years until they reach the twenty-eighth year of service, after a maximum of seven assessments.[104] Consequently, high-ranking positions, which had been permanent since the CSM came into being, have now become temporary and subject to periodic scrutiny.[105]

The Italian case is similar to the French case, although the Italian council is more dependent on the executive, with narrower competences, and reflects relatively slower decline of the influence of judicial hierarchy. Both cases fit well into our dynamic model, which first predicts excessive politicization as a result of granting extensive independence to the judicial power and next predicts that serious accountability issues will be raised once judicialization of party politics becomes notable (in both Italy and France, due mostly to political scandals). New judges with media attention (Garzón in Spain, Jean-Pierre in France, and Di Pietro in Italy) have pushed judicialization of politics as never seen before in these countries. Thus, in the immediate future, the problem will be the extent to which the judicial agenda is sustainable once it does not coincide with the media agenda.

The Netherlands

The Netherlands' model has differed from that of France and Italy. The government has recently introduced important reforms to ensure more transparency and accountability, but these did not result from high-profile political scandals. Historically, the Dutch judiciary has been very restrained; judicial review doctrines in the Netherlands were similar to the British principle of parliamentary sovereignty. But constitutional reforms in 1953 and 1956 paved the way for more judicial activism. The purpose of these reforms was to accommodate the developments in European Economic Community law at the time, and the consequences were far-reaching. As a result, the main source of judicial activism has been the enforcement of the European Convention on Human Rights.[106]

The selection of judges in the Netherlands combines the appointment system typical of common and civil law: half of the judges are young university graduates and the other half experienced members of the legal profession.[107] The Ministry of Justice shares the power of selecting the members of the judicial selection boards with both the judiciary and the legislature.[108]

The judicial system in the Netherlands was substantially reformed in January 2002. A significant change was the creation of the Council for the Judiciary (Raad voor de Rechtspraak),[109] a committee primarily responsible for organizing and financing the Dutch judiciary. However, these roles of the council are limited by the Dutch Supreme Court (Hoge Raad) and the Administrative Jurisdiction Division of the Council of State (Afdeling Bestuursrechtspraak Raad van State). And while the council has only five members, it maintains an office to assist it in its activities that employs around 135 people.[110] The acts of the council are not subject to any control. The council was granted certain administrative powers previously in the hands of the Ministry of Justice, in an effort to reinforce the independence of judiciary authority with respect to the legislature, the Parliament, and the government.[111]

The Dutch case is a good example of a judicial system in which no serious concerns about excessive politicization have arisen, and yet certain reforms have sought to introduce more accountability and better allocation of resources. Perhaps this results from its proximity to several other jurisdictions that are deeply engaged in judicial reform.

The United Kingdom

In the United Kingdom, the Act of Settlement 1701[112] confirmed the independence of the judiciary, and since then, strong norms of judicial immunity have made the removal of judges quite difficult. However, appointments remained in the hands of the lord chancellor.[113] The traditional view was that the lord chancellor represented the judiciary in the government and the government in the judiciary and hence was a unique office well placed to represent the view of each side.[114] Although the lord chancellor's position became an exclusively political office, by convention, he was drawn from the ranks of senior lawyers. The process of judicial selection increasingly emphasized professional experience; few judges appointed to English higher courts had any political experience.[115] Although the independence of the English judiciary was not perceived to be significantly affected by this arrangement, some lord chancellors have been seriously criticized in the press for having policies that were too politically oriented.[116] At the same time, the senior judiciary sitting at the House of Lords participated in lawmaking, and so the roles of legislator and judge were combined.[117] England's version of the separation of powers did not challenge the combination of roles in a single office. The English judiciary was never perceived as a separate branch of government in the American sense.[118] The lord chancellor could sit in on cases, and the last one to do so (at the time of this writing) was in 2001.[119] In practice, however, the system that developed under the lord chancellor created a unified and hierarchical judiciary. The chancellor became perceived as the guardian of judicial independence and a voice of the senior judiciary, rather than a constraint on it. Such structure did not promote diversity of opinions, since someone who did not conform to the views of the establishment was not likely to be chosen by the lord chancellor.[120] In this sense, the judiciary became self-governing.

The increasing importance of the English judiciary reflected changes in the political environment after the 1960s. These changes include the expansion of the welfare state, the Labor government's creation of a specialized Industrial Relations Court under Edward Heath, and the arrival of Margaret Thatcher and her legal reforms.[121] Europe also played an important role in transforming British public law. European integration in 1973 and the development of EU law have progressively empowered the English judiciary to review legislation in the light of EU directives or regulations, sometimes against the will of the government. This has contributed to a bolder judiciary, confronted with the enlargement of the scope of judicial review and power over public policy.[122] Senior judges challenged the doctrine of parliamentary sovereignty.[123] Furthermore, the new role of the judiciary in the face of the domestic and international challenges of the late 1970s and 1980s raised concerns about the extent to which the English judiciary was up to the tasks expected of it.[124] This led to gradually increasing demands for accountability in a self-regulating, independent judiciary.

Several issues in the late 1990s brought these tensions to a head. Sentencing policy came under scrutiny in the aftermath of the passage of the

Human Rights Act 1998.[125] The Pinochet case in 1999 raised serious questions about the wisdom of having the most senior judiciary sitting in the House of Lords.[126] In addition, Europe played a major role in encouraging transformation of the institutional structure. In the 1990s, the Council of Europe encouraged eastern European countries to enhance judicial independence by reducing the role of politicians, but the UK system remained a stubborn anachronism in that the head of the judiciary was a government minister. Then the case of *McGonnell v. UK*[127] in the European Court of Human Rights, regarding the Bailiff of the island of Guernsey, gave impetus to movements to reform the judicial structure. In that case, the court decided that a judge who also plays an administrative role violates Article 6 of the European Convention of Human Rights, which requires a fair trial. Although in England and Wales, the lord chancellor traditionally avoided sitting on cases where there might be a conflict of interest, the European Court of Human Rights applied a somewhat formalist approach, finding that theoretical blending of functions violated norms of judicial independence.[128] The formal separation of powers, it seems, is now a constitutional requirement in Europe.

More generally, judges' extrajudicial activities, including leading commissions and inquiries and producing reports, have been the source of controversy. In many important cases, the appointed judges encountered politically sensitive issues. Judge-headed commissions included those on the Profumo affair in 1963,[129] industrial relations in Northern Ireland in the 1970s,[130] the Nolan committee on standards in public life in the aftermath of sleaze scandals (1994–95), the Scott inquiry on exports of military equipment to Iran and Iraq (1995–96), and the Hutton inquiry on the death of an employee of the Ministry of Defense and the weapons of mass destruction in Iraq (2003–4).[131] We have seen the risks of judicial involvement in extrajudicial functions in chapter 3.

From a reputation perspective, in the United Kingdom we observe a small judiciary that had, through internal self-governance, developed over many centuries a powerful collective reputation for independence. External developments, however, put greater pressure on the system as judicial decisions began to play a more prominent role in public life. The long-standing reputation of judicial independence led, as our dynamic model suggests, to greater demands for judicial involvement, including in extrajudicial activities that place individual judicial reputations at risk. In 2003, Prime Minister Tony Blair's government announced its intention to alter the system for appointing judges in England and Wales.[132] The political forces were frustrated with the incumbent lord chancellor, who opposed judicial reform, and abruptly dismissed him in 2003.

Two goals justified the reform: improving judicial independence and enhancing accountability and public confidence in judicial offices.[133] In fact, Lord Falconer, the new secretary of state for constitutional affairs, declared that it was no longer acceptable for the executive branch to control judicial appointments. Accordingly, he revealed the intention to establish an independent Judicial Appointments Commission (JAC), responsible for recommending candidates for judicial appointments on a more transparent basis and based solely on merit.[134]

The Constitutional Reform Act 2005[135] introduced several substantive changes in the English and Welsh judiciaries, including a statutory prohibition on government members seeking to influence judicial decisions. Two reforms were especially far-reaching: First, the act abolished the centuries-old judicial role of the lord chancellor, the most senior judge in England and Wales, and transferred his judicial functions to the president of the courts of England and Wales (formerly known as lord chief justice of England and Wales).[136] (The lord chancellor retains a role in judicial management.) Second, the act created a new Supreme Court, consisting of twelve judges independent of and removed from the House of Lords, with its own independent appointment system.[137]

Alongside the JAC,[138] the Constitutional Reform Act of 2005 established two new bodies: the Judicial Appointments and Conduct Ombudsman (JACO)[139] and the Directorate of Judicial Offices for England and Wales (DJO). The JAC is composed of fifteen commissioners drawn from the judiciary, the legal profession (one barrister and one solicitor), the lay magistracy, and the lay public. The chairman of the commission is required to be a lay member. In 2007, further reforms established a Ministry of Justice, which would incorporate some of the lord chancellor's functions and be responsible for criminal justice policy, among other areas. Yet more reforms occurred in 2008 and 2013, modifying the composition of the JAC slightly and ensuring that a lay member would head the committee to select the president of the Supreme Court. The purpose of this latter change (in the Crime and Courts Act 2013) was to guard against the perception of the panel selecting judges on the basis of their own preferences.

The constitutional reform emerged in a context of enhanced influence of the judiciary in Britain. The Human Rights Act of 1998 has allowed the courts to review acts of Parliament for the first time ever (by assessing compliance with the European Convention of Human Rights, for all legislation passed after and before 1998).[140] Although courts tend to follow a general doctrine of deference to the legislature, the Human Rights Act of 1998 considerably increases the weight of external audiences.[141]

Some of these behavioral changes were already being developed since the European Community Act of 1972.[142] The fine line between law and politics has been blurred since the late 1970s, straying from the traditional arrangement and posing a serious problem from the perspective of the reformers.[143]

It seems the most important issue in the United Kingdom discussion has been enhancing accountability through more formal processes. As predicted by our model, the growth of judicial review and the perception that judicial interference in politics has significantly increased has raised concerns about accountability.[144] One concern was the lack of minorities and women in the bench, which suggests a sense of gender and racial bias in the appointments mechanism.[145] There has been a general feeling that a small clique from Oxford and Cambridge dominates the appointments.[146] Furthermore, there have been indications of personal and corporate bias in judicial profiles.[147] We observe defensive actions on the part of the judges, as when the lord chief justice argued that the JAC, "like a recruitment agency, must respond to the needs of the client's business; and those needs must be judged and articulated by the business, not the recruitment agency."[148] But we also see continued pressure to open up. In 2010, an advisory panel to the lord chancellor proposed a shift to a judicial career, with the aim of achieving greater diversity within the judiciary. Only later was it clarified that this was not meant as a call for a career judiciary, where judges are appointed after graduating from university and trained for the bench, but rather as a call to the legal profession to bring about further changes in its composition.[149] The Parliamentary Joint Select Committee expressed its disappointment with the lack of measurable progress toward increasing diversity within the judiciary. While more women, black, and minority candidates are in fact applying for judicial roles than before the JAC, and more women are being selected (with five women high court judges appointed between April 2008 and June 2009, the highest number ever), the number of successful minority candidates has remained constant and rather low.[150]

Our model predicts that reforms aimed at improving accountability might sacrifice independence. Not surprisingly, in the United Kingdom, the extent to which current reforms actually improve judicial independence seems to be a matter of debate.[151] The formalist version of independence would view the restructuring of the office of lord chancellor as an improvement, but many members of the senior judiciary were opposed to reform and sought to ensure that their independence was retained.[152]

What is clear is that the judiciary now is subject to much greater scrutiny from external audiences. The traditional audiences were other judges, in the self-policing clubby world of the senior judiciary and the political forces that appointed the lord chancellor. Today, a wide range of political and administrative actors, including the rump office of the lord chancellor, the new Supreme Court and Lord Chief Justice, a new Judicial Office, the Court Service, the Judicial Appointments Commission, a Judicial Appointments and Conduct Ombudsman, and an Office for Judicial Complaints, as well as a parliamentary commission, all play a role in managing and interacting with the judiciary. For example, Professor Robert Hazell and his team counted 148 appearances by 72 judges before 16 different parliamentary committees from 2003 to 2013.[153] Multiple audiences might provide the judicial agents with freedom to maneuver but also create much more scrutiny. We expect that the public will be the ultimate beneficiary in that judges will seek to cultivate public opinion with well-reasoned, prominent cases.

The Spread of Councils

One of the interesting things about judicial councils is that they have spread all over the world. The French-Italian model has been exported to Latin America and other developing countries.[154] One motivating concern for adoption of councils in the French-Italian tradition was ensuring independence of the judiciary after periods of undemocratic rule. To entrench judicial independence, most of these countries enshrined a judicial council in their constitutions.

A major factor was that the World Bank and other multilateral donor agencies have made judicial councils part of the standard package of institutions associated with judicial reform and rule of law programming.[155] Efforts to produce model "best practices" have ensured much replication and refinement of the judicial council model. For example, the Association of European Magistrates for Democracy and Freedom (MEDEL) produced a draft additional protocol to the European Convention on Human Rights called the Elements of European Statute on the Judiciary (known as the "Palermo Declaration"). This model statute states that there shall be a supreme council of magistracy, composed of judges and also including appointees of the parliament.[156] The model statute also declares that the supreme council will produce a budget for the courts; manage their administration; and control recruitment, assignment,[157] and discipline of judges,[158] thus guaranteeing judicial independence. The Council of Europe made a similar recommendation in a document published in 1994.[159] Other international organizations have followed suit.[160] The next section analyzes the factors behind the adoption in greater depth.

Empirical Data on Councils

Why Do Countries Constitutionalize Judicial Councils?

We have developed a small database on judicial councils. The sample consists of the councils in 121 different nation-states, listed in appendix B. Data were gathered for the most recent iteration of the judicial council available. (The omissions are in no way related to the explanatory variables.) For ninety-three countries, the judicial council is mentioned and described in the country's constitution, so we gathered our information from there.[161] For twenty-eight other countries, the constitution provides no detail on the composition and powers of the judicial council. In these countries, the judicial council is left to ordinary law. We gathered data on these countries from an array of sources, including the 2002 study of Linn Hammergren,[162] the Comparative Constitutions Project,[163] and a number of country-specific sources. Figures 4.2a and 4.2b provide some indication of the trends over time and space.

Note that the issue of whether or not a council is constitutionalized is itself important. If the composition and powers of the council are left to ordinary law (as they are in twenty-eight countries in our dataset), they are subject to enhanced manipulation by the government and legislature and hence have a weaker guarantee of independence. Presumably those councils lean more toward the accountability pole than the independence pole. Conversely, when the council structure is entrenched in the constitution, it is beyond the reach of ordinary politics and hence likely to reflect a desire for greater levels of judicial independence and insulation. In the results that follow, we find systematically lower independence scores for countries with nonconstitutionalized councils.[164]

What predicts whether a country will constitutionalize a judicial council or not? Casual observation of figure 4.2 suggests both a time trend and some regional variation. These factors affect all countries and so are a bit different from the local political variables that we have been emphasizing in our account. Ideally, we would like to understand the relative importance of these factors with the local conditions that might drive demand for judicial councils.

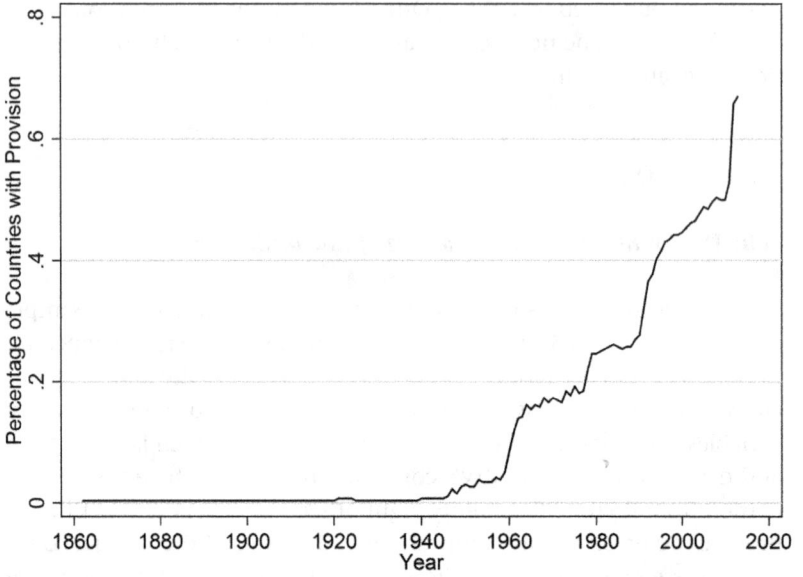

4.2a Constitutionalized judicial councils over time Source: Comparative Constitutions Project, http://www.comparativeconstitutionsproject.org

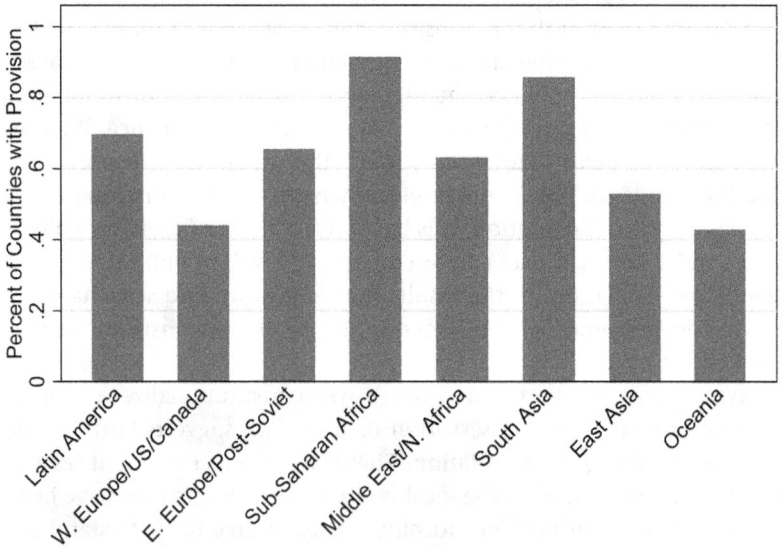

4.2b Constitutionalized judicial councils by region, 2010 Source: Comparative Constitutions Project, http://www.comparativeconstitutionsproject.org

We run a series of fixed-effect probit models in which the dependent variable is the "onset" of a judicial council, meaning the first year in which it is adopted.[165] The unit of analysis is the country-year. As predictive factors, we include region, the level of democracy (as measured by the POLITY2 index), wealth, and whether or not the country is a common law jurisdiction.[166] We model time by looking at the duration between the country's first constitution and the year in which it adopts a judicial council. (As is standard, we include squared and cubed terms in modeling duration.) Our hypothesis is that, if there is indeed a time trend, countries will be more likely to adopt a judicial council, the longer they have been "waiting" to do so. In each regression, we include fixed terms for countries, which of course will capture the region the country is in.

We are particularly interested in whether variables that predict political motives for expanding judicial power play a role in driving the adoption of judicial councils. We might predict that more powerful judiciaries—say, those with the power of constitutional review—would be greater targets for political control. After all, there is little reason to adopt a new institution to manage an unimportant set of government actors. We also include an indicator of judicial independence drawn from recent work by Professors Drew Linzer and Jeffrey Staton, lagged in one-, five-, and ten-year periods (in models 1, 2, and 3, respectively).[167] If judicial councils are always designed to enhance judicial independence, we should see a negative correlation between judicial independence at t-1 and the adoption of a council. Conversely, if judicial councils are instituted to control the judiciary, we should see a positive correlation: more independence at t-1 will correlate with the adoption of a council at time t.

Our results—presented in table 4.3—confirm some of our hypotheses. We find a strong correlation between the prior presence of judicial review and the adoption of a council. Judicial councils are adopted when judges have formal power. But this correlation disappears when we lag the variable by five and ten years. We interpret this to indicate that the adoption of a judicial council is likelier when judicial review has itself been recently adopted and that both trends are codetermined by other factors. Figure 4.3 illustrates the effect graphically.

We do not observe any significant correlation between prior levels of judicial *independence* and council adoption. This is consistent with, or at least does not disconfirm, our theory that judicial councils are sometimes adopted to enhance independence while other times designed to enhance accountability. It is, of course, also possible that the councils

Table 4.3 Probit models predicting constitutional adoption of a judicial council

Variables	(1) 1-year lag	(2) 5-year lag	(3) 10-year lag
Democracy (POLITY2)	0.169**	0.143***	0.151***
	(0.0785)	(0.0402)	(0.0454)
GDP per capita	-1.73^{e-06}	-2.15^{e-06}	-2.44^{e-06}
	(1.40^{e-06})	(2.32^{e-06})	(2.46^{e-06})
Common law	−5.393	−10.89*	−8.780
	(3.300)	(5.890)	(6.003)
Time from first constitution	0.124**	0.121	0.150
	(0.0589)	(0.0856)	(0.135)
Time squared	−0.000685	−0.000514	−0.000964
	(0.000880)	(0.00125)	(0.00175)
Time cubed	1.45^{e-06}	1.46^{e-06}	2.69^{e-06}
	(3.12^{e-06})	(4.03^{e-06})	(5.57^{e-06})
Judicial review at t-1	4.586***		
	(1.128)		
Judicial independence at t-1	−1.619		
	(2.844)		
Judicial review at t-5		0.0533	
		(0.421)	
Judicial independence at t-5		−2.262	
		(1.676)	
Judicial review at t-10			0.348
			(0.577)
Judicial independence at t-10			−0.805
			(2.127)
Constant	−7.029***	−5.052**	−5.726*
	(2.041)	(2.188)	(3.427)
Observations	1,158	997	823

All regressions are fixed-effects probit models, with fixed effects for countries.
Robust standard errors in parentheses.
*** $p<0.01$, ** $p<0.05$, * $p<0.1$

are simply adopted as part of a kind of trend or fashion, like many other constitutional institutions. Either way, the claim that judicial councils always enhance independence does not seem to be supported by the evidence.

Our results also show that democracy is an important predictor of judicial councils, which is hardly surprising because authoritarian regimes have many collateral institutions for controlling judges. In unreported specifications, we examine more precisely the political incentives for the adoption of judicial councils. A line of literature has shown that when a dominant party is in control of the political system, there is little incentive to empower the judiciary; conversely, where multiple parties vie for power, there is a greater incentive to adopt powerful and

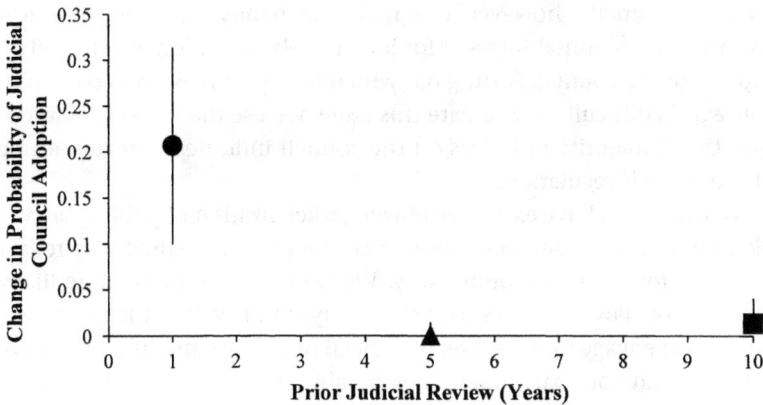

4.3 Effect of prior judicial review on council adoption

independent courts.[168] If councils indeed enhance independence in all cases, we should see that demand for "political insurance" will correlate with the onset of a council. But we find no such relationship in multivariate models. Finally, the common law does not predict the adoption of judicial councils.[169]

What Features Do Judicial Councils Have?

We next wish to examine the particular features of judicial councils. First, we developed a simple ordinal index of powers/competences ("power index"). Each judicial council was rated depending on the extent of its competences. A council that had purely administrative or housekeeping functions council was coded as 1 (n = 8), and a council with a role in appointment, transfer, and discipline of judges was rated a 3 (n = 68). The intermediate rating of 2 was given to councils that had a limited role either because they could appoint but not discipline judges or because their role was limited in performance-relevant variables (n = 34). For example, a council that only had a role in recommending judges for appointment or minimal role in discipline would be rated a 2. We also include information on countries *without* judicial councils, an important control group. These are denoted with a score of 0 on the power index. A complete coding of countries with judicial councils is in appendix B.

Our first prediction was that competences, as captured in the power index, would vary systematically depending on the institutional problem being faced. Extensive competences correlate with stronger councils.

Stronger councils, however, can reflect demands for strong political control and accountability—or for judicial self-regulation effectuated by capture of the council. Sorting out which motivation exists in particular contexts is difficult. To evaluate this issue, we use the working assumption that a majority of judges on the council indicates a greater degree of judicial self-regulation.

When judges have extensive power, judicialization of public policy is likely to follow. In such environments, the judicial council may reflect pressures for greater accountability. We expect this may be more likely in common law countries as well as any country in which ordinary judges can engage in the power of judicial review. We might also observe that, in such contexts, judges may be able to secure a majority of the positions on the judicial council. In other situations, however, accountability concerns might lead to efforts to reduce the number of judges.

Composition also interacts with competence. To understand the relationship between composition and competence, we want to understand whether an assignment of more extensive powers is associated with a higher percentage of judges on the council. We run a series of regressions in which the dependent variables are, first, our four-point power index, and, second, the percentage of judges on the council. These two things, competence and composition, are typically decided together at the time of institutional design, though each may be subject to later tinkering as new problems arise. For each of our dependent variables, we run two models: a baseline model in which the only predictors are common law, democracy, presence of judicial review, and level of judicial independence, along with regional dummies (with Latin America as the omitted category), and an additional model with the other dependent variable as an additional predictor. That is, we use the percentage of judges to predict powers and the power index to predict the percentage of judges. This will help us understand if the two design features go together. We use an ordered probit model for the power index, which is appropriate because it is an ordinal variable, and an ordinary least squares regression to predict the percentage of judges on the council.

Our results, presented in table 4.4, confirm many of our hypotheses: we find that stronger councils are associated with judicial review but not judicial independence (column 1). The common law result is unstable: when we add the percentage of judges as a predictor (column 2), we lose statistical significance and the sign switches. In examining the predictors of composition on the council (columns 3 and 4), we observe that judicial independence measures are *negatively* correlated with more

Table 4.4 Predictors of judicial council power and composition

Dependent variable	(1) Council powers index	(2) Council powers index	(3) Percentage of judges on council	(4) Percentage of judges on council
Model	Ordered probit	Ordered probit	OLS regression	OLS regression
Democracy (POLITY2)	0.0201	0.0225	−0.00635	−0.00704
	(0.018)	(0.0262)	(0.00546)	(0.00538)
Common law	0.442*	−0.473	−0.0513	−0.0371
	(0.250)	(0.436)	(0.0840)	(0.0828)
Judicial independence	0.0003	−0.000419	−0.00408*	−0.00404*
	(0.009)	(0.00999)	(0.00207)	(0.00203)
Judicial review	0.553**	0.105	−0.0151	−0.0233
	(0.264)	(0.385)	(0.0770)	(0.0758)
Percentage of judges on council		1.228**		
		(0.532)		
Judicial council power index				0.0591**
				(0.0295)
Western Europe / North America	−0.0558	0.145	0.344***	0.331***
	(0.473)	(0.607)	(0.116)	(0.114)
Middle East	−0.574	4.524	0.337*	0.294
	(0.489)	(283.9)	(0.199)	(0.197)
South Asia	−1.226**	−1.139	0.650***	0.688***
	(0.603)	(0.783)	(0.148)	(0.147)
East Asia	0.0469	0.922	0.287**	0.251**
	(0.459)	(0.696)	(0.120)	(0.119)
Eastern Europe / Post-Soviet	0.0562	0.234	0.158	0.139
	(0.435)	(0.588)	(0.115)	(0.114)
Sub-Saharan Africa	−0.322	0.562	0.158	0.131
	(0.402)	(0.541)	(0.107)	(0.106)
Oceania	−0.633	0.168	0.111	0.114
	(0.834)	(0.889)	(0.182)	(0.179)
Time	−0.000876	−0.00199	0.00116	0.00114*
	(0.00275)	(0.00358)	(0.000700)	(0.000688)
Constant	−0.401	−0.810	0.324***	0.200
	(0.412)	(0.533)	(0.107)	(0.122)
Observations	97	97	97	97
R^2			0.326	0.357

Standard errors appear in parentheses.
*** $p<0.01$, ** $p<0.05$, * $p<0.1$

judges. At a minimum, this result should help debunk arguments that judicial majorities on the council are necessary for securing judicial independence. Instead, it seems like relatively dependent judiciaries are being rewarded for political loyalty with seats on the councils.

Columns 2 and 4 help us identify the relationship between competence and composition. It appears that greater competences are correlated with a higher percentage of judges on the council. Figure 4.4 captures the

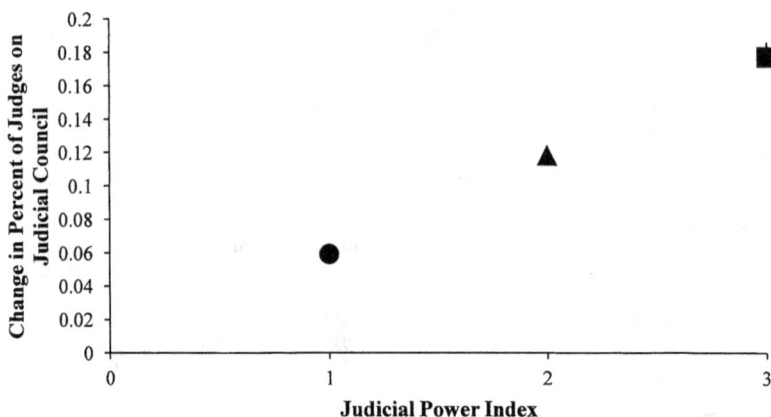

4.4 Relationship between judicial power index and change in percentage of judges on council

relationship graphically. Perhaps these councils are the ones in which the senior judiciary is given a powerful role in controlling lower court judges, on behalf of political principals. This is consistent with the argument of Professors Mark Ramseyer and Eric Rasmusen about the Japanese judiciary.[170] Although the Japanese judiciary does not have a judicial council, it does feature extensive control of the lower judiciary by higher levels. Ramseyer and Rasmusen argue that this institutional configuration of hierarchical judicial control suits the politicians that run Japan. If the senior judges are loyal, they can be trusted with the task of governing lower judges.

Another interesting result comes from the regional variables. It appears as if there is a particularly South Asian style of judicial council—one with many judges but relatively few competences. East Asian and Western European councils are likely to have a higher percentage of judges than those in Latin America (the omitted category), where political configurations may be less stable.

In earlier work, we established that correlations between the presence of a judicial council and levels of judicial independence (using various measures available before the creation of the Linzer-Staton measure) were very low.[171] One might think, however, that these results fail to specify the proper relationship between judicial councils and judicial independence. After all, if introducing a judicial council is supposed to enhance judicial independence, we would observe an improvement only some years later. We can explore this conjecture by looking at the

Table 4.5 Predictors of judicial independence

	Judicial independence	Judicial independence t+5	Judicial independence t+10
Years since first constitution	−.018 (0.005)***	−.015 (0.005)***	−0.016 (0.006)***
Onset of judicial council	−3.63 (1.48)**	−3.33 (1.54)**	−3.24 (1.57)**
Democracy	0.27 (0.04)***	0.25 (0.04)***	0.024 (0.042)***
GDP per capita	1.43^{e-07} (3.29^{e-07})	-7.48^{e-08} (3.56^{e-07})	-1.27^{e-07} (4.62^{e-07})
Constant	6.03 (0.56)***	5.65 (0.57)***	5.71 (0.58)***

Standard errors appear in parentheses.
*** $p<0.01$, ** $p<0.05$, * $p<0.1$

trend in judicial independence scores some years after the adoption of a judicial council. Judicial independence is generally improving around the globe, and there is also a trend toward adoption of judicial councils. Therefore, we need to control for time and for the impact of factors like democracy and wealth, commonly thought to be drivers of judicial independence. We estimate a series of ordinary least squares regressions, again using the Linzer-Staton metric of judicial independence in the year in which the council is adopted, then five and ten years later (see table 4.5).

Again, we observe that time and levels of democracy are important factors that correlate with judicial independence. Judicial councils tend to be associated with low levels of judicial independence, suggesting that they are intended to be part of the solution to the problem. We indeed observe that the negative relationship decreases over time, suggesting that, on average, judicial councils may improve independence over time. The effect is quite small, and the explanatory power of the models is low (with R^2 only about 0.01).

The above results suggest that there is little if any evidence that judicial councils promote judicial independence. If they do so, the effect is small and takes many years to realize. Our argument is consistent with other recent studies. Stefan Voigt and Nora El-Bialy, using a forty-seven-country dataset produced by the European Commission for the Efficiency of Justice (CEPEJ) find that countries with judicial councils have judiciaries that are *less* efficient and resolve fewer cases than those without.[172] Together with our analysis, this suggests that judicial councils are not a best practice, even if they are treated as such. To some degree, this may reflect that best practices are contingent on the institutional problem being faced.

How then did judicial councils become a "best practice" in the first place? While we do not attempt a complete analysis, there is a hint about the motive in the recommendation of international organizations that judicial councils always have a majority of judges. This view implicitly assumes that the only threat to judicial performance is from outside the judiciary, particularly the executive branch. But our analysis of reputation and audiences suggests that sometimes judges will excessively value their internal audience to the detriment of their ultimate societal principal. Indeed, a recent study of Slovakia by David Kosar has indicated that a council headed by the Ministry of Justice may better establish checks and balances than one headed by the chief justice, particularly when the chief seeks to exercise dominant control over lower judges.[173] Perhaps, then, a combination of armchair institutional reasoning by donors and interest-group activities by judges themselves best explains the spread of a new form. One can view the strong pressure from the European Union on Eastern European countries as a kind of alliance in which judges on both sides of the former Iron Curtain allied to empower themselves in the new institution.

Conclusion

Judicial councils are an important new phenomenon that has spread all over the world and become a global best practice, yet we know little about them and their consequences. The conventional wisdom is that they enhance judicial independence, but we are skeptical of this claim. From an economic perspective, councils are designed to resolve principal-agent problems. As an intermediate body between the principal (the public) and the agent (judges), the judicial council aims to reduce agency costs due to the possible capture by a minority that may distort the judicial process for its own purposes. From this point of view, a judicial council is an expert monitor designed to ensure accountability rather than independence.

We recognize that the diversity in council structures across countries reflects local conditions. We have canvassed institutional designs in both common law judicial appointment commissions, including the merit plans in the United States and the Canadian and British experiences, and civil law high judicial councils, including the French-Italian model. We have argued that the different designs aim at achieving the appropriate balance between independence and accountability in the face of two recurrent phenomena—the politicization of the judiciary and the judicialization of politics—that are reflected in different degrees around the world.

Our empirical observation of patterns of institutional design show that competence and composition interact in complex ways to respond to particular institutional problems. We also found little evidence in favor of the widespread assumption that councils increase quality or independence in the aggregate. Therefore, we emphasize the complexity of the role of a judicial council and reject the simplistic view that importing or transplanting certain types of judicial council is likely to have a decisive impact on the quality of the judiciary. We thus reject the views of international organizations that assert that judges should always and everywhere form the majority of members on the council.[174]

Our framework also explains why it is that councils persist as institutions. Because they involve actors from multiple arenas, the councils themselves promise that no one institution can easily dominate the judiciary. The councils, once created, provide an arena for competition and the eternal struggle to calibrate independence and accountability. We thus predict that councils themselves will frequently become the targets of institutional reform, as examples from Italy, Brazil, and elsewhere demonstrate.[175] We also can understand why they have been widely adopted, notwithstanding little support for claims that they enhance independence: councils allow a wide number of stakeholders to participate in discussions of judicial governance.

There is also a branding component to the spread of the institution. Judicial councils, in particular, are championed by donor organizations; for example, in Rumania, the adoption of a judicial council was a condition of accession to the EU.[176] In Europe, an association of judicial councils has been formed. It seems that judicial councils may reflect the efforts of a kind of transnational movement, seeking to advance a particular model, regardless of whether or not they actually achieve their desired goals. Judicial independence, in this process, becomes an idea to be wielded in debates rather than a real tangible good.

Finally, we introduce the notion of the politically accountable but strong judiciary. In many ways, this ideal is more desirable than the conventional view that judicial independence is an unqualified good. Those who emphasize judicial independence too often do not articulate the need for accountability, which provides the crucial other side of the proverbial coin.

These findings have important implications for the ongoing debate on judicial appointments in the United States. Rather than assume that merit commissions, the American counterpart to judicial councils, always enhance independence, scholars should conduct more thorough empirical research to understand the precise determinants of independence and accountability. Our case studies suggest that these determinants are highly context specific and not susceptible to one-size-fits-all solutions.

We have seen that judicial councils have become increasingly fashionable since the early 1990s, but they do not seem to provide universal solutions to the issues of finding the appropriate mix of judicial accountability and independence. While councils become managers of reputation, their skill in regulating judicial behavior varies widely. In some cases, they become loci of their own political conflicts, in which external and internal audiences compete over judicial management. As in so many areas of institutional reform, popular solutions sometimes generate their own set of problems. In chapter 5, we will turn to another increasingly popular mechanism, constitutional courts, and document the struggles they have with ordinary courts in the battle for reputation.

FIVE

When Courts Collide: Intracourt Relations and the Problem of Audiences

One of the great developments in judicial design in recent decades has been the spread of specialized constitutional courts all over the world. Originally adopted in Austria and later in postwar Germany and Italy, designated constitutional courts have expanded to southern Europe, Asia, eastern Europe, and more recently Latin America during subsequent waves of democratization. Initially, France adopted a body, the Conseil Constitutionnel, empowered with a much narrower power of judicial review in accordance with French traditions of parliamentary sovereignty, but this court has also come to resemble the specialized model of institutional design.[1] At this writing, some ninety-two countries have some version of a constitutional court—nearly half of all the countries in the world (see figure 5.1).[2]

The design of specialized constitutional courts in the Western world has been influenced by the ideas and legal theories of Hans Kelsen and his model of the court as a "negative legislator."[3] Kelsen believed in a strict hierarchy of laws, in which ordinary judges are mandated only to apply law created by the parliament. To effectively restrain the legislature and ensure the compatibility of law with the higher normative order of the constitution, he proposed a special extrajudicial organ. The Kelsenian model establishes a centralized body outside the structure of the conventional judiciary to exercise constitutional review and

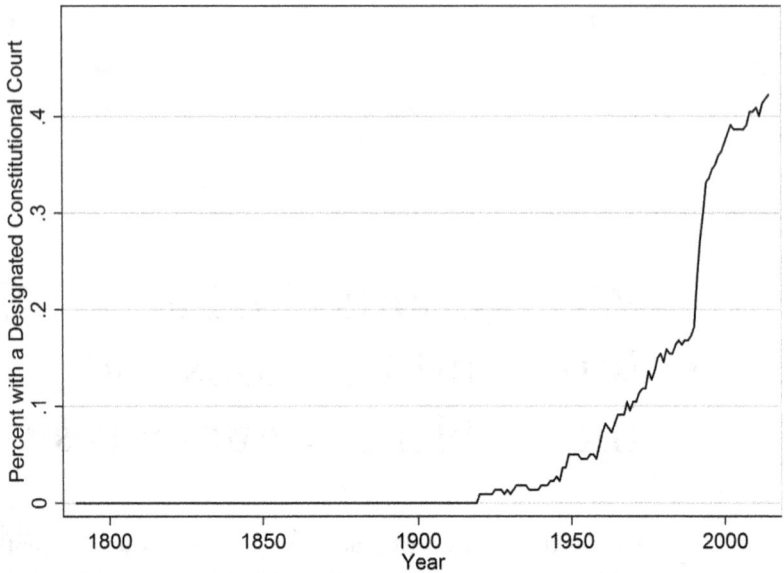

5.1 Percentage of constitutions in force with a designated constitutional court

act as the guarantor of the constitution. This body, typically called a constitutional court, operates as a negative legislator because it has the power to reject legislation but not propose it. Because this design sets up two alternative high courts that may compete for reputation, there is a great potential for conflict, which is the subject of this chapter.

The application of the Kelsenian model in each country varies, and the general trend has been toward expanding the competences of constitutional courts over time well beyond Kelsen's simple model of the "negative legislator." In the narrowest cases, constitutional courts only have the power of ex ante abstract review of legislation, in which the court makes a decision on a law before promulgation and framed outside of a specific case. More often, courts have the power of ex post abstract review, with the ability to strike a law after promulgation. Over time, in many countries, abstract review has been conjoined with concrete review, allowing individual citizens to access the constitutional courts, either directly or indirectly through the ordinary courts. At the same time, most constitutional courts have been granted ancillary powers in different but important areas, such as verifying elections, regulating political parties, and supervising states of emergency.[4] To some degree, this expansion of power reflects a successful reputation for the institution, both in general and in specific countries. After all, no constitutional designer would assign an important power to an institution that was perceived by everyone as weak or incompetent.

Scholars consider the development and spread of the Kelsenian model of constitutional review to be one of the most important transformations of legal systems in the last fifty years.[5] Even as it has led to increased judicialization of politics, some argue that these courts have largely been able to avoid the politicization and polarization of the US Supreme Court.[6] Constitutional judges in the Kelsenian model do not seem to develop "ideologically distinct public personalities" like their American counterparts.[7] Moreover, even if the appointment process for constitutional court judges is political in nature, there is no process of campaigning for positions nor a public confirmation process that focuses on judicial philosophy.[8] In our terms, these courts have been able to cultivate and maintain a collective reputation rather than a set of individual ones.

In this chapter, we focus on the reputational effects of internal consensus and fragmentation within the constitutional court as a function of the need to cultivate reputation among external audiences. There are two different audiences that we focus on. One can be characterized as the "political" audience: other branches of government and the political establishment more generally. Interaction with this audience takes place in the shadow of the ultimate principal, the general public. In this vein, we recognize that constitutional courts are inevitably political actors. Even in the narrow sense of a Kelsenian "negative legislator," they have the power to reject legislation, and hence their decisions have political consequences. The interaction of constitutional judges and what we call the political audience is not fully understood, but scholars have proposed several hypotheses. Some believe that judges seek to advance the preferences of their appointers in the realm of constitutional interpretation. Others view judges as primarily concerned about their future once their term in the court is over. Even if they have life tenure, they might care about what happens once they retire in terms of prospective appointments for other prestigious posts in government, international organizations, or the private sector. The interaction between politics on the one hand and constitutional and statutory interpretation on the other has been the focus of much literature, both theoretical and empirical, on the US Supreme Court and many other constitutional courts.[9] A major focus has been to demonstrate the extent to which judges advance their own ideology, rather than simply following formalism.[10] Others have considered the judicialization of the political branches, in which legislators or executives try to anticipate the decisions of courts and adjust legislation to avoid confrontation or rejection.[11] In short, the political dimension of constitutional review has been acknowledged and is subject to an intense legal and scholarly debate.

A second audience that a constitutional court must face is other courts, and the legal community more broadly, whose cooperation is needed to effectuate constitutional decisions in ordinary cases. The relationship between constitutional courts and this judicial audience has not been subject to extensive analysis. In civil law countries, constitutional courts have been inserted as a "special court" into a legal system with an already established judicial hierarchy.[12] While some civil law countries may have different specialized courts with well-defined jurisdictions (such as administrative, tax, or labor courts), these tend to be depoliticized and are clearly within the judicial branch; they have traditionally been fairly deferential toward other branches of government. This is not so with constitutional courts, which appear more political in nature and are qualitatively different from ordinary courts. This greater political profile is hardly surprising, since the insulation of ordinary courts from politics was one of the corollaries of the Kelsenian theory. However, the resulting politicization of the constitutional court may create a problem in terms of deference by the higher judicial courts. Furthermore, there may be institutional rivalries between the top court (or courts) of the ordinary jurisdiction, accustomed to holding a superior place in the judicial hierarchy, and the new constitutional court. One might think of the introduction of a new constitutional court as a legal irritant, to use Gunther Teubner's pithy phrase, causing a reaction from the traditional courts.[13] Conflict can lead to legal incoherence and gridlock, which tend to harm collective reputation.

Such conflicts between the supreme court and the constitutional court have taken place in many countries, usually arising when the supreme court rejects the supremacy of the constitutional court in a particular case.[14] These conflicts are typically exacerbated once concrete constitutional review is developed to its full extent, since the interaction between judicial courts and the constitutional court is more intense, and coordination between the two systems is essential. The natural goal for the constitutional court in this context is to achieve normative supremacy as the highest court in the country; in other words, the court aims to establish a degree of control over a traditionally depoliticized and deferential judicial system.[15] In contrast, the supreme court may wish to preserve its reputation as the final court on matters within its jurisdiction.

We might expect that a constitutional court that needs to establish and enhance its reputation before the ordinary courts would develop a significant aversion to dissent, with its concordant emphasis on individual reputation. Too much dissent will signal to the legal audience that the law is unsettled and may undermine the collective reputation of the constitutional court, inviting resistance from the ordinary courts. Not surprisingly, constitutional courts tend to be quite consensual when they are first formed and become increasingly polarized as time goes by; judicial activism and judicial boldness take some time to emerge. Constitutional courts that are relatively weak vis-à-vis their supreme courts, such as those in France and Italy, take a long time to become polarized (and even now these two courts still preserve the façade of unanimous decisions by not publishing dissents). Even though the long-run trend seems to be toward increasing polarization, cycles are observable in all countries; these cycles seem to be related to political instability or transition in the party system—in particular, the power of the constitutional court relative to other branches. Reputation is power, and a court that builds up a stock of reputation can insulate itself from political pressures.[16]

This chapter explicitly addresses the interaction between the political and the judicial dimensions of Kelsenian constitutional courts. We focus on jurisdictions with a distinct constitutional court sitting alongside a supreme court, though of course there are also intrajudicial politics within any unified court system. However, the problem is of much less importance in a unified court system since a clear hierarchy mitigates conflict, and there is no potential conflict over supremacy between the supreme court and the constitutional court. A unified system allows better cultivation of reputation for the judiciary as a whole, as judges will share common socialization, a single appointment process, and a disciplinary hierarchy. Essentially, the problem is that a two-headed court system creates competition for reputation, which can end up hurting both bodies.

Our emphasis is on dissent as a measure of internal polarization, which is tied to individual reputation building. Other literature has stressed the internal incentives to disfavor dissent, such as the value of a pleasant workplace or the costs of writing a separate opinion.[17] Our approach emphasizes external incentives for constitutional judges, not only in terms of providing consistent legal doctrines, but also in terms of obtaining the approval and respect of judicial courts. Moreover, in accordance with recent work, Kelsenian constitutional courts tend to satisfy the conditions for dissent aversion, in that they are relatively small in composition and have a significant workload (unlike the US Supreme Court).[18]

The approach we develop to explain the behavior of the Kelsenian constitutional judges is broadly inspired by the distinction between policy preferences and dispositional preferences.[19] Policy preferences are associated with the court's opinion, while dispositional preferences reflect an ideal position associated with the judge's opinion. Constitutional judges sometimes have to trade policy losses (whether or not a constitutional judge supports the court's opinion) against dispositional losses (whether or not a constitutional judge delivers an opinion consistent with the most preferred solution). Policy losses are determined by the interaction between the constitutional and the supreme courts, whereas dispositional losses are independently determined in each court (since they are fully determined by individual judges). In a broader view, this kind of analysis belongs to the literature on strategic judicial decision making. Rather than relying on mere attitudinal inclinations, courts in that literature are modeled as behaving in anticipation of reactions by the other branches of government (in our case, the supreme court).[20]

A final preliminary comment is in order. Our concepts of judicial and political audiences are ideal types. We recognize that constitutional courts also interact with other audiences, including losing parties who need to be convinced of the legitimacy of unfavorable court decisions, legal scholars, and the general public. However, in this chapter, we focus primarily on the political and judicial audiences to isolate the countervailing forces that we believe constrain or influence a Kelsenian-type constitutional court.

The first part of this chapter motivates the question under discussion—namely, the importance of the relationship between the constitutional court and the supreme court in jurisdictions that have both institutions.[21] In the second part, we extend the discussion to consider the importance of abstract versus concrete review, the existence of opportunities for court confrontation, and other institutional factors. The last part introduces an empirical analysis that supports our approach.

Motivation

We focus on the tension between the political and judicial audiences for constitutional jurisprudence. Most of the judicial behavior literature addresses these two sets of constraints on decision making as implicitly separate, and the judicial dimension has not attracted the same scholarly attention as the political dimension. This may be because the literature has been developed most extensively in the United States, in which there is only one highest court, and where political scientists have focused attention on the Supreme Court for more than fifty years.[22] But the two dimensions are necessarily interrelated and generate a complicated trade-off between advancing the political agenda of the constitutional court and competing with the higher courts for judicial supremacy. In some cases, the goals might coincide. For example, promoting human rights might simultaneously enhance the reputation of the constitutional court with both judicial and political audiences. However, in many circumstances, these two goals conflict.

Some literature has identified the trade-off faced by American courts in terms of ideological activism and institutional activism.[23] Appealing to a political audience in our context can be seen as a form of ideological activism, in the sense of a propensity to strike down legislation that is incompatible with the ideology of the court. However, interacting with a judicial audience is a specific form of institutional activism in our terms, a form that has less to do with being deferential to other branches of government and more to do with achieving the *judicial* supremacy of the constitutional court.

Our approach is to consider the internal decision making of a constitutional court confronted with potentially conflicting external audiences. The key variable we are trying to explain is whether decision making on the court will be unified or fragmented—that is, whether or not there will be separate opinions. We argue that fragmentation is a function of which particular audience the court is targeting. We assume that the court is composed of individual judges with a range of ideological and legal preferences. We consider the work of the court as a whole to require the kind of team production we discussed in chapter 1. Individual judges might prefer to emphasize their individual contributions to the quality of decision making, but the court as a whole will also have a reputation for quality that sometimes requires suppressing the individual reputations of the judges. Here, we assume that the court can resolve internal collective action problems to the extent it wishes to produce unified opinions, but it might also prefer to reveal the internal preferences of its individual members.

In particular, we imagine that there are two strategies available for the court. On the one hand, the court can follow a *consensual decision-making* approach: decisions in the court are taken by unanimity and negotiated to achieve a consensus of all judges. This makes the constitutional court look like the other high courts in the careerist tradition.

Alternatively, the court can follow a strategy of *fragmentation*: decisions in the court are taken by majority, with concurring and dissenting opinions, if allowed, directly or indirectly revealing division in the constitutional court.[24] In keeping with the framework developed in chapter 1, consensus favors collective reputation while fragmentation favors individual reputation.

In a struggle for judicial supremacy, political fragmentation of the constitutional court is an impediment; a fragmented court does not look like the prototypical judicial court in civil law systems, where unanimous decision making prevails.[25] The top ordinary courts may thus resist implementing decisions that appear fragmented.

The source of political division within a constitutional court is easily understood, given the recognition mechanism of judicial appointment. But that contrasts heavily with the ordinary courts in a civil law system. As the introduction argued, the career model of the ordinary courts is accompanied by an ideology that each legal issue can only have one correct answer.[26] If there are many possible answers, then the underlying question is not legal but political in nature: the answer involves making choices that will advance some values and interests over others. Under the conventional theory, the personality and the ideology of the judge is irrelevant since there is only one correct answer.[27] As a consequence, dissenting and concurring opinions are rare and not welcome in civil law courts. The practice of allowing dissent in constitutional courts, where it exists, signals that they are political and not entirely judicial in nature.[28] When separate opinions are allowed, unanimous voting is a costly signal of a judicial nature, since specific ideological goals are sacrificed.

Consensus in a constitutional court thus expresses "legal" decision making rather than "political" decision making. Legal decision making enhances legitimacy in the eyes of the other higher courts. It also may help maintain judicial legitimacy in the eyes of the general public, thus enhancing the prestige of the court. At the same time, consensus could deter more explicit intervention by political actors. By enhancing the perception that decision making is legal, a constitutional court raises the costs (in terms of public opinion) for political bodies attempting to discipline or manipulate judges. A fragmented decision does not usually produce a formal constitutional precedent, in the sense of *jurisprudence constante* or *doctrina jurídica*, and even less in the common law sense of *stare decisis*. Therefore, a fragmented decision presumably leaves the constitutional court in a weaker position vis-à-vis the supreme court.

At the same time, fragmentation may be desirable from the point of view of individual judges. A judge appointed by a particular political actor may maximize her own reputation by signaling loyalty, even if in the minority view in a particular case. A credible ability to dissent also allows individual judges to push the outcomes of collective deliberations in a favorable direction. Fragmentation can also undermine the precedential value of decisions, which may be desirable when the law is in transition. The political audience favors fragmentation, even as the legal audience favors unanimity.

We should emphasize that our discussion applies to "strategic" unanimity and fragmentation. In many constitutional courts, such as those of France and Italy, no separate opinions are allowed (in keeping with the style of court decisions in alignment with the civil law tradition), so all decisions are formally unanimous. However, it is well known that even in these formally consensual courts, there are significant opportunities to expose division and signal dissent if needed.[29]

Institutional Factors

As we have argued, Kelsenian constitutional courts have to consider two different audiences in exercising constitutional review. Nevertheless, there are significant institutional factors that are relevant in determining the balance between the two audiences.

Abstract and Concrete Review

The first important institutional aspect is the balance of abstract and concrete review in the workload of the court.[30] In abstract review, the court exercises influence through screening legislation and shaping policy making. It involves, as Professor Alec Stone Sweet has put it, governing with judges.[31] Naturally, the political audience is more directly relevant to this activity than the judicial audience. This is not to say that the other courts are irrelevant. In many cases, the constitutional court might actually need the judicial courts to enforce its decisions. Nevertheless, the judicial audience is relatively more important in concrete review cases, since implementation often (though not always) requires cooperation between the constitutional court and ordinary courts.[32] Clearly, concrete review, whether it is initiated by incidental referrals from ordinary judges or direct constitutional complaints, blurs the separation between the constitutional court and the rest of the judiciary. It induces the constitutional court to participate in the resolution of individual cases, either substituting or complementing ordinary dispute resolution. The constitutional court substitutes for ordinary courts when it decides cases that would otherwise be within the judicial province; it complements them when it serves to resolve constitutional questions that are then implemented by ordinary courts. Neither function was intended in the original Kelsenian model, and apparently Kelsen himself was opposed to any form of concrete review by constitutional courts. The consequence is a less transparent delimitation of jurisdictions and the potential emergence of conflicts of competence between the constitutional court and the higher judicial courts.[33]

Abstract review (and in particular preventive or ex ante promulgation) by its very nature provides a weak mechanism for a constitutional court to try to condition other courts. There is no obvious relation between the review of legislation in the abstract and the work of courts. However, given the importance of the constitutional court, creative techniques can be developed to achieve influence over ordinary judges. For example, the French idea of a "conforming interpretation," in which national law is interpreted in a way that conforms as much as possible to European law, is conceptually influential and can be used to require ordinary judges to interpret the law to avoid a constitutional conflict.[34] Yet where abstract review is very limited (such as in Italy), the ability to shape legislative outcomes is reduced and constrains the political influence of the court.[35]

The possibility of a conflict between the two major court systems has substantive implications. First, it puts pressure on constitutional judges to achieve a coherent and prestigious body of constitutional jurisprudence so as to convince the ordinary courts of the legal integrity of constitutional decision making.[36] Therefore, it transforms the nature and scope of constitutional review by creating pressure for a façade of apolitical decision making, even if there is in fact internal disagreement. The constitutional court must be a better legal craftsman when it relies on ordinary courts to implement its decisions. Second, conflict or competition among the courts increases the political value of constitutional review because it can provide an indirect mechanism for influencing both policy and the judiciary (if politicians use the constitutional court to interfere with the ordinary courts). The natural inclination for the constitutional court is to expand competences that make it politically more relevant; the progressive constitutionalization of private law in several jurisdictions is just one example. Third, the balance of power is shaped by the constitution itself—that is, the extent to which a constitutional court is conceived of as not only a negative legislator but a positive legislator with formidable powers of statutory interpretation.[37] As a positive legislator, the court not only strikes laws but actively interprets the conditions under which they can be implemented. If a constitutional court has a role as a positive legislator, it can act either as a counterweight against the parliamentary majority or as a substitute if no stable parliamentary majority exists.[38]

Concrete review is not immune from politics. However, the capacity to advance an ideological agenda through concrete review is more limited than through abstract review. Concrete review requires the constitutional court to develop specific legal reasoning in terms of rhetoric and judicial syntax that makes it similar to a decision of an ordinary court while at the same time advancing a particular ideological agenda. Since ordinary courts do not engage in abstract review, the constitutional court is not under pressure to use similar specific legal reasoning in those cases.

Another type of review is preventive (abstract) review, in which a court merely blocks unconstitutional policies *before* implementation. Whereas concrete review "judicializes" constitutional courts, preventive review has the opposite effect. Mere preventive review makes a constitutional court less judicial and more political—indeed legislative—in nature.[39] Constitutional courts as idealized by Kelsen are political in nature. Their work, albeit judicial in form and procedure, is fundamentally political. Hence they should not be part of the traditional judiciary or court structure. The point is that constitutional law is political in nature, and constitutional adjudication is a necessary part of the political process. If law is the mere formalization of politics, then constitutional review is necessarily political. The distinction between law and politics is likely not to be clear in constitutional review.[40]

The double role of the constitutional court as a political and a judicial institution creates pressures for "judicialization" of politics for two reasons. First, the goal of expanding institutional power affects the delicate balance between the judicial and the political structures. As the court becomes more politically involved, other political agents will became aware of it and respond. Second, fragmented party systems make the role of a constitutional court more important, as disparate political groups seek a third party to resolve disputes and the policy space for the court to work in expands. The "judicialization of politics" necessarily politicizes the court. Hence politics inside the constitutional court become unavoidably contaminated by party politics. The stakes are simply too relevant and important for political parties not to interfere.[41]

At the same time, the ongoing skirmishes between the two major courts can actually contaminate the supreme court, leading it to depart from traditional decision making, style, and content of decisions. The process of replacing literal statutory interpretation through the embracing of general principles of law invented and created by courts in Europe has been explained as a byproduct of the interaction between the two higher courts. One particular striking case is France. Traditionally, the French higher courts insisted on judicial deference to the legislative and executive branches and favored the administrative review of legality and good governance over the judicial review of constitutionality.[42] The slow development of constitutional principles applied to individual rights and liberties by the French Conseil Constitutionnel after the 1970s, coupled with other external factors, resulted in significant changes in the legal culture of the other French courts.[43] Recently, the French higher courts have shifted toward the use of fundamental principles at the expense of code law. Partially, this trend has responded to more individual capacity for participation in the judicial process (by making use of individual rights). Inevitably, the higher courts have been more frequently asked to deliberate on these (largely uncodified) general principles that affect public policy.[44] Although this shift has been criticized by many French legal commentators for undermining legal security, this form of judicial activism by the Cour de Cassation and the Conseil d'État is arguably a response to the activist approach taken by the Conseil Constitutionnel since the early 1980s.

Opportunity, Structure, and Other Factors

Inevitably, a constitutional court is not likely to be fragmented all the time or consensual all the time. In that sense, we expect a "mixed" strategy that responds to the relative importance of both political and judicial audiences in a given context. The implementation of a "mixed" strategy will depend on a number of factors.

One immediate aspect to consider is the opportunity for exercising constitutional review. This is partly a function of institutional design. Usually abstract review must be triggered by political actors (other branches of government, opposition, other political actors), and therefore the court has little control over its occurrence. As to concrete review, there are different possibilities. Direct constitutional complaints are generated by private actors and citizens in general. In many countries, however, ordinary citizens can access the constitutional court only through incidental referrals by ordinary courts in the context of concrete cases.

Relative to the US Supreme Court, then, most constitutional courts have relatively little control over their dockets.

A second important aspect is the extension of competences of the constitutional court relative to nonconstitutional jurisdiction.[45] Formally, the extension of constitutional law is explicitly defined by the constitution. But a constitutional court engaging in maximizing supremacy and jurisdiction will use case law to increase the scope of constitutional law. It could also influence the other branches of government to promote constitutional amendments that further consolidate the role of constitutional law. For example, the inevitable instability of federal arrangements might empower the constitutional court to interfere in areas that were not anticipated in earlier periods. (Spain and Germany provide good examples here, as does, arguably, the history of the European Union.)[46] So the extent to which the delimitation of constitutional vis-à-vis infraconstitutional matters is expressed in the constitution is an important exogenous variable that constrains courts.

Inevitably the enlargement of constitutional law and the reduction of infraconstitutional law will result in clashes with the higher courts. Formally most legal systems allocate to the constitutional court the monopoly over the decision of which matters are constitutional. The so-called *Kompetenz-Kompetenz* question (i.e., who has the power to decide who has the power) has been resolved in most legal systems, and therefore conflicts should not exist—at least in theory. However, such a formalistic approach ignores the practicalities of judicial decision making and disregards the ingenious abilities of higher courts to undermine formal solutions to conflicts, should they wish to.

Another relevant variable for understanding the extent to which a constitutional court cares about achieving supremacy is its composition. Limited tenure certainly reduces the incentives for long-run court-specific investments in reputation while incentivizing judges to be concerned about outside employment opportunities after their terms in the court are finished. Career magistrates who are sitting on the constitutional court (as in some countries) might be less interested in sacrificing the influence and scope of powers of the supreme court, since they will presumably return there after their term is over. Life tenure certainly may foster more judicial concern about achieving supremacy and may increase the willingness of the constitutional judges to trade off short-run goals against gains in the future.

At the same time, court turnover affects the ability to generate consensus. It could be that there is a "period of acclimation" during which new constitutional judges avoid confrontation and are more willing to sacrifice ideological preferences.[47] However, as we have argued previously, consensus requires stability in the composition of the court, which is incompatible with high turnover. This effect is likely to be more relevant if the appointment process is politically divisive.

Empirical Analysis

In this section, we provide some suggestive quantitative evidence that supports our analysis and then discuss several examples. We have collected data on twenty-two constitutional courts (including France, where before 2009 only ex ante promulgation abstract review existed). Table 5.1 summarizes the findings in terms of reported incidence of conflicts between constitutional and supreme courts (as reported in the press and in legal journals) and the stability of the court majority (as measured by a stable allocation of seats to political parties—that is, a quota system by which political parties have a relatively fixed number of seats in the constitutional court).

Table 5.2 presents an econometric analysis relying on previous empirical work by the authors as well as specialized local reports. We operationalize stability in a slightly different way; we consider the existence of a quota system and whether there have been any reported conflicts over appointments to the constitutional court. For additional data, we relied on reports from the Twelfth European Conference of Constitutional Courts, which focused on relations between the constitutional courts and other national courts, including conflicts.

Our account predicts that there is an important relationship between court stability and conflict between the constitutional court and the supreme court. We expect to see more conflicts between the constitutional

Table 5.1 Conflict and stability in constitutional courts in twenty-two countries

	Stable party composition	Variable party composition
Low incidence of conflicts	Germany (after 1970s), Austria, Belgium, Portugal, Taiwan (before 2000s), Hungary, Lithuania, Turkey, South Africa	France (before 2009), Chile, South Korea, Slovakia, Slovenia, Latvia, Ukraine
Occasional incidence of conflicts	Germany (before 1970s), Poland, Russia	France (after 2009), Spain, Italy, Colombia, Czech Republic, Taiwan (after 2000s)

Table 5.2 Probit analysis of intercourt conflict

Variable	Coefficient
Instability (coded by authors)	0.46** (0.17)
Rule of law (using world governance indicators)	−0.10 (0.07)
Population (using Penn world tables)	2.17^{e-06} (4.73^{e-06})
GDP per capita (IMF)	1.24^{e-07} (2.10^{e-07})
N	28
Pseudo R²	0.30

Marginal effects are reported; robust standard errors are in parentheses.
**p<0.05
Log likelihood is −12.85.

and the supreme courts when there is court instability, all else equal. To assess this, we first produced two dummy variables for twenty-eight courts, one representing instability in the allocation of seats on the court and the other representing the existence of occasional confrontation between the supreme court and the constitutional court. Our hypothesis is that there is positive correlation between these two dummies, and we indeed find a correlation of 0.4.

Ideally, of course, we would be able to conduct a serious multivariate analysis. However, the paucity of data (and the fact that we could only find reliable information for twenty-eight different countries) presents a challenge to conducting serious estimates. Nevertheless, we provide a simple probit analysis in which the dependent variable is the existence of conflict among courts and the independent variable is the level of instability of the court majority, as well as country-level controls for GDP per capita, population, and the World Bank's rule of law indicator.[48] These controls are standard in cross-country regressions (and, due to the limited number of observations, we have excluded other standard regressors such as the region dummies). We report marginal effects. The regression shows that the coefficient for instability is statistically significant and has the correct (positive) sign. The probability that there are occasional conflicts between supreme and constitutional courts increases by a value in the order of 46 percent when the court majority is instable. While our small sample and the fact that our measures of stability and conflict are crude make it difficult to draw strong conclusions, the relationship is surely worth further investigation. The next section explores this and the other hypotheses outlined above through a series of case studies of prominent jurisdictions.

Cases

Germany

The Federal Constitutional Court of Germany was established in 1951. It is composed of sixteen judges and divided into two senates of eight constitutional judges each, based in specialization of areas of constitutional law.[49] The sixteen constitutional judges are appointed by Parliament, eight by the lower house (the Bundestag) and eight by the upper house (the Bundesrat). As a consequence of the appointment mechanism, which requires a supermajority in Parliament, there is a need for a consensus between major political parties.[50] Over time, a norm has developed so that constitutional judges are effectively appointed on party tickets without public hearings.[51] The fact is that the supermajority requirement (a two-thirds majority) has created a de facto quota system.[52] Traditionally, the two major parties divide the seats, with the occasional appointment of a judge from one of the minor parties to reflect parliamentary composition and ongoing governmental coalitions. As a consequence, we can conclude that the majority in the German court is reasonably stable.

Dissenting opinions were always regarded as inappropriate by many German constitutional judges, who had been trained in the civil law orthodoxy of a single correct answer to legal disputes. Dissent was formally introduced in 1970. In the early 1970s, however, many constitutional judges resisted the idea of separate opinions, as they seemingly proved the court to be more political in nature than the rest of the German courts.[53] Many constitutional judges, particularly career magistrates, refused to file dissenting opinions.[54]

The relationship between the German Constitutional Court and the rest of the courts has not always been smooth, but overall, explicit conflicts are rare. Cooperation is required to effectuate constitutional decisions: constitutional questions that arise in ordinary disputes are referred to the Constitutional Court through the incidental reference mechanism, after which the interpretation of the Constitution is sent back to the originating court to apply. Although the German Constitutional Court was inserted into a complex structure with a five-headed supreme court, the ordinary courts were in a weak position in the early 1950s, given their failure to oppose the Nazi regime and their history of enforcing despicable Nazi laws. Clearly, the new German Constitutional Court was untainted by any Nazi past and was perceived as the guarantor of the new democratic regime.[55] Therefore, as predicted by our approach, the court focused its early decisions on the political audience, deciding many important issues about the political process and achieving administrative and budgetary autonomy in 1952. The confrontation with the other courts only emerged later.[56]

By the late 1950s there were some skirmishes over procedural rules—in particular when the German Constitutional Court decided that the supreme courts could not submit their own opinions about constitutionality in the context of incidental review and later abolished their participation in judicial referrals. The supreme courts protested. However, more was to come. In landmark decisions in 1957 and 1958, the court extended a general right to "individual liberty," therefore effectively subjecting all private law to constitutional review. Inevitably this caused the supreme courts to lose exclusive jurisdiction over many areas of the law. Clear refusals by ordinary courts to follow the doctrines of the Constitutional Court are rare, given the legal status of the Constitutional Court, but scholars have identified areas where divergences have been taking place (for example, the "expropriation" clause concerning property or compliance with rules on the length of detention). Occasionally, one of the supreme courts is more vocal against doctrines developed by the German Constitutional Court (for example, the supreme court in civil and criminal matters, the Bundesgerichtshof), but by and large, the courts appear to accommodate them.[57]

Despite these skirmishes, legal scholars argue that the situation in Germany is less confrontational than in other jurisdictions.[58] Our approach explains this path by emphasizing the historically weak position of the supreme courts, both in terms of their limited jurisdiction (each of them vis-à-vis the other four supreme courts) and the Nazi period. On the other hand, the stabilized political appointment processes in the German Constitutional Court have allowed the development of doctrines that emphasize the judicial role at the expense of advancing particular short-run ideological gains.[59] Stability has led to the effective subordination of the ordinary courts.

France

The Conseil Constitutionnel is a specialized body separated from the judiciary and the other branches of government.[60] Formally, the duty of the council is to ensure that the principles and rules of the constitution are upheld.[61] It was established in 1958 to act as a watchdog of the legislature on behalf of the executive branch, given the well-known

French antipathy to judicial interference in governmental affairs.[62] It is sometimes considered more like a fourth branch of government, or a third house of the legislature, rather than a judicial court.[63] The French council was conceived originally as a political body that progressively has evolved more judicial competences. Not surprisingly, given its nature, the political audience has been important for the court from its early stages.

The council is composed of nine members who serve a nine-year, nonrenewable term. The council is renewed in thirds every three years. Three of its members are named by the president of the republic, three by the president of the national assembly, and three by the president of the senate. In addition to the nine members, former presidents of the republic are members of the Constitutional Council for life.[64] The appointments to the council are not always judges (and in a few rare cases are not even legally trained)[65] but rather are predominantly professional politicians.[66]

Individual behavior cannot be monitored due to the collegiality of the council. The secret nature of judicial deliberations, the façade of unanimity, the lack of dissenting opinions, the lack of methods for detecting division, and the lack of public discussion or hearings are impediments to analyzing the case in our framework.[67] Nevertheless, there are clues that provide some support for our position.

First, the court majority has been unstable. The council was overwhelmingly dominated by the right for a long time while Gaullists were in government. The rising influence of the socialists in the 1980s was reflected in a left-wing majority for the period from 1986 to 2002.[68] Since 2002, the council has again been dominated by the right.

Given the nature and formal role of the court, it is not surprising that the political audience seems to have played a larger role than in other countries. At the same time, the particularities of the institutional arrangements have not helped streamline the interaction between this court and the other major courts (Cour de Cassation and Conseil d'État). To start with, the council is not formally a part of the French judiciary. Until 2009, the decisions of the council were addressed exclusively to the legislature. France had a form of abstract and preventive constitutional review with no formal access procedure for individuals other than specific political actors.[69]

Still, there is some indication that the French constitutional judges have been concerned with the judicial branch. There has been an effort to provide coherent and consistent case law.[70] At the same time, the shift to more general (uncodified) principles of law has significantly influenced the Cour de Cassation, which has tended to align the legal doctrines developed by both courts. Traditionally, the Conseil d'État was less accommodating to the cooperative mode, but this has changed in recent years. The informal sharing of clerks among the three top courts has also contributed to the harmonization of procedure and sentencing.[71]

The recent reforms of 2009 introducing concrete review inevitably reinforced the importance of judicial audience, and we can expect some significant skirmishes in the future. In fact, the immediate reaction of the Cour de Cassation to the new mechanism of preliminary reference to the Conseil Constitutionnel has been quite problematic. By April 2010, the Cour de Cassation involved the European Court of Justice in a dispute concerning the validity of the preliminary reference to the Conseil Constitutionnel within EU law (under Article 267 TFEU).[72] By 2011, the Cour de Cassation ruled on police custody powers in open contradiction with the Conseil Constitutionnel.[73]

Italy

The Italian Constitutional Court was established in 1955. There are fifteen judges selected by three different actors who appoint five judges each. The five judges appointed by the parliament require a supermajority (in a joint vote of the two chambers, by a two-thirds majority for the first three rounds, and thereafter a three-fifths majority). As expected, this has resulted in a structural arrangement that corresponds to a de facto quota system. However, the five judges appointed by the president and the five judges elected by the judiciary disrupt the existence of a stable court majority.

Several mechanisms have been implemented to avoid explicit party alignments, including the writing of single opinions, secret votes, and the disallowance of concurring or dissenting opinions. The confrontation between the Constitutional Court and the other top courts in Italy has been widely documented.[74] The main source for the difficult relationship between the Italian Constitutional Court and the ordinary courts is the process of submission of "legal questions." Once an ordinary court submits a "question," the court decides on constitutional interpretation, and the ruling is an important part of law applied to the case by the ordinary court.[75] The Constitutional Court has developed particular techniques of interpretation that occasionally collide with the doctrines developed by the ordinary courts. There were major clashes between the Italian Constitutional Court and the Italian Court of Cassation in 1965.[76] More skirmishes followed in the 1970s and in the 1980s. In the late 1990s, new confrontations took place in the area of criminal law and criminal procedure, with the refusal of the Court of Cassation to apply interpretative developments advanced by the Constitutional Court.[77]

A particular source of conflict is the trend toward "interpretative decisions" by the Italian Constitutional Court in the last few decades, in which the court says that only a particular reading of the legislation is constitutional. However, under Italian law, only decisions concerning unconstitutionality are formally binding. "Interpretative decisions" demand express cooperation of the judicial courts.[78]

The difficult coexistence of top courts in Italy is well explained by our approach. The dockets of the Constitutional Court rely heavily on questions interposed by ordinary courts.[79] Hence there is a direct relationship that creates tension, since the decisions by the Constitutional Court immediately affect the outcomes of the cases heard by the ordinary courts, hence limiting the influence of the Court of Cassation. The *application* of the law is still a monopoly of the ordinary courts, so the Constitutional Court has to convince the ordinary courts that a cooperative mode is better for all. Inevitably the judicial audience plays a very important role in explaining the behavior of this court. Instability in the composition of the Constitutional Court has limited its ability to effectively discipline the lower courts, and conflict has continued.

Other Examples

Spain

The Spanish Constitutional Court was established by the 1978 Constitution, which introduced a parliamentary regime under a constitutional monarchy after almost forty years of dictatorship led by General Franco. The court is composed of twelve judges. They are nominated for a nine-year nonrenewable term. The mixed appointment mechanism involves the government, the two chambers of Parliament, and the judicial council and has diluted the possibility of a de facto stable quota system. Significant skirmishes between the Spanish Constitutional Court and the Spanish Supreme Court have been widely documented. Tension with the Spanish Supreme Court, the highest court for infraconstitutional matters, has been observed due to the leading role of the Spanish Constitutional Court in guiding lower courts in interpreting laws that affect individual rights and liberties.[80]

More recently, the incapacity of the Constitutional Court to decide on the constitutionality of the Catalan Constitution due to its internal polarization has contributed to a serious deficit of reputation.[81] At the same time, the ongoing conflict with the Spanish Supreme Court has not been reduced.[82] The resulting loss of credibility of the Spanish Constitutional Court has been widely discussed by the media. We again see internal fragmentation harming the external supremacy of the Constitutional Court.

Portugal

The Portuguese Constitutional Court was inaugurated in 1982 (after the first constitutional reform) and exercises constitutional review according to the 1976 Constitution. There are thirteen constitutional judges. Ten of the judges are elected by Parliament, requiring a two-thirds majority (elected judges), and the remaining three are chosen by the elected judges (appointed judges). In practice, the elected judges are extracted from a unique list of names negotiated by the parliamentary leadership of the main parties. Moreover, a *de facto* quota system exists, which allocates party seats to the major parties, thus explaining the stability of the court majority. There are six right-wing judges and six left-wing judges, the thirteenth being a personality perceived to be politically neutral.[83] Constitutional judges are elected for nonrenewable terms of nine years. (The mandate was for six years and renewable for a second period in office before the 1997 reform.) The political structure of the court is thus fairly stable and predictable.

There have been very few conflicts between the Portuguese Constitutional Court and the Portuguese Supreme Court. This is in part a result of the hybrid system by which lower courts can also perform constitutional review in concrete cases (a design of US influence that reached Portugal through the 1891 Brazilian Constitution).[84] Under our approach, the stability of the court majority might have helped the constitutional judges defer particular ideological gains when exercising concrete review, focusing on consolidating the position of the court vis-à-vis the ordinary courts (thus entertaining many appeals on constitutional issues from lower courts), while using abstract review to signal party allegiance.[85]

Taiwan

The Republic of China (Taiwan) Constitution is one of the oldest constitutions currently in force, dating from its adoption on the mainland in

1947. Similarly, the Taiwanese Constitutional Court (known as the Grand Justices of the Judicial Yuan) predates almost all the other specialized Kelsenian constitutional courts. Although composition and competences have been reformed in the last fifty years, the Taiwanese Constitutional Court is not a new institution, like its counterparts in many third-wave democracies, but an institution that has persevered throughout the authoritarian period and the more recent emerging democracy. The age and role of the Taiwanese Constitutional Court make it quite different from other constitutional courts around the world.

Prior to 2003, the court was composed of seventeen judges who were appointed by the president with approval of the Control Yuan (1948–92) or the National Assembly (1992–2000) and served for renewable terms of nine years.[86] Since 2003, the number of constitutional judges has been reduced to fifteen. They are now appointed by the president with the majority consent of the Legislative Yuan and serve nonrenewable terms of eight years.

Dissent was unusual in the authoritarian period. From the transition to democracy in the late 1980s to today, there have been three presidents, two affiliated with the traditional KMT (Chinese Nationalist Party; Kuomintang) and one supported by the opposition (Democratic Progressive Party; DPP).[87] The disproportional influence of the KMT-appointed judges is clear, although we should not take the KMT to be a monolithic party. The court majority has been stable even after the election of DPP President Chen.

Taiwan's court exercises exclusively abstract power: it requires ordinary courts to refer concrete cases to it, and decisions in such cases require implementation by the ordinary courts. Until 1993, this referral power was concentrated in the Supreme Court of the Republic of China and the Supreme Administrative Court: lower courts could not refer cases. Furthermore, in the initial design of the Constitutional Court, it was not seen as having the power to review Supreme Court decisions that might potentially conflict with the Constitution. Just as democratization was beginning in 1986, the Constitutional Court moved to assert jurisdiction over Supreme Court decisions.[88] It later ruled that lower court justices could refer cases directly to the Constitutional Court, empowering the lower ranks of the judicial hierarchy and securing supremacy over the Supreme Court.[89] With the need to communicate unity to the judicial audience resolved, the court became more involved in political matters, adjudicating major policy questions. Dissent rates increased from a low base, though the court still insists on unity in certain important cases.[90] The political audience became primary.

South Korea

The South Korean Constitutional Court was established in late 1988 as part of the establishment of South Korea's Sixth Republic. Though expected by the constitutional drafters to be a relatively quiescent institution, the court has become the embodiment of the new democratic constitutional order of South Korea. The court consists of nine justices who serve six-year renewable terms, now staggered so that justices are appointed in sets. Three justices each are appointed by the Supreme Court, the National Assembly, and the president. As a consequence, there is no stable majority in the court.

The South Korean Constitutional Court has been engaged in occasional struggles with the Supreme Court over jurisdiction. The distinction between administrative and legislative interpretation is not as clear or straightforward as might be imagined. The question of the constitutionality of an administrative regulation frequently requires interpretation of the relevant statutory text. A restrictive interpretation of a statute will tend to void on constitutional grounds any administrative actions taken under it, where those actions rely on a broad reading of the statute. So the Constitutional Court is able to shape Supreme Court constitutional interpretations where the Constitutional Court is able to issue a prior decision on the statute underlying administrative action. But if it acts second, it cannot always do so.

The problem is caused in part by the design flaw that ordinary court decisions are not explicitly included within the jurisdiction of the Constitutional Court.[91] At the same time, the law provides that rulings of the court on unconstitutionality are to be respected by ordinary courts, other state agencies, and local government bodies.[92] This means that while ordinary courts must abide by Constitutional Court decisions, they are themselves the sole determiners of what those decisions require. Ordinary courts cannot be corrected by the Constitutional Court for failure to apply its decisions correctly. Rather, the Supreme Court is the sole body able to overrule lower court decisions. Therefore, much is at stake on the question of whether Supreme Court decisions can be appealed to the Constitutional Court.

In 1990, the Constitutional Court unilaterally decided that it had implied jurisdiction over administrative regulations issued pursuant to statutes and that the assignment of administrative review in Article 107(2) to the ordinary courts was not exclusive.[93] In response to that decision, the Supreme Court issued a statement to all ordinary judges condemning the Constitutional Court decision and stating that it had "gone beyond its domain."[94] Later, in 1995, the Constitutional Court declared a tax law partially unconstitutional and dictated that it could only be applied if given a particular narrow interpretation by ordinary courts.[95] The Supreme Court responded that, since the Constitutional Court had no authority over ordinary court judgments, its decision could only be taken as an expression of opinion regarding constitutionality and had no binding force over ordinary courts. The ordinary courts then proceeded to apply the controversial tax law in the manner that the Constitutional Court had criticized. In December 1997, the original petitioner again sought relief from the Constitutional Court, and the court obliged by annulling the Supreme Court judgment, even though it had no explicit power to do so in the Constitutional Court Act. The court also voided the portion of the Constitutional Court Act that excluded ordinary court decisions from constitutional review, saying that Constitutional Court decisions must be binding on all. The Supreme Court responded by holding a press conference, asserting that it would reply through a judgment.[96] Subsequently, the Constitutional Court continued to consider ordinary court judgments in certain cases, and it now appears that the theory of the Constitutional Court has been accepted de facto.

Colombia

The Constitutional Court of Colombia was established in 1992. It is formed by nine judges selected by the Senate under the proposal of the president, the Supreme Court of Colombia, and the Colombian Supreme Administrative Court (with each selecting three candidates) for a term of eight years. The resulting composition of the court is not ideologically stable and has led to well-documented conflicts between the Colombian Constitutional Court and the Supreme Court. Because the Supreme Court and Supreme Administrative Court (Consejo de Estado) traditionally rendered *res judicata* rulings (thus without any revision or appellate process available), inevitable conflicts of power arose after the new constitutional mandate was in place. The bolder doctrines developed by the Colombian Constitutional Court on personal rights conflicted with the approaches taken by the higher courts. The inevitable antagonism between these institutions led to legislation in 2000 to subordinate the higher courts to the decisions of the Constitutional Court.[97] This is an example of how a political audience ultimately had to intervene to ensure the supremacy of a constitutional court after costly conflicts.

Conclusion

In earlier chapters, we introduced the construct of reputation as a tool for understanding forces involved in the structure and supervision of ordinary courts. This chapter has extended that model to constitutional courts, focusing on the different audiences before which courts seek to develop reputation.

This chapter has proposed a reputation-based explanation for why Kelsenian constitutional courts may be less fragmented than the attitudinal model would suggest. Like attitudinalists, we argue that constitutional judges want to advance their ideological agenda. But institutional structures are crucial for understanding how they can do so. In this chapter, we focus on the fact that constitutional courts face competition from other higher courts in terms of influencing the law and lower court judges. In order to advance their ideological agenda, constitutional judges need to have influence over other high courts, requiring them to sacrifice immediate ideological goals in order to demonstrate unity. They sometimes invest in collective reputation, sacrificing individual reputation, in the early years after creation of the court. When the composition of constitutional courts becomes unstable or divided, however, this unity is more difficult to achieve, and one result is conflict among jurisdictions.

Our analysis has provided preliminary empirical evidence and reviewed several important cases from the perspective of our theory. The case studies provide examples of significantly politicized constitutional courts that seek to cultivate reputation before the political audience. With regard to judicial audiences, there is more variation. In Italy, Spain, Colombia, and South Korea, we observe more tension between the constitutional court and other higher courts, whereas Germany and Portugal exhibit a more collaborative mode. Taiwan represents both patterns at different periods in its history: a cooperative attitude during dictatorship and a struggle for supremacy during democracy, ultimately resolved by the victory of the constitutional court. France traditionally exhibited a collaborative mode that has now evolved toward more tension after the introduction of concrete review in 2009. We have identified factors to account for the varying developments observed in these jurisdictions— namely, a stable and consistent court majority and the legal and judicial prestige of the constitutional court. When the constitutional court is stable, it is better able to overcome tendencies toward internal fragmentation and thus better able to assert superiority over other courts.

Constitutional courts operate at the junction of jurisprudence and politics. Where intercourt rivalry is low, reputational concerns may be less visible. As rivalry increases, courts may try to maintain and increase reputation by engaging in power struggles to an extent seldom seen among ordinary courts. Power and politics may in fact become more important than pure reputational concerns with regard to the primary audiences involved. Reputation sometimes appears to be an effect that is secondary to the consideration and behavior of the audiences.

SIX

The Rule of Lawyers: Globalization, International Law, and Judicial Reputation

We live in an era in which the determinants of judicial reputation are rapidly changing as a result of globalization. The intensified cross-border interaction and dramatically lower information costs that result from new technologies have changed the mechanisms by which courts and judges communicate with each other and their key audiences. Intensified economic competition, combined with a global emphasis on the rule of law as a determinant of economic performance, has increased the stakes involved in reputation but also the ability to learn. At the same time, the expansion of international arbitration has produced significant competition for public systems of dispute resolution. And at the level of public international law, a major proliferation of judicial institutions has expanded the field, providing both opportunities and challenges.

One way to think about these developments is that the reputation of judges is now determined globally and in an increasingly competitive environment. Globalization changes both the demand and the supply curves of judicial reputation. In the era of the nation-state, a judiciary's reputation was determined primarily by its interaction with domestic audiences—mainly other branches of government and the national public. In the twenty-first century, in contrast, a judiciary's reputation may in part be determined by the global reputation of law as a field. Law competes with other devices for social ordering; judges compete with other producers of law for authority. In short, judges now have some stake in the products of their brethren in other states.

This chapter describes some of the changes that affect the nature, supply, and demand of judicial reputation. We argue, broadly speaking, that both supply and demand curves have shifted upward and that new technologies of monitoring and communication are facilitating the expansion of judicial reputation. We focus our attention on what is known as the rule of law project, a global multisectoral effort to promote the rule of law. By its nature, this project also involves the rule of lawyers and, specifically, the rule of judges. We then discuss the expansion of international courts and tribunals and their impact on national judicial reputation.

The Nature of Reputation and the Possibility of Global Teams

In chapter 1, we considered judicial reputation as a problem of team production, in which individual judicial reputation was in part a function of the work of other judges and collective reputation required securing investment from individuals. The possibility of global audiences means that, to some extent, there is an overall *global* reputation of judges. One might think of this as a team production problem, in which the task is to maximize the total reputation of all individual courts, each of which faces its own team production problem. These courts may consist of national judiciaries, constitutional courts, and international tribunals, all of which have a stake in the overall rule of law project.

For any particular national judiciary, the global project may not be very important. If the judiciary already occupies a strong position in its domestic political and legal order, it may care little about what happens in other countries or at international courts, as these actors will not affect its reputation much. On the other hand, if the judiciary is relatively weak, it may gain credibility by associating with judges in other jurisdictions and emphasizing that a country's national development hinges in part on the rule of law. This could help it in terms of national audiences and status.

While this implies that judges in developing countries, or smaller countries that benefit more from international trade, might be the greatest beneficiaries of globalization, even judiciaries in advanced industrial societies have some opportunities that arise from the global rule of law project. One feature of judicial globalization is a set of increasing opportunities for judges to travel abroad to deliver lectures, meet their colleagues, and contribute to promoting judicial independence in developing countries. Individual judges may value these opportunities more than others—former US Supreme Court justice Sandra Day O'Connor, for example, has traveled abroad with some frequency, while her erstwhile colleague David Souter seems to prefer New Hampshire. Nevertheless, for those who do wish to engage in these nonjudicial functions, individual reputation will matter, as will the reputation of the court on which they serve.

For these reasons, there is a real sense that judges in many countries have an interest in the global rule of law project. And their ability to participate in it may depend on their individual and collective reputations. The problem of team production at the national level is replicated to some extent at the international level.

In terms of our theory of judicial reputation, it is notable that the internationalization of judicial reputation relies more significantly on the collective aspects than on the individual aspects. While the Singaporean judiciary is regarded as extremely skilled in commercial litigation, few commentators mention the actual names of Singaporean judges. Belgium and Spain have received significant attention among human rights scholars due to their efforts to utilize universal jurisdiction. However, with few exceptions (such as Spanish former judge Baltasar Garzón), individual Belgian and Spanish judges do not become famous for their handling of human rights cases. At the same time, the multiple existing surveys of judicial quality across the world—produced by organizations like the World Bank, the Organisation for Economic Co-operation and Development (OECD), and the World Justice Project—focus international attention primarily on the collective reputation of national judiciaries. Governments have designed legal policies to boost their country's performance in these surveys; these policies inevitably focus on improving collective judicial reputation, rather than the individual reputations of judges. For all these reasons, the market for collective reputation has been enhanced.

Demand for Reputation

To begin the analysis of the demand side, let us consider a truism: globalization has increased cross-border transactions and interaction. This means that there will be more cases in which judges are, for example, asked to enforce a judgment from abroad, extradite a defendant, or cooperate with another court to provide evidence. The more opportunities there are for judges to confront foreign legal systems, the more they will have to evaluate the quality of those systems and compare them with their own. Many judicial doctrines require judges to evaluate the quality of foreign legal systems. Judges in common law countries will, for example, grant "comity" to judicial systems they evaluate as of equivalent quality to their own; they will decide a motion for forum non conveniens to allow a case to be transferred to another jurisdiction but sometimes will want to make sure basic aspects of fairness are met. Functionally similar doctrines are found in civil law countries as well. In the United States, scholars have noted both the increase in claims based on actions that occurred abroad and the increasing use of forum non conveniens motions by defendants.[1] In short, globalization produces demand for global reputation.

More generally, globalization increases the probability that courts in different contexts will indeed face common issues, and a natural response is to see how other courts have handled similar questions. Common substantive problems create demand for learning and practical experience. Reputation will matter when a judge must decide which other courts to look at. And borrowing doctrines and approaches can serve to enhance the reputation of the judge.[2]

As supply rises to meet demand, we observe new opportunities for the cultivation of reputation. Some years ago, Professor Anne-Marie Slaughter called attention to the increasing propensity of judges and other state officials to engage with each other across borders.[3] She noted that judges were increasingly likely to cite to each other across borders. In a globalized era, international regulatory networks and other institutions increasingly impinge on domestic decision making of all types, including decisions made by judges. As judges face common problems, it is only natural that they will look abroad to see how other judges have sought to solve similar problems. An individual judge who writes a successful opinion will now be not only known in her own polity but potentially cited around the world. And even judiciaries that do not formally cite others' decisions now look to how others have solved problems.[4] In some cases, internal management structures have been overhauled to enhance engagement with foreign law.[5]

Consider some prominent examples. The Constitutional Court of South Africa in its early years was a frequent referent to other countries' jurisprudence, a process facilitated by explicit permission granted in the Constitution for judges to look at other countries' law in interpreting the Bill of Rights. A judge on the Canadian Supreme Court has said that citing nonbinding foreign sources contributes to a "community of interpretation" among judges.[6] Justice Anthony Kennedy has drawn both scorn and praise for his citation of cases from the European Court of Human Rights in his decision to find the juvenile death penalty unconstitutional in the United States.[7] And former chief justice Aharon Barak of Israel became known as both a prominent borrower and an author whose opinions were frequently analyzed and borrowed abroad.[8]

There is some evidence that a court's reputation for quality and overall integrity is important for drawing attention—perhaps more important than the true relevance of its case law. Jurisdictions cited tend to be from a fairly narrow set of rich industrialized countries, and if judges stray too far afield, as when Justice Stephen Breyer cited a decision from Zimbabwe in a case involving denial of certiorari in death penalty matters, they may be subjected to criticism.[9] In an important recent book, Professor Ran Hirschl argues that judges use citations strategically to define their reference group.[10] For example, when dealing with problems of religion and law, Israeli judges do not cite countries like Malaysia that deal with similar challenges of pluralism and accommodation. Instead, they look to European jurisdictions, which are arguably less substantively relevant but are seen as better models for the values the judges want to promote. In this interaction, reputation works two ways: the European judicial reputation as advancing the rule of law makes European judiciaries desirable courts to cite, and the Israeli judges seek to advance their own reputations by treating reference societies as peers. Similarly, Professor Johanna Kalb has argued that judges in developing countries refer to foreign sources to signal their own independence and legitimacy to the outside world.[11] This function, she argues, is particularly important in new democracies, in which the judges can signal a break from the past and strategically enhance their own image as servants of the new order.

Relatedly, Professors Martin Gelter and Mathias Siems show that European higher court decisions exhibit strong clusters of citations based on language and legal tradition.[12] At the same time, smaller countries (Austria and Ireland) often cite larger countries (Germany and Britain) but not vice versa, showing a complicated network of citation styles. It seems that cross-border reputation affects different higher courts in different ways, with a few courts playing leading roles. And a courts' role in the "market" of citation and influence is determined by its overall reputation.

The surge in transnational citation has, for the most part, been uncontroversial. Only in the United States has it become a major source of political contention. A conservative movement—led by the caustic pen of Supreme Court Justice Antonin Scalia—has attacked the citation of foreign cases. "We must never forget," he notes in a twist on a classic phrase of Chief Justice John Marshall, "that it is a Constitution for the United States of America that we are expounding. . . . Where there is not first a settled consensus among our own people, the views of other nations, however enlightened the Justices of this Court may think them to be, cannot be imposed upon Americans through the Constitution."[13] Similarly, in 2010, the citizens of the state of Oklahoma, in their infinite wisdom, passed a referendum forbidding state courts from applying international law (or Sharia law) in cases before them. Notwithstanding the likely unconstitutionality of the referendum (and an injunction declaring so by an Oklahoma state judge was upheld by the Tenth Circuit Court of Appeals in 2012), it illustrates the strong reactionary feelings of some Americans to the judicial practice of citing foreign cases.[14] And it has led some individual judges, such as Scalia, to cultivate a counter-reputation for resistance to this trend.

At the same time that transnational judicial communication enhances the incentive to cultivate reputation, the process has consequences for the collectivity of judges as a whole. Professors Eyal Benvenisti and George Downs, for example, provide a fascinating interpretation of a recent trend in democracies toward judicial constraint of executives in foreign affairs matters.[15] Placing this development in the broader context of interjudicial cooperation and globalization, they argue that courts are increasingly coordinating across borders to constrain their national executives. This requires resolution of a transnational collective action problem among judges.

The process of looking abroad is facilitated by the increasing number of fora in which judges meet to discuss matters of mutual interest. Horizontal judicial networks, such as the International Association of Judges, the Consultative Council of European Judges, or the francophone high court association (with the impossibly long name of the Association des Hautes jurisdictions de cassation des pays ayant en partage l'usafe du francais), facilitate the sharing of information of all kinds. (There is even a network for judicial councils in Europe.) There are also a large number of bilateral judicial delegations visiting each other: the Supreme Court of Canada, for example, reports receiving about twenty-five visits per year.[16] This increasingly intense interaction has obvious effects on incentives to invest in reputation. And the various organizational attempts to bring judges together help enhance their collective status and reputation, perhaps protecting them from institutional attacks. The

Venice Commission for Democracy through Law, for example, is an intergovernmental body based in Europe that promotes constitutionalism and now regularly brings together national judges in World Conferences of Constitutional Justice. As the commission puts it, "As these judges sometimes find themselves in situations of conflict with other state powers due to the decisions they had to hand down based on the Constitution, being part of the World Conference provides them with a forum that not only allows them to exchange information freely with their peers, but where judges from other countries can also offer moral support. This can be important in upholding constitutional principles, which the judges are called upon to defend in their line of work."[17]

The Supply of Reputation

We now observe increasing worldwide attention to the actions of judges in many countries. When Egypt's judges sentenced several hundred people to death in 2014 for participating in a riot in which a policeman died, criticism of the court came in from around the world. In contrast, when the Supreme Court of Pakistan stood up to President Pervez Musharraf in 2009, judges and jurists around the world celebrated. Decisions by the German Constitutional Court are now debated across the European Union by constitutional judges. The rule of law is now seen as a global public good, to which everyone has a right to contribute. Of course, the rule of law frequently comes down to the rule of lawyers—namely, judges. How judges exercise their rule affects the legitimacy of them all.

Increased demand tends to create incentives to enhance supply. In some cases, we observe judges and judiciaries that invest in their "brand" on the global stage. One British judge was described by his colleagues as an "extreme networker" because of his active travel schedule.[18] The famous Spanish "superjudge" Baltasar Garzón was so effective at cultivating an international reputation that he earned twenty-one honorary doctorates abroad.[19] When he was indicted for corrupting the law to investigate Franco-era crimes, the *New York Times* published an editorial in his defense, and the prosecutor of the International Criminal Court offered to hire him as a consultant.[20] Though ultimately suspended from the judiciary by the Spanish Supreme Court in 2012, he has remained prominent as a member of Julian Assange's defense team. Garzón remains an international superstar, even though he has lost his day job.

At the collective level, judiciaries can promote their reputation by making their decisions easily available to outsiders. English is becoming the de facto lingua franca, and so judiciaries that want to enhance their reputation may translate their leading decisions into English and make them publicly available. Note also that courts can select the decisions to translate, allowing them to manage their image abroad. We do not, however, see the Supreme Courts of the United States or United Kingdom translating their decisions into German or French.

A particularly powerful example of collective reputation building is that of the Constitutional Court of South Korea, created in 1988 as part of that country's democratization process. The country as a whole has engaged in a development strategy focused on globalization, and the South Korean Constitutional Court is no exception. Consider how the court has invested in its brand in recent years: The court has been a leader in its development of a website to announce its decisions, translating the most important into English. In 2011, on the proposal of the Constitutional Court, the legislature created a Constitutional Research Institute under the court; the court's website announced that South Korea was "the first among some 80 countries having specialized and independent constitutional adjudication bodies to have created a research institution under the authority of a constitutional court." The goal, reportedly, was to make the court into a model for constitutional adjudication in Asia. Professor David Law notes this would help "to fashion a viable jurisprudential alternative to the traditionally dominant European and American models."[21] Some evidence of the success of the South Korean "brand" is the adoption, by Indonesia, of a very similar model for its own constitutional court in 2003.

In addition, the South Korea Constitutional Court has sought to play a leading role in transnational judicial organizations. South Korea is the only Asian country to join the Venice Commission on Democracy through Law. In 2010, the Constitutional Court established an Asian Association of Constitutional Courts to bring together judges in the region.[22] The website of the new organization states that it was "a good opportunity for Korea to enhance its international status . . . and also to promote to the world about its economic development and judicial advancement."[23] Judicial reputation can enhance national reputation more generally.

Another global factor affecting the supply of reputation is the increased movement toward transparency in government decision making, which affects courts as well as other bodies. Take constitutional courts, for example. Of constitutions that established constitutional courts before the year 2000, 17 percent (23 out of 131) provided for opinions of the court; of those set up in year 2000 or later, the comparable figure was

31 percent (12 out of 38). We also see an increase in the number of constitutional systems that require explicit judicial opinions of high courts after 2000—the comparable figures are from 12 percent (81 out of 698 total constitutional systems, as some countries have multiple constitutions in their histories) to 19 percent (11 out of 57). An increasing supply of explicit judicial opinions provides opportunities for cultivation of reputation. This reflects a change from an earlier era and puts pressure on traditional conceptions of the judicial role as an invisible technocrat. In short, judges are playing an increasing role in shaping their reputations in many jurisdictions.

The Rule of Law Movement and the Production of Metrics

Nearly two decades after Thomas Carothers noted the "Rule of Law Revival,"[24] the global effort to promote the rule of law shows no signs of abating. The UN General Assembly adopted a Declaration on the Rule of Law in 2012, and the World Economic Forum, sponsor of the famous meetings at Davos, declared that the rule of law "made its appearance on the global agenda."[25] National governments, foundations, and nongovernmental organizations have devoted significant resources toward improving the performance of judiciaries in developing countries. These judiciaries, in turn, are targets precisely because of their historically bad collective reputation. Institutional tinkering is designed to reduce corruption, improve efficiency, and promote judicial quality. On its face, this seems like a part of an effort to enhance the collective reputation of *all* judiciaries by providing resources and improving management. In a global era, perhaps the network of judicial interaction is only as strong as its weakest link.

The rule of law movement has several components. One is the self-conscious effort on the part of states to export their own legal systems and institutions.[26] One can see this as a kind of market process in which the prestige of the "sellers" of law will depend on the quality of their legal systems but also on their reputation. This in turn may encourage the managers of legal systems to make them more attractive for transnational borrowing. The recipient countries—the "buyers" in this market—depend on information about developed countries' legal systems. Sometimes this is simply the result of a general sense that the legal system of a rich country must be good or else the country would not be rich. Furthermore, buyers are typically not as well situated with regard to information about legal system quality—they are not able to make the most informed choices necessarily. In such cases, reputation may be influenced by self-conscious efforts to promote a brand, as the South Korean example above reflected.

The active market in legal reforms has been accompanied by cultural shifts that have led to the adoption of similar reforms in diverse countries in an apparently uncoordinated pattern. The spread of judicial councils, discussed in chapter 4, and the spread of constitutional courts, discussed in chapter 5, provide some examples. The adoption of mechanisms of lay participation in judicial decision making, which tend to be motivated by concerns for transparency, provides another example. These reforms, which may or may not be the result of active interventions, are nevertheless facilitated by globalization and transborder interaction.

More attention to the quality of justice has spawned an array of external monitors, willing to bear the costs of generating information about judicial quality. We live in an era of measurement and quantification, in which both the supply and demand of numerical indicators is greatly expanding. We rank cities for their level of global integration,[27] universities and law schools for their overall quality,[28] businesses for their environmental practices,[29] and countries on a wide range of development measures.[30] Naturally, the multibillion-dollar effort to promote the rule of law has been part of this trend, as scholars and policy makers have sought to generate and utilize relatively objective measures of legal phenomena. We now have a host of different indicators—some say more than 150—purporting to capture "governance" and related aspects of institutional quality, including the rule of law.[31] For example, the European Commission releases a biannual "Justice Scoreboard," rating judiciaries from Finland (highly independent) to Slovakia (not so much). These rating systems have been the target of much critique, both methodologically and substantively.[32] The veritable thicket of measures—and the fact that they are not always tightly correlated—poses challenges to social scientists and to policy makers who would like to use them to make comparative judgments about the quality of different legal systems and governance structures.[33] For present purposes, however, the point is that there are a good number of metrics by which to evaluate judicial quality.

The World Justice Project is an important recent effort in this regard. Initiated by William Neukom, a former general counsel of Microsoft and president of the American Bar Association, the project is designed to use state-of-the-art social science techniques to measure the rule of law cross-nationally. It has produced a multidimensional indicator based on surveys of elites and masses in developing countries and has now measured nearly a hundred countries on such factors as the quality and speed of civil justice, the fairness of the criminal justice process, the availability of alternative dispute resolution, and other aspects relevant to judicial quality. Its proponents believe that countries are taking specific reform steps in response to the measures produced by the project. This is a good example of how an information-rich environment can encourage judiciaries to invest in reforms that will enhance their reputation and how the global reputation of the judiciary is being produced through a kind of collective action by those in the profession. Monitoring technology tends to enhance attention to reputation, and there is some evidence that countries take ratings very seriously.[34]

Cross-national ratings such as the World Bank's Rule of Law Measure can induce the managers of the judiciary to ensure that there is sufficient investment into collective reputation. Because the managers ultimately work for the public, high-profile ratings can capture public attention and lead to pressures on the managers to improve performance. It can also motivate the government to expend resources on the judiciary, empowering judges in the internal competition for funds. It should be recognized, though, that any simple metric risks inducing new pathologies into the system as managers and judges try to "fool" the system. Suppose, for example, that a cross-national metric of time to disposition is used to rank judiciaries, just as the World Bank's *Doing Business Report* measures administrative procedures required to set up a firm. This could lead to an emphasis on speed over quality, which might in turn hinder the overall reputation of the judiciary.

This is not to say that these efforts to improve the rule of law will certainly succeed. Consider the problem of judicial corruption. The nature of corruption makes it difficult to observe. Scholars who study judicial corruption tend to rely on perceptions of businessmen or citizens, which are not perfect measures of the actual behavior in question. Technical problems of measurement might lead to distorted perceptions of corruption, either over- or underestimating its prevalence. This would lead to a distorted global reputation for the judiciary. Metrics are, by their nature, imperfect proxies for actual quality, and there is a risk of putting too much weight on them.[35]

It is also possible for the name-and-shame strategy to backfire. If a citizen perceives corruption in her country to be a mild problem but is then confronted with a sudden change in the externally reported assessment of the extent of corruption, the citizen will update her perceptions as to the likelihood of the problem and perhaps become more willing to pay a bribe. Publicizing corruption can, perversely, encourage it.

This is not a case for keeping measures secret—far from it. But it does reiterate the importance of getting the measures right. Suppose, for example, that there is a country in which citizens, for reasons of culture or history, are systematically willing to report that levels of corruption are higher than they really are. This could be because citizens' perceptions are wrong or because there is a "culture of complaint" whereby citizens are happy to criticize government officials. Giving wide voice to an inaccurate report of actual levels of corruption might induce those citizens who do think the government is trustworthy to weaken their faith. In this way, we can imagine that measures can undermine efforts to improve things. The major point, though, is that the information tends to be produced at the level of the judiciary as a whole. Globalization encourages investment in collective reputation.

It is not at all clear yet whether the production of metrics has led to genuine improvements in judicial management. A parallel effort to rate national regulators for the ease of doing business has generated a good deal of reforms, but it remains controversial as to whether these improve society's overall welfare.[36] Too often, crude reforms have unanticipated consequences, and measuring this impact is challenging. Furthermore, there is no lateral market for judges. The vast majority cannot go to other jurisdictions and sell their services (though there is an important but limited exception of international judging opportunities, noted below). This makes it difficult to figure out how much we should value judges' efforts. Nevertheless, the existence of comparative data might induce the judicial leadership to make sure that individuals are contributing appropriately to the collective reputation of the judiciary.

International Tribunals

Another level at which globalization affects judicial reputation is through the proliferation of international tribunals. There are now more than two dozen international courts operating, including many that are specialized in particular areas of law such as the law of the sea, criminal law, or international trade law. These vary greatly in terms of their function and mandate and the degree to which they have been able to exercise power.[37] Each of them has strategic considerations in managing its own collective reputation.[38]

The proliferation of tribunals necessitates a proliferation of judicial appointments. We estimate there are over four hundred international judicial positions at present.[39] This does not count the possibility of serving on lists of arbitrators for private arbitration, or the World Bank's International Center for the Settlement of Investment Disputes.[40] Having a strong international reputation and good personal connections abroad can make a huge difference for a judge seeking to obtain an international post. Furthermore, judges who seek international appointments also have to rely on the overall reputation of their judiciaries, bolstering investment in collective reputation as well. While nationals of over a hundred countries are represented in the international judiciary, more than half come from Europe, North America, Australia, or New Zealand.[41]

International bodies tend, by their nature, to be "recognition" structures in which judges are appointed by nation-states from among senior lawyers, diplomats, and academics.[42] They serve limited terms and are not promoted (although there are some exceptions, such as the European Court of Justice, in which judges may be subject to reappointment). In this sense, international judges resemble those of the US federal judiciary rather than the prototypical French judiciary, even though many of them are drawn from civilian systems. On the other hand, the fact that the terms are limited, unlike those of federal judges, provides judges with incentives to signal to external audiences that can provide post-judicial opportunities. For example, a former judge at the International Court of Justice, H. E. Awn Shawket Al-Khasawneh, recently served as the prime minister of the Hashemite Kingdom of Jordan, and his former colleague on the court, Mohammed Bedjaoui, served as Algeria's foreign minister from 2005 to 2007. Furthermore, lateral movement across international regimes is possible and even common. Judge Bruno Simma, for example, moved from the International Court of Justice to a position at the Iran–United States Claims Tribunal. A number of judges of the International Criminal Court have served in other international tribunals (while many have been prominent judges in national high courts beforehand).[43] In addition, many retired international judges, such as former president of the International Court of Justice Stephen Schwebel, develop active practices in international arbitration. All of these positions involve audiences external to the judiciary, and many involve audiences external to the nation-state, freeing the individuals from some of their traditional constraints.

International courts themselves vary in terms of the emphasis on individual or collective reputation. For virtually all international courts, the initial appointment is made on the basis of a "recognition" type of system. Judges are nominated by their nation-state and will usually be voted upon by members of the particular treaty regime to sit in the relevant court. Support from one's home country is necessary but not sufficient, as the applicant must also reach audiences in other voting countries. For judges from weaker and smaller states, this often involves appealing to other countries in the region and to foreign affairs departments in rich and powerful countries.

The International Court of Justice (ICJ) allows separate opinions, and judges frequently invest in their individual reputations; virtually every case has at least one separate opinion and often several. The European Court of Justice (ECJ), in contrast, seems better designed to pursue collective reputation. Public unanimity is the norm, and there are no dissenting opinions. One powerful reason for the difference might be that individual reputation building would have rendered the ECJ too weak during its early years, when it was playing a role of disciplining member states in service of harmonizing a uniform market.[44] The judges appointed to the European Court of Justice defend the need for secrecy and unanimity because their appointments were only for six-year renewable terms and not life: if they were to sign separate opinions, member states could check whether their judges were voting for or against the national interest and refuse to reappoint judges who did not vote appropriately, thereby compromising their independence.[45] (Protocol 14 of the European Convention modified this to a single nonrenewable nine-year term.) This is an excellent example of how provision of individual information might be detrimental and how judges have decided to act collectively to preserve the quality of their product. Over time, and the role of the ECJ has greatly expanded to cover diverse topics from citizenship to human rights; there has been some discussion of enhancing transparency, even to the extent of adding individual opinions.[46]

Other trade courts modelled after the ECJ also do not have separate opinions. These include the Court of the European Free Trade Association (EFTA), the Andean Tribunal of Justice, and several others. On the other hand, the European Court of Human Rights (ECHR) does have individual opinions, and roughly 80 percent of its cases are non-unanimous.[47] This likely reflects the fact that, unlike the harmonizing ECJ, the ECHR is an international body whose role is to uphold a minimum set of standards across a very diverse set of nations. By its nature, it reviews state decisions of governments and courts of its member states in which a balancing occurs between individual and social interests. Balancing, by its nature, involves assigning different weights to different interests, and making alternative opinions public might enhance the overall legitimacy of the project.

Support for this conjecture is found in table 6.1, which lists all the major international tribunals. Jurisdictions focused on human rights or criminal law often issue separate opinions. In contrast, when the tribunal in question is focused on trade, there is public unanimity.

The ECHR is a very large court, with one judge from each of its forty-seven member states. This makes it a bit more akin to a supreme court in the civil law tradition, in which the judges are faceless and the courts are large. In recent years, the ECHR has faced a number of institutional challenges caused by its tremendous workload. The innovations it has adopted—more cases decided by smaller panels rather than the grand bench, administrative rejection of some appeals by small three-judge panels, and pilot cases that are meant to apply beyond the facts of the individual case—have a managerial flavor. Still, it is best to think of it as a recognition superjudiciary ensconced over a set of career judiciaries. In this sense, it is similar to the ECJ or the Inter-American Court of Human Rights. These supranational courts, by nature, are heavily involved in quasiconstitutional review of national court decisions and form increasingly dense "vertical networks" in which judges interact not only across borders but across levels of a globalized judicial system.

The relationship between "recognition" supranational courts and the national career judiciary in Europe has not always been straightforward. The development of EU law has been driven by the expansionary character of the European Court of Justice, whose active judicial lawmaking has resulted in profound transformations in the governance of the union.[48] This was largely advanced through a kind of alliance between national judges, on whom the ECJ was dependent both for enforcement and to refer cases to it and the supranational body. The national judges were a crucial audience for the ECJ, and national judiciaries saw an opportunity to enhance their own reputations through enforcing European law. It is unlikely that the role of the European Court of Justice would be the same if it had been designed as a conventional career judiciary or, conversely, national courts had primarily been organized on the recognition model.[49]

At the same time, national courts have reacted to the ECJ in different ways. Initially, national courts were cautious about the interventions of these "recognition" supranational courts into their own hierarchies, and some constitutional courts resisted expansionist European doctrines. However, as the European courts established a good reputation among the national judges in relevant areas, the conflicts have been managed,

Table 6.1 Separate opinions in international tribunals

Court name	Primary subject matter	Dissenting opinions?	Separate opinions?
African Court on Human and Peoples' Rights	Human rights	Yes	Yes
Andean Justice Tribunal	Trade	No	No
Benelux Economic Union Court of Justice	Trade	No	No
Caribbean Court of Justice	Mixed	Yes, but only in Appeals Chamber	Yes, but only in Appeals Chamber
Central American Court of Justice	Interstate disputes	Yes	Yes
Common Court of Justice and Arbitration of the Organization for the Harmonization of Corporate Law in Africa	Trade	No	No
Court of Bosnia and Herzegovina (Section I—War Crimes Chamber)	Criminal	Yes	Yes
Court of the Eurasian Economic Community	Trade	Yes	Yes
Court of Justice of the Central African Monetary Community	Trade	No	No
Court of Justice of the Common Market for Eastern and Southern Africa	Trade	No	No
Court of Justice of the West African Economic and Monetary Union	Trade	No	No
East African Community Court of Justice	Mixed	Yes	No
Economic Court for the Commonwealth of Independent States	Trade	Yes, but not disclosed	Yes, but not disclosed
European Court of Justice	Trade and now EU Constitutional Law	No	No
Court of Justice of the Economic Community of West African States	Trade	No	No
European Free Trade Association Court	Trade	No	No
European Court of Human Rights	Human rights	Yes	Yes
Extraordinary Chambers in the Court of Cambodia	Criminal	Yes	Yes
Inter-American Court of Human Rights	Human rights	Yes	Yes
International Criminal Court	Criminal	Yes, but only in Appeals Chamber	Yes, but only in Appeals Chamber
International Court of Justice	Mixed	Yes	Yes
International Criminal Tribunal for the Former Yugoslavia	Criminal	Yes	Yes
International Criminal Tribunal for Rwanda	Criminal	Yes	Yes
International Tribunal for the Law of the Sea	Law of the sea	Yes	Yes
Permanent Review Tribunal of the Mercosur	Trade	No	No
Special Court for Sierra Leone	Criminal	Yes	Yes
Special Tribunal for Lebanon	Criminal	Yes	Yes
World Trade Organization Appellate Body	Trade	No	No

if not completely abated. Some have argued that national courts have themselves become more aware of the importance of general principles of law over codification and shifted from an emphasis on social control to more active lawmaking. Such a change has raised concerns about judicial activism and the judicialization of public policy in many countries.[50]

Some scholars emphasize that the result of all these developments is to render the European Court (along with the European Court of Human Rights) into a new kind of superagent—a trustee, in their parlance.[51] A trustee court is one that is the authoritative interpreter of the treaty regime, with compulsory jurisdiction, in which it is practically impossible (because of unanimity requirements or some other reason) to overrule a decision.[52] For our purposes, this level of autonomy might mean that reputation may become *less* important, in the sense that audiences are less able to discipline wayward courts. Still, the development of so-called trustee courts requires a long period of building up an effective reputation and is the exception rather than the rule.

There is some tendency in international legal scholarship to put Europe at the center of the analysis of global courts.[53] Drawing on the generally cooperative relationship between national judges and those sitting on supranational courts in Europe, many believed that judges would serve as key instruments of integration all over the world. In our framework, this implied that alliances with other courts would always enhance national judicial reputation and that internationalist audiences would be the most important. But a number of recent studies have called this teleology into question. Professor Alexandra Huneeus, for example, has identified a series of instances in which Latin American courts have rejected rulings of the Inter-American Court of Human Rights.[54] In Venezuela, this involved a local rejection of an attempt by the Inter-American Court to defend judicial independence in the face of Bolivarian politicization. In Chile, the Inter-American Court stepped into a very delicate navigation of transitional justice by calling for invalidation of the 1978 Amnesty Decree, which had been used by General Augusto Pinochet to absolve the military for the 1973 coup. Huneeus emphasizes the desire of Chilean judges to retain control of and take credit for the prosecutorial turn in Chilean politics, and this put them into some tension with the demands of the international court. Courts, in other words, do not always cooperate. This is because, for any particular judiciary, a local audience might be more important than a global one. Reputational concerns may be the root of these relationships, and there is no necessary dynamic requiring that all judges cooperate to advance their collective reputation.

The Rise of Private International Arbitration

The rise of international commercial arbitration has channeled many relevant cases away from the public system of conflict resolution to private tribunals. To a large extent, global trade demands global commercial law, and in its absence, parties have opted for private tribunals that can deal with such concerns.[55] These tribunals—typically staffed by private lawyers picked by the parties themselves—are facilitated by a supportive international regime that minimizes the scrutiny that national judges can exercise in enforcing awards.[56]

Typically, parties to a commercial contract will include a clause specifying that, in the event of a dispute, they will submit to arbitration. Well-drafted clauses also include provision for the national law that will be applied by the arbitrators, as well as the rules that will govern the arbitration. Parties will usually identify a specific arbitration institution—a private body—that will facilitate the conduct of the arbitration. A growing international competition among these institutions for business itself reflects reputational concerns in so far as they affect revenue. In addition, some jurisdictions have sought to make their legal systems more arbitration-friendly so as to seem more probusiness. In recent years, the whole regime has spread as a result of felt demand and the successful entrepreneurial activity of lawyers and arbitral institutions.

These tribunals are not only deciding commercial cases. In the past two decades, there has been a massive growth in so-called investor-state arbitration, facilitated by a dense network of bilateral investment treaties. These treaties typically guarantee the nationals of each state party the right to take claims to an international arbitral body (typically that associated with the World Bank's International Center for the Settlement of Investment Disputes). These arbitral panels are now routinely deciding cases that involve national regulations that are challenged as discriminatory by foreign investors. International arbitration thus reaches deeply into the traditional regulatory capacities of states.

All this has also allowed more choice of law and induced what some legal scholars call the market for law.[57] Not surprisingly, this market for law exists in areas that are more subject to globalization and less so in areas that are still dominated by national values and culture (for example, family law). At the same time, certain jurisdictions have more influence than others in shaping global law.[58] Jurisdictions with more influence will inevitably have more familiarity with global law (since it is not so different from their local law), whereas other jurisdictions will feel more estranged by international arbitration (those that see their legal tradition replaced by alien global law).

Given the asymmetric impact of international arbitration across fields of law and jurisdictions, national courts and the public system of dispute resolution have been affected in different ways. Reactions by national judges have been mixed. Some jurisdictions, such as Britain, have made an effort to integrate arbitration into their own legal systems (in the British case through the Arbitration Act of 1996), therefore redesigning their courts as significant appellate institutions to deal with private tribunals (in the case of Britain, even in family law). Other jurisdictions have been less sympathetic and have not dealt elegantly with this new challenge.

Notwithstanding, we have not observed full outsourcing of dispute resolution, since national judicial authorities tend to be quite protective of their roles.[59] Enforcing national law is still understood as a prerogative of sovereignty; thus there is a general reluctance to allow foreign courts and foreign law to shape a public system of dispute resolution. It also raises practical questions if judges have to deal with different laws when there is a general tendency to use domestic law to fill in the gaps.

Furthermore, there are signs of backlash. The investment arbitration regime, as a whole, has acquired a reputation among developing countries as being biased toward rich capital exporters.[60] There have been some attempts to evaluate these claims with data, but the studies so far are inconclusive.[61] Even though the empirical studies of the issue are not definitive, the very existence of the perception is creating a backlash against the investment arbitration regime, as several Latin American countries have withdrawn from it in recent years. India recently announced a comprehensive program of renegotiating its bilateral investment treaties in the wake of adverse decisions rendered by an international tribunal.[62] Indonesia has followed suit in reviewing its own investment commitments. Reputation, it seems, exists at the level of not only individual judges or national legal systems but entire international regimes of law.

Conclusion

Globalization provides both challenges and opportunities for judges. Global competition is a major factor in every field, including law, and national judiciaries find themselves competing for material and symbolic resources with many other actors. Judiciaries now operate in a far more complex regulatory environment, in which the old certainties of national legal systems are being replaced with a pluralistic matrix of norms, systems, and actors. The currency of this new world is persuasion and reputation, and so investment in judicial reputation is becoming ever more important. While the new set of global audiences provides opportunities for certain judges to distinguish themselves as true superstars, it also places importance on the development of collective reputation for judiciaries, legal systems, and even areas of law. Our framework provides a helpful lens through which to make sense of these dynamics.

We have argued that in this messy new world, judges everywhere are engaged in a larger problem of team production, replicating dynamics that occur in any given judiciary. National judiciaries compete for reputation with each other but in the process may also contribute to an enhanced global reputation of judges and law. The willingness of states to support judicial solutions to international problems, in the form of an increasing number of international courts, both reflects this enhanced global reputation and provides new arenas for the cultivation of individual judicial reputation.

The rule of law project can also be understood in this light, in which technologies of monitoring judges help advance reputation. The development of international surveys and metrics about the quality of judiciaries by organizations such as the World Bank, OECD, the Council of Europe, and others in the last thirty years has pushed the focus to collective reputation of national judiciaries. Legal reforms to enhance a country's performance in these rankings inevitably impact judicial collective reputation; furthermore, most of these surveys are based on perceptions for which collective reputation is an important determinant.

SEVEN

Conclusion: The Shift toward the External Audience and Lessons for Reform

Our basic argument in this book has been that judges are agents of society, hired to perform a set of tasks. The particular tasks they are given are complicated and vary across contexts: they include making rules, resolving disputes, engaging in routine administrative application of rules to particular cases, and watching other agents (like politicians). Furthermore, unlike someone you hire to paint your house or serve you a cup of coffee, a judge's job involves the exercise of judgment, and so it is difficult for outsiders to tell when judges are performing their jobs properly. Furthermore, many of the tasks assigned to judges need to be done in teams, requiring cooperation and making it difficult to evaluate how much each judge is contributing.

Society, of course, is not monolithic. Various audiences have an interest in how judges are performing, but most of them lack the sophisticated knowledge to monitor judges effectively. This basic problem has several important consequences. First, judges need to provide information to their audiences; we have used the concept of reputation as a way of capturing this. Second, the difficulties of monitoring create some room for judges to ignore the demands of their principals.

Reputation is power and allows judges to advance their

myriad goals. Crucially, reputation requires team production: judges have to care about the collective reputation of the judiciary in order to maximize their individual reputations. The institutional structures in which judges operate incentivize investment in either individual or collective reputation to different degrees, and these structures themselves may be transformed as different audiences compete over information. We have not asserted any universal optimum, because the importance of different audiences will differ across time and space. But we can say that an ideal structure will provide sufficient incentives to invest in both individual and collective reputation, and we believe that systems that stray too far in one direction will not be able to deliver efficient, neutral justice. When too little of one type of information is provided or made available, pressure will arise for legal reforms to try to reverse the situation.

Our sense is that we are in an era in which audiences outside the judiciary have gained importance relative to internal audiences. No doubt this has to do with the increasing visibility of the law and the global rise in judicial power: as judicial cases involve higher stakes, everyone has more of an incentive to learn more about the judiciary. It might also, more speculatively, have to do with the relatively poor reputation of legislatures around the world.[1] One observes, in both national and cross-national surveys, that legislatures are held in low esteem, particularly in democracies. Judicial reputation is relatively higher. Greater media access is also a source of pressure. Finally, there may be secular trends toward greater transparency for all government institutions, which affect judges as well as others.

An implication of the analysis is that incentive systems are subject to change and that traditional structures are under some pressure. Tinkering with various aspects of judicial incentive structures produces novel configurations different from the ideal typical civil and common law systems. Broadly speaking, these trends seem to have pushed toward greater use of recognition systems for appointing judges. While common law jurisdictions might be considered better situated to adjust to this world, they have hardly been immune from judicial reforms, as the major overhaul at the top of the British judiciary makes clear.

Legal reforms often affect the environment for producing judicial reputation. We have shown that all systems, even those of classic "careerist" judiciaries such as in France and Japan, have witnessed subtle shifts toward external audiences. These might increase the incentives for judges to invest in their individual reputations rather than the reputation of the judiciary as a whole. In France, the shifts have initially occurred at the apex of the judiciary, but the changes seem particularly significant, given longstanding French resistance to government du juges. In Japan, the Justice System Reform Council of the late 1990s can be seen as an effort to open up the process of judicial decision making to greater public scrutiny, most apparent in the adoption of a system of lay assessors to assist judges in deciding serious criminal cases. This is likely to increase public attention to the judicial process and may have more unanticipated consequences down the road. We have already begun to observe increases in separate opinions in Japan, as documented in chapter 1.

The Italian case discussed in chapters 3 and 4 demonstrates how relatively minor institutional changes led to a complete restructuring of the role of the judiciary in society, so that external audiences became much more important. In Italy, lower level judges banded together to capture the judicial council and then undermined both performance evaluation and hierarchical controls. The judges' unions became very political, and ultimately this led some of them to topple the entire Italian political order. The positive feedback and support from public opinion and the magistrates' individual reputation and visibility born from it further encouraged the individualistic incentives of judges.[2] Gradually judges were elected to both the Italian Parliament and the European Parliament and served as government ministers and city mayors. And political attempts to constrain judicial powers—from Benito Craxi to Silvio Berlusconi—were largely ineffectual.

This story also cautions against one-size-fits-all solutions. As we demonstrated in our analysis of judicial councils in chapter 4, sometimes new ideas about judicial organization can become "best practices" on the basis of little or no evidence. But institutions always interact with local environments, and so it is very unlikely that a single model of judicial design would be appropriate for all places and all times. Some environments will be characterized by judiciaries that are too beholden to political audiences; others will be characterized by judges that are beholden to none and so impose their own preferences on society. Audiences compete with each other to influence the institutional environment of judges, and these politics will largely determine the particular configurations in which judges operate. Judicial councils are a prime arena for these political fights.

We started our analysis with the conjecture that judges engaged in high-profile lawmaking functions would be more likely to be subject to external monitoring, in the form of recognition appointment systems, separate opinions, and the like. The trends we observe with regard to judicial system design reflect this conjecture. The greater responsibility of the judiciary for major decisions affecting society, captured in the notion of judicialization, has naturally led external audiences to be more interested in judicial decision making. Greater media scrutiny, and a secular social interest in high-profile cases, also contributes to demand for transparency from outside the judiciary.

While we do not assert a universal optimum, our account does have implications for certain kinds of reforms. We first consider proposed reforms that are designed to induce more investment in individual reputation and then reforms designed to enhance collective reputation.

Reforms to Induce Greater Individual Effort

Variable Pay

One might wonder whether variable compensation based on performance would be a good idea to motivate judges. In an ideal world, we would compensate judges for their marginal contribution to judicial reputation, which would require some proxy for individual judicial performance. There are, however, three substantive problems that need to be considered, some of them already detected in previous chapters. First, individual performance measures might disrupt teamwork and raise agency costs—that is, given the existence of a nonseparable component, it might not be possible to approximate the individual marginal contribution. Second, inadequate individual performance measures might distort activities, hence generating strategic adjustments by the judiciary in order to boost the potential gains. For example, we might see judges invest insufficient time in hard cases or seek to hear only easy ones. Relatedly, judges might try to adjust decisions to conform to the metrics used for evaluation or the preferences of the evaluators. Finally, there might be a crowding-out effect between intrinsic and extrinsic motivation. Many professional norms among the judiciary (regarding, for example, judiciousness and precedent) are established by prestige and status, and they could be undermined by the introduction of high-powered market incentives that result in differential pay.[3]

Fee-for-service has some history in the common law. Until 1799, judges in the English monarchical courts were paid a salary and were also allowed to charge fees that ranged from 8 to more than 54 percent of total judicial income.[4] Professor Daniel Klerman has argued that these fee-for-service arrangements facilitated competition among judges and courts to produce quality rules—particularly those that favored plaintiffs.[5] There is some evidence that courts with institutional structures that concentrated authority were better able to produce innovative rules in this process of competition.[6] The English system thus seems to have provided some incentive for both individual and collective reputation.

The system, however, was controversial in the United States.[7] Though fee-for-service arrangements were common in colonial America, there was concern about the potential for judicial corruption, and many state constitutions banned the practice.[8] Article 3 of the US Constitution seems to frown upon (and probably ban) the practice for federal judges, referring as it does to payment for services "at stated Times."[9] The Judiciary Act provides for salaries rather than fees, and when one early district court judge insisted on charging fees for admiralty cases, Congress responded by forbidding the practice.[10] In short, the US experience has shied away from fees for ordinary judges. Specialized courts and some lower level magistrates, however, have received variable pay. For example, bankruptcy judges were paid by size of case until the 1890s.

The only modern experiment with variable pay of which we are aware was in Spain. A controversial law allowed for the possibility of performance-based salaries for the judiciary (*Ley 15/2003*). The judicial council (Consejo General del Poder Judicial) implemented that new system of compensation in 2004 (*Reglamento 2/2003*), but the Spanish Supreme Court nullified part of it in March 2006 (*Sentencia de la Sala de lo Contencioso Administrativo 17/2004*). Aside from procedural issues, the substantive arguments provided by the Supreme Court included that the estimation of individual productivity is contrary to the very nature of judicial activity and that the work of the judiciary is not compatible with quantitative assessments of productivity. We view this decision as privileging collective reputation over individual reputation.[11]

In theory, adequate performance measures should be able to avoid all these shortcomings (minimizing the costs of disrupting team work, deterring inefficient strategic substitution of activities, and avoiding crowding-out effects with intrinsic motivation), but it might be unfeasible for practical purposes to develop such measures. Furthermore, the most obvious performance measures as embraced by the Spanish legal policy makers are likely to be insufficient and even detrimental. Compensation based on the number of cases or the speed of case disposition is likely to induce judges to spend too little time on cases and to seek to avoid complex cases. Using productivity in terms of the number of pages drafted is likely to lead to wordy opinions that are too long. In conclusion, although ideal individual performance measures would be the optimal instrument to improve individual reputation from an economic perspective, we are quite skeptical that such devices can be utilized effectively. Still, we encourage scholars to consider workable proxies for judicial performance that might facilitate the creation of new incentive structures for judiciaries.[12]

Transparency

Another reform that may be workable involves introducing greater transparency into the operations of the judiciary, particularly when identifying the performance of individual judges. Simply informing the public of the judges who sit in on a particular case will induce marginal investment into individual reputation while encouraging accountability. Currently, such information is hard to come by, particularly in many developing countries, although judicial councils and ministries of justice provide information in some systems.

One idea here is to encourage competing sources of information. There would be some cost in terms of duplication, but there may also be corresponding benefits in accuracy. In Israel, for example, an ombudsman of the judiciary was established in 2003 to investigate complaints about judges. In many developing countries, nongovernmental "judicial watch" programs have been established, often with the help of foreign donors. The thought is that the judiciary, like any other administrative agencies, requires monitoring. Because of concerns about judicial independence, hiring another state agency to watch the courts might be inappropriate in some countries, and so civil society and the media may be better situated to play a role in watching individual cases. If working well, transparency tends to enhance investment in both individual and collective reputation.

Competition and a Market for Individual Judges

It is well known that forum shopping naturally introduces competition among courts, which might pressure judges to build individual reputation in order to attract litigants. One might go even further and allow judges to compete in offering their services. Allowing litigants to more freely choose their judge would induce more investment in individual reputation. While traditionally concerns about witness and litigant access to the court drove judicial decisions about geographic venue, such concerns matter less in an era of improved communications technology, and there is less need for geographic proximity to the judge. This means that judges might compete *across* courts and even jurisdictions for particular cases.

There may also be ways to exploit competition among judges in assignments to courts and promotion. The relevant audiences might be internal, external, or a combination of both. In Europe, for example, one could allow judges from one country to adjudicate EU law cases in another. In the United States, imagine that all federal judges had to compete for positions every few years and could be reassigned by an appointments committee within the court. Criteria for evaluation could include a survey of lawyers about the judges' quality (which have been used in both Israel and the United States, among others), as well as performance metrics. This type of institution, which has been well documented within the Japanese judiciary by Professor Mark Ramseyer, would enhance the judges' responsiveness to internal audiences, but with the additional factor that they would be competing with other high-powered judges for plum spots.

To some degree, there is precedent for judges serving in other courts. Some African countries will allow judges from other jurisdictions to hear cases. For example, Sanji Mmasenono Monageng, a judge from Botswana, served as an acting judge of the High Courts of Gambia and Swaziland before she was appointed to the International Criminal Court in 2009. This kind of extrajurisdictional sitting is now actively promoted by the British Commonwealth and perhaps can be seen as a legacy of the old idea of a unified common law. Today, it has a very different meaning and might be used to promote disinterested adjudication in contexts where judicial independence is under threat. The key factor in obtaining these assignments, of course, would be the reputation of the individual judge for integrity.

Reforms to Induce Greater Collective Effort

Unlike individual reputation, investment in collective reputation requires collective action on the part of the judiciary as a whole. When senior judges have a supervisory role, they may be the focus of reform efforts. How might the senior managers of the judiciary be induced to foster higher levels of investment in collective reputation?

Random De Novo Appeal

As we have seen, systems with de novo appeal tend to have a greater emphasis on collective reputation than those without such appeals. This might lead one to propose an expansion of de novo appeal as a way of ensuring judicial quality. The problem is that de novo appeal is expensive, and many judiciaries that do not allow it also have a relatively small number of judges.

One way to obtain the benefits of de novo appeal without incurring all the costs would be to use a randomization method to draw a certain number of cases into a de novo review. Just as random drug testing deters drug use beyond those immediately subjected to it, so randomization of appeal could induce judges to be more mindful. If trial judges know that there is some chance that their fact finding would be reviewed in detail, this might induce them to invest more resources into individual cases, which presumably would enhance the overall quality of fact finding. The number of de novo appeals could be calibrated to balance the marginal cost against the marginal deterrence benefit in heightened quality. We know of no system that utilizes random audit methods for reviewing judicial cases, but it seems an elementary innovation, with potential beneficial effects in countering corruption as well as producing more careful decisions.

Renting Judiciaries?

We discussed the idea of a market for individual judges above. One might go further to allow countries to rent out their judges to hear disputes in other countries. As Professors Jens Dammann and Henry Hansmann argued with regard to commercial litigation, it would be ideal for countries with poorly performing judiciaries to reform their institutions.[13] But reform is difficult and often produces unintended consequences. An alternative that they propose would be to allow litigants to hear their disputes in the courts of countries with better judiciaries. Trials could easily be held remotely, obviating the need for parties and witnesses to travel. Such a scheme might induce countries to compete for cases.

We can accept that there are practical restrictions to renting judiciaries in the way Professors Dammann and Hansmann have envisaged, due to language, cultural, and sovereignty issues. However, the mechanisms they propose clearly fit with our analysis. Some judiciaries have better collective reputation than others (in their case, with respect to commercial litigation). Therefore, countries with an interest in exporting judicial services have an incentive to enhance collective effort across their judiciary. Allowing governments to profit on the collective reputation of their judiciaries could induce investments in judicial quality.

To be sure, there might be a perverse unintended consequence in judicial systems that are already of low quality because of a substitution effect. As one of us has argued with respect to investment arbitration, the availability of high-quality alternatives to judicial decision making deprives the local courts of a potential source of political support for improvement—namely, foreign investors.[14] Drawing on Albert Hirschmann's classic framework of "exit, voice, and loyalty," whenever exit is possible, there may be fewer loyal customers remaining and less incentive to exercise voice to improve the system.[15] A poor-quality judiciaries may wish to improve its collective reputation, but that reputation may depend on resources from the central government, which will have less incentive to provide such resources if high-stakes disputes can be outsourced. We do not know which effect would prevail but believe there is scope for experimentation.

Cleaning House

What can a poor-quality judiciary do to avoid a self-reinforcing cycle of a poor reputation leading to less resources, encouraging judicial corruption and sloth? This is the billion-dollar question of the rule of law industry discussed in chapter 6. To date, we have precious few examples of judiciaries that have significantly improved their reputations.

First, we should state clearly the nature of the problem from our perspective. When a judge is corrupt or politicized, she has favored her individual reputation before particular, narrow audiences at the expense of the broad public audience, which is the ultimate principal. This in turn undermines the collective reputation of the judiciary. Managers of the judiciary in such circumstances face severe problems in restoring the collective reputation.

Enhancing judicial disciplinary systems is one way to grapple with reputational concerns. But too often these systems are not effective because the ultimate judges of judges are, and to some extent must be, other judges. Furthermore, disciplinary systems may be challenging when many judges are corrupt. By nature, they deal with one case at a time.

One approach that is promising is to have a process of reviewing the entire judiciary with the goal of removing bad judges. The recent experience of Kenya provides a nice model. After massive election violence in 2007 and 2008, the international community and Kenyans came together to support the drafting of a new constitution, adopted in 2010. One of the institutions that it established was a Judges and Magistrates Vetting Board, with the constitutional mandate of reviewing every judge and magistrate to determine whether they were "suitable" to remain in office. It was part of an overall package of reforms, including a reappointed Supreme Court, designed to improve the functioning of the Kenyan judiciary as part of the "new Kenya." The vetting board included three foreigners, including renowned human rights activist Albie Sachs of South Africa, Chief Justice Georgina Wood of Ghana, and Justice Fredrick Chomba, a retired member of the Zambian Supreme Court. These were the only judges on the nine-member board; all the Kenyans came from other spheres and so represented exclusively external audiences. One might think of this combination of foreigners and Kenyan nonjudges as being best positioned to consider the external reputation of the judiciary and to do so in an independent fashion.

The vetting board proceeded sequentially, starting at the top and working their way down to magistrates.[16] This allowed the judiciary to continue functioning during the process. The inquiry focused not on narrow legal violations of the law, but on overall suitability, and so included matters of character, taking into account the judges' records, as well as contrition for those judges who had committed wrongs in the past. In at least one case, medical reasons were given in finding a judge unfit to serve. Altogether, some fourteen senior judges were found unfit to serve, though some were reinstated after further vetting. The results of this effort are remarkable. Whereas the judiciary was always considered one of the most corrupt institutions in all of Kenya, its public image has improved dramatically after the vetting process, as of this writing. While such processes may only be politically feasible during political transitions, they offer an example of creative institutional thinking, driven ultimately by reputational concerns.

Media Management

The trend toward a more open media environment has not bypassed the judiciary. In some countries, such as Brazil and Mexico, the supreme court has created television channels. Brazil's may have been the first supreme court with a YouTube channel, and many courts now have Twitter feeds.

Judiciaries may find it beneficial to take a more active role in managing their brands, both locally and internationally. We have seen some examples of courts, such as the South Korean Constitutional Court discussed in chapter 6, that have developed a significant web presence as a way of advancing its global reputation. American state judiciaries use websites for similar purposes.[17] Another recent development is the emergence of media offices within courts, which can issue press releases and manage the collective "brand" of the judiciary. In the United Kingdom, for example, there is a new Judicial Communications Office; the lord chief justice now holds annual press conferences for the media.[18] We know of no major study of these developments, but there seems little doubt that a proactive approach to brand management is appropriate in an era of media saturation.

Note that, as in so many areas we have covered, there is a potential tension between the individual judge and the collective judiciary as a whole. The intensive media environment provides opportunities not just for collective branding but for individual investment in reputation as well. Judges, like others, may wish to express themselves on Twitter, write blogs, or set up Facebook pages. But managers of the judiciary may be concerned about damage to the collective reputation if these expressions are seen to be representative of the group as a whole. (Not surprisingly, Facebook pages by judges have been the focus of regulation and judicially imposed limitations in several jurisdictions.) For this reason, some judiciaries have limited judges' ability to tweet and blog about their jobs and even subjected them to potential discipline.

Conclusion

Traditional comparative law focused on problems of legal families—an approach revived in recent years by the "legal origins" school of comparative economics. While traditional comparative law had some room for studying transfers and change, the economists tend to rely on strong theories of path dependency. Neither school provides a comprehensive theory to explain the causes and consequences of changes in judicial organization. In this book, we have argued that the simple device of treating judges as agents, along with the concept of reputation, helps gain purchase on these questions.

Judges work for the rest of us. To maintain their position and influence, like any other agent, judges need to make sure they have a good reputation. As Joseph Hall once said, "A reputation once broken may possibly be repaired, but the world will always keep their eyes on the spot where the crack was."[19] As we move to an era of enhanced reputation for judges, it helps to understand how institutional structures facilitate their good names and how we might induce judges to invest more in their collective reputation. Ultimately, the goal is to make sure that judges are not only acting as a team but acting on the same team as the rest of us.

Appendix A

List of Courts Included in the Dataset

Country	Court
Albania	Constitutional Court
Albania	Supreme Court
Argentina	Corte Suprema de Justicia
Australia	High Court
Austria	Oberster Gerichtshof (Supreme Court of Justice)
Austria	Verfassungsgerichtshof (Constitutional Court)
Austria	Verwaltungsgerichtshof (Administrative Court)
Bangladesh	Appellate Division of the Supreme Court
Belarus	Constitutional Court
Belarus	Supreme Court
Belarus	Supreme Economic Court
Belgium	Constitutional Court
Belgium	Council of State
Belgium	Court of Cassation
Bosnia-Herzegovina	Constitutional Court
Bosnia-Herzegovina	Court of Bosnia and Herzegovina
Brazil	Superior Tribunal de Justiça
Brazil	Supremo Tribunal Federal
Bulgaria	Constitutional Court
Bulgaria	Supreme Administrative Court
Bulgaria	Supreme Court of Cassation
Canada	Supreme Court
Chile	Corte Suprema de Justicia
Chile	Tribunal Constitucional
Colombia	Consejo de Estado
Colombia	Corte Constitucional
Colombia	Corte Suprema de Justicia
Croatia	Constitutional Court
Croatia	Supreme Court
Cyprus	Supreme Court

(*continued*)

Country	Court
Czech Republic	Constitutional Court
Czech Republic	Supreme Administrative Court
Czech Republic	Supreme Court
Denmark	Supreme Court
Estonia	Supreme Court
Finland	Supreme Court
France	Conseil Constitutionnel
France	Conseil D'État
France	Cour de Cassation
Germany	Bundesarbeitgericht (Federal Labor Court)
Germany	Bundesfinanzhof (Federal Finance Court)
Germany	Bundesgerichtshof (Federal Court of Justice)
Germany	Bundessozialgericht (Federal Social Court)
Germany	Bundesverfassungsgericht (Federal Constitutional Court)
Germany	Bundesverwaltungsgericht (Federal Administrative Court)
Greece	Chamber of Accounts
Greece	Council of State
Greece	Court of Cassation
Greece	Special Supreme Tribunal
Hong Kong	Court of Final Appeal
Hungary	Constitutional Court
Hungary	Supreme Court
Iceland	Haestirettur (Supreme Court)
India	Supreme Court
Ireland	Supreme Court
Israel	Supreme Court
Italy	Consiglio di Stato
Italy	Corte Constituzionale
Italy	Corte Suprema di Cassazione
Japan	Supreme Court
Jordan	Court of Cassation
Jordan	High Council
Jordan	Special Council
Kenya	Supreme Court
Latvia	Constitutional Court
Latvia	Supreme Court
Liechtenstein	Administrative Court
Liechtenstein	Constitutional Court
Liechtenstein	Oberster Gerichtshof (Supreme Court)
Lithuania	Constitutional Court
Lithuania	Supreme Administrative Court
Lithuania	Supreme Court
Luxembourg	Administrative Court
Luxembourg	Constitutional Court
Luxembourg	Court of Cassation
Macedonia	Constitutional Court
Macedonia	Supreme Court
Malawi	Constitutional Court
Malawi	Supreme Court of Appeal
Malaysia	Federal Court
Malta	Constitutional Court

Country	Court
Malta	Court of Appeal
Mexico	Suprema Corte de Justicia
Moldova	Constitutional Court
Moldova	Supreme Court
Monaco	Supreme Court or Tribunal Supreme
Montenegro	Constitutional Court
Montenegro	Supreme Court
Netherlands	High Council
New Zealand	Supreme Court
Nigeria	Supreme Court
Norway	Supreme Court
Pakistan	Supreme Court
Peru	Corte Suprema de Justicia
Peru	Tribunal Constitucional
Philippines	Supreme Court
Poland	Constitutional Tribunal
Poland	Supreme Administrative Court
Poland	Supreme Court
Portugal	Supremo Tribunal Administrativo
Portugal	Supremo Tribunal de Justiça
Portugal	Tribunal Constitucional
Romania	Constitutional Court
Romania	High Court of Cassation and Justice
Russia	Constitutional Court
Russia	Supreme Arbitration Court
Russia	Supreme Court
Serbia	Constitutional Court
Serbia	Supreme Court of Cassation
Singapore	Court of Appeal
Slovakia	Constitutional Court
Slovakia	Supreme Court
Slovenia	Constitutional Court
Slovenia	Supreme Court
South Africa	Constitutional Court
South Africa	Supreme Court
South Korea	Constitutional Court
South Korea	Supreme Court
Spain	Tribunal Constitucional
Spain	Tribunal Supremo
Sweden	Supreme Administrative Court
Sweden	Supreme Court
Switzerland	Federal Supreme Court
Turkey	Constitutional Court
Turkey	Court of Cassation
Uganda	Supreme Court
Ukraine	Constitutional Court
Ukraine	Supreme Court
United Kingdom	Supreme Court
United States	Supreme Court
Venezuela	Tribunal Supremo de Justicia
Zambia	Supreme Court
Zimbabwe	Supreme Court

Appendix B

Data on Judicial Councils

Country	Year created	Number of members	Percentage of judges	Power index
Algeria	2002			3
Albania	1998	15	67	3
Andorra	1993	5	20	2
Angola	1992	19	58	3
Argentina	1994		25	2
Armenia	2005	9	55	3
Bahamas	2002	4+		3
Bangladesh	1996	3	100	2
Barbados	1995	5	20	3
Belgium	2005		50	2
Belize	2002	4	25	3
Benin	1990			2
Bolivia	2009			3
Bosnia-Herzegovina	2004	15	40	3
Botswana	2006	6	33	3
Brazil	2009	15	60	3
Bulgaria	2003	25	52	3
Burkina Faso	1997			2
Burundi	2004	15	47	3
Cape Verde	1992	9	33	
Chad	1996	2+		3
Chile	2001		0	
China	2004			
Columbia	2005	13	100	3
Costa Rica			60	2
Cote D'Ivoire	2000	14+		2
Croatia	2010	11	64	3
Cyprus	1967	13	100	3
Democratic Republic of the Congo (Kinshasa/Leopoldville)	2003			2
Dominican Republic	2010	5	100	2
East Timor	2002	5	40	3
Ecuador	2011	5		3

(*continued*)

Country	Year created	Number of members	Percentage of judges	Power index
El Salvador	2003	6	0	2
Equatorial Guinea	1995	7	0	
Eritrea				2
Ethiopia	1994	12	41	3
Fiji	2009	5	40	3
France	2008	16	37	3
Gabon	1997	7	57	3
Gambia	2001	6	33	2
Ghana	1996	18	38	1
Greece	2002	5	100	3
Guatemala	1993	5	60	2
Guyana	1995	3+		3
Hungary	2011	15	100	1
Indonesia	2002		0	2
Iraq	2004	26	100	2
Israel	2003	9	33	2
Italy/Sardinia	2003	2+	60	3
Jamaica	1994	6	33	1
Kazakhstan	2007	3	0	2
Kenya	2010	11	45	3
Latvia				3
Lebanon	1995	15	53	
Lesotho	1993	4	25	3
Lithuania				3
Macedonia	1998	7	0	3
Madagascar	1998			1
Malawi	1999	2+		3
Malaysia	1994	2+	0	3
Mali	1992			2
Malta	2001	10	50	2
Marshall Islands	1979	3	33	3
Mauritius	2003	4	50	3
Mexico	2011	7	57	3
Moldova	2003	11	55	3
Mongolia	2001	14		2
Morocco	2011	19	68	3
Mozambique	2004	16	56	2
Namibia	1998	4	25	2
Nepal	2008	5	60	3
Nigeria	1999	23	69	2
Pakistan	2002	5	100	
Palau	1992	7	14	
Panama		8	63	1
Papua New Guinea	1991	5	40	
Paraguay	1992	8	13	2
Peru	2005	7	14	2
Philippines	1986	7+	22	2
Poland	1997	25	68	3
Portugal	2004	17	47	3
Republic of the Congo (Brazzaville)	2006	20+		3

Country	Year created	Number of members	Percentage of judges	Power index
Romania	2003	19	79	3
Rwanda	2010	16+	75	3
Saint Vincent and the Grenadines	1979			2
Samoa/Western Samoa	2001	3	33	3
Senegal	2001			2
Seychelles	1996	3	0	2
Sierra Leone	2002	7	50	3
Singapore	2007	6	40	3
Slovakia	2006	18		3
Slovenia	2004	11	55	2
Solomon Islands	2010	6	16	3
Somalia	2012	9	22	3
South Africa	2003	23	13	
Spain	1992	22	59	
Sri Lanka (Ceylon)	1984	3	100	3
Sudan	1999		0	3
Sudan	2005			1
Tajikistan	2003		0	2
Tanzania/Tanganyika	1995	6	50	3
Thailand	1997	15	87	3
Togo	2002	9	78	3
Trinidad and Tobago	2000	5+	40	3
Turkey	2010	22	67	3
Uganda	1995	9	33	3
Ukraine	1996	20		3
Uruguay		7	43	3
Vanuatu	1983	4	25	2
Venezuela		8	50	3
Zambia	2012	15	33	3
Zimbabwe (Rhodesia)	2013	13	38	3

Key: Power index has value 1 for purely administrative functions, value 2 for involvement in appointments, and value 3 for roles in appointment, discipline, removal, and promotion of judges.

Notes

INTRODUCTION

1. National Federation of Independent Business v. Sebelius, 567 U.S. ___ (2012); see Lawrence B. Solum, "How *NFIB v. Sebelius* Changes the Constitutional Gestalt," *Washington University Law Review* 91, no. 1 (2013): 1–58.
2. Avik Roy, "The Inside Story on How Roberts Changed His Supreme Court Vote on Obamacare," *Forbes*, July 1, 2012, http://www.forbes.com/sites/aroy/2012/07/01/the-supreme-courts-john-roberts-changed-his-obamacare-vote-in-may.
3. Alexander Hamilton, "Federalist No. 78," in *The Federalist Papers*, ed. Benjamin Wright (Cambridge, MA: Harvard University Press, 1961), 461.
4. Richard Posner, *Reflections on Judging* (Cambridge, MA: Harvard University Press, 2013).
5. Terry Moe, "The New Economics of Organization," *American Journal of Political Science* 28, no. 4 (November 1984): 739–77.
6. Gregory D. Miller, "Hypotheses on Reputation: Alliance Choices and the Shadow of the Past," *Security Studies* 12, no. 3 (2003): 40–78.
7. Anne-Marie Slaughter, "A Global Community of Courts," *Harvard International Law Journal* 44 (2003): 191–219.
8. Barry Moody, "Knox Case Puts Spotlight on Italy's Dysfunctional Legal System," *Reuters*, March 27, 2013, http://www.reuters.com/article/2013/03/27/us-italy-knox-law-idUSBRE92Q0ZO20130327; see also Julia Grace Mirabella, "Scales of Justice: Assessing Italian Criminal Procedure through the Amanda Knox Trial," *Boston University International Law Journal* 30, no. 1 (2012): 229–59.
9. Gianluca Esposito, Sergi Lanau, and Sebastiaan Pompe, "Judicial System Reform in Italy—A Key to Growth,"

International Monetary Fund Working Paper No. 14/32, February 13, 2014, http://www.imf.org/external/pubs/cat/longres.aspx?sk=41313.0.

10. See Mabel Azcui, "Bolivia suspende a dos magistradas del Constitucional que detuvieron una ley," *El Pais*, July 30, 2014, http://internacional.elpais .com/internacional/2014/07/30/actualidad/1406733535_345999.html.

11. See David Fontana, "The People's Justice?" *Yale Law Journal Online* 123, no. 447 (2013), http://www.yalelawjournal.org/forum/the-peoples -justice; see also David G. Savage and Michael A. Memoli, "Sotomayor Scheduling Conflict Leads to Biden's Early Swearing-In," *Los Angeles Times,* January 18, 2013, http://articles.latimes.com/2013/jan/18/news /la-pn-sotomayor-biden-inauguration-20130118.

12. Scheutte v. Coalition to Defend Affirmative Action, 134 S. Ct. 1623 (2014).

13. See Nicholas Georgakopoulos, "Independence in the Career and Recognition Judiciary," *University of Chicago Law School Roundtable* 7 (2000): 205–25.

14. Rafael La Porta, Florencio Lopez-de-Silanes, and Andrei Shleifer, "The Economic Consequences of Legal Origins," National Bureau of Economic Research Working Paper 13608, November 2007, http://www.nber.org /papers/w13608.pdf.

15. For an excellent introduction, see Ralf Michaels, "Comparative Law by the Numbers? Legal Origins Thesis, *Doing Business* Reports, and the Silence of Traditional Comparative Law," *American Journal of Comparative Law* 57 (2009): 765–96; Holger Spamann, "Large-Sample, Quantitative Research Designs for Comparative Law?" *American Journal of Comparative Law* 57 (2009): 797–810.

16. See, among others, William M. Landes and Richard A. Posner, "The Inde-pendent Judiciary in an Interest Group Perspective," *Journal of Law and Economics* 18 (1975): 875–901; Robert D. Tollison and W. Mark Crain, "Constitutional Change in an Interest-Group Perspective," *Journal of Legal Studies* 8 (1979): 165–76; W. Mark Crain and Robert D. Tollison, "The Executive Branch in the Interest-Group Theory of Government," *Journal of Legal Studies* 8 (1979): 555–67; and McNollgast, "The Political Origins of the Administrative Procedure Act," *Journal of Law Economics and Organization* 15 (1999): 180–217.

17. Zachary Elkins, Tom Ginsburg, and James Melton, *The Endurance of National Constitutions* (New York: Cambridge University Press, 2009).

18. The implication is that some change in the balance between internal and external constituencies is caused by legal reforms and therefore presumably the output of an intended plan. However, some of the changes in the bal-ance between internal and external could be unintended and the conse-quence of external factors uncontrolled by reformers.

19. See "Trust in Professions 2014," GFK Verein, 2014, http://www.gfk.com /Documents/Press-Releases/2014/GfK_Trust%20in%20Professions_e.pdf.

20. "Evaluation Report on European Judicial Systems," European Commission for the Efficiency of Justice, 2012, http://www.coe.int/t/dghl/cooperation /cepej/evaluation/2012/Rapport_en.pdf.

21. We found that twenty-nine of thirty-five countries surveyed in 2010 showed improvement with regard to measures of impartial civil justice by 2012; twenty-five out of thirty-five showed an improvement in corruption. Criminal justice, which of course involves many actors besides the judiciary, showed decreased quality in twenty-five out of thirty-five nations.

22. Eyal Benvenisti and George Downs, "National Courts, Domestic Democracy, and the Evolution of International Law," *European Journal of International Law* 20 (2009): 59–72.

23. Anne-Marie Slaughter, *A New World Order* (New Jersey: Princeton University Press, 2004); Joachim Bornkamm, "The German Supreme Court: An Actor in the Global Conversation of High Courts," *Texas International Law Journal* 39 (2004): 415–27.

24. Cf. Andrew Guzman, *How International Law Works: A Rational Choice Theory* (New York: Oxford University Press, 2008).

CHAPTER ONE

1. Jeffrey Toobin, "Justice O'Connor Regrets," *The New Yorker*, May 6, 2013, http://www.newyorker.com/online/blogs/comment/2013/05/sandra-day -oconnor-shift-on-bush-v-gore.html.

2. Bush v. Gore, 538 U.S. 98 (2000) (Breyer, J. dissenting).

3. Herbert Kritzer, "The Impact of Bush v. Gore on Public Perceptions and Knowledge of the Supreme Court," *Judicature* 85, no. 1 (2001): 32–38.

4. We follow closely here the standard economic approach: see David M. Kreps and Robert Wilson, "Reputation and Imperfect Information," *Journal of Economic Theory* 27 (1982): 253–79; and Paul Milgrom and John Roberts, "Predation, Reputation, and Entry Deterrence," *Journal of Economic Theory* 27 (1982): 280–312.

5. Bayesian updating refers to an idea in rationalist theories of human behavior, according to which individuals change their beliefs by rationally adjusting expected probabilities whenever new information is revealed.

6. Martin M. Shapiro, *Courts: A Comparative and Political Analysis* (London: University of Chicago Press, 1981); Martin M. Shapiro, "The United States," in *The Global Expansion of Judicial Power*, ed. C. Neal Tate and Torbjorn Vallinder (New York: New York University Press, 1995). Shapiro makes the point that only reputable courts can defend rights from infringements by the majority.

7. The foundational papers on team production include Armen A. Alchian and Harold Demsetz, "Production, Information Costs and Economic Organization," *American Economic Review* 62, no. 5 (1972): 777–95; Bengt

Holmstrom, "Moral Hazard in Teams," *Bell Journal of Economics* 13, no. 2 (1982): 324–40; Masahiko Aoki, "The Contingent Governance of Teams: Analysis of Institutional Complementarities," *International Economic Review* 35, no. 3 (1994): 657–76; and Raghuram G. Rajan and Luigi Zingales, "Power in the Theory of the Firm," *Quarterly Journal of Economics* 113, no. 2 (1998): 387–432.

8. The distinction in this paragraph comes from Shapiro, *Courts*. See also Mirjan Damaska, *The Faces of Justice and State Authority: A Comparative Approach to the Legal Process* (New Haven: Yale University Press, 1986).

9. For a similar approach, see Gillian Hadfield, "The Levers of Legal Design: Institutional Determinants of the Quality of Law," *Journal of Comparative Economics* 36, no. 1 (2008): 43–73; and Gillian Hadfield, "The Dynamic Quality of Law: Judicial Incentives, Legal Human Capital and the Adaptation of Law," *Journal of Economic Behavior and Organization* 79 (2011): 80–94.

10. The vast literature on legal origins is associated with Rafael La Porta, Florencio Lopez-de-Silanes, Andrei Shleifer, and Robert W. Vishny, "Law and Finance," *Journal of Political Economy* 106 (1998): 1113–55; Rafael La Porta, Florencio Lopez-de-Silanes, Andrei Shleifer, and Robert W. Vishny, "Legal Determinants of External Finance," *Journal of Finance* 52, no. 3 (1997): 1131–50; Simeon Djankov, Rafael La Porta, Florencio Lopez-De-Silanes, and Andrei Shleifer, "Courts," *Quarterly Journal of Economics* 118 (2003): 453–517; and Rafael La Porta, Florencio Lopez-de-Silanes, Cristian Pop-Eleches, and Andrei Shleifer, "Judicial Checks and Balances," *Journal of Political Economy* 112 (2004): 445–70.

11. Gregory D. Miller, "Hypotheses on Reputation: Alliance Choices and the Shadow of the Past," *Security Studies* 12 (2003): 40–78.

12. On individual judicial preferences, see Richard A. Posner, "What Do Judges and Justices Maximize? (The Same Thing as Everybody Else)," *Supreme Court Economic Review* 3 (1993): 1–41; Richard A. Posner, "Judicial Behavior and Performance: An Economic Approach," *Florida State University Law Review* 32 (2005): 1259–79; Richard A. Posner, "The Role of the Judge in the Twenty-First Century," *Boston University Law Review* 86 (2006): 1049–68; and Richard A. Posner, *How Judges Think* (Cambridge, MA: Harvard University Press, 2008). See also Frank H. Easterbrook, "What's So Special about Judges?" *University of Colorado Law Review* 61 (1990): 773–81; Mark Cohen, "Explaining Judicial Behavior, or What's 'Unconstitutional' about the Sentencing Commission?" *Journal of Law, Economics, and Organization* 7 (1991): 183–99; Mark Cohen, "The Motives of Judges: Empirical Evidence from Antitrust Suits," *International Review of Law and Economics* 12 (1992): 13–30; Dan Simon, "A Psychological Model of Judicial Decision," *Rutgers Law Journal* 30 (1998): 1–142; Frederick Schauer, "Incentives, Reputation, and the Inglorious Determinants of Judicial Behavior," *University of Cincinnati Law Review* 68 (2000): 615–36; Gordon

R. Foxall, "What Judges Maximize: Toward an Economic Psychology of the Judicial Utility Function," *Liverpool Law Review* 25 (2004): 177–94; and Chris Guthrie, Jeffrey J. Rachlinski, and Andrew J. Wistrich, "Blinking on the Bench: How Judges Decide Cases," *Cornell Law Review* 93 (2007): 1–43. For a different perspective, see Lawrence Baum, "What Judges Want: Judges' Goals and Judicial Behavior," *Political Research Quarterly* 47 (1994): 749–68; Lawrence Baum, *Judges and Their Audiences: A Perspective on Judicial Behavior* (Princeton: Princeton University Press, 2006); and Lawrence Baum and Neal Devins, "Why the Supreme Court Cares about Elites, Not the American People," *Georgetown Law Review* 98 (2010): 1516–81.

13. Stephen Burbank, S. Jay Plager, and Gideon Ablavsky, "Leaving the Bench, 1970–2009: The Choices Federal Judges Make, What Influences Those Choices, and Their Consequences," *University of Pennsylvania Law Review* 161 (2012): 1–102, at 15.

14. For the different possible goals of the judiciary, see Lawrence Baum, *The Puzzle of Judicial Behavior* (Ann Arbor: University of Michigan Press, 2004); and Jennifer K. Robbennolt, Robert J. MacCoun, and John M. Darley, "Multiple Constraint Satisfaction in Judging," Illinois Public Law Research Paper No. 08-22, UC Berkeley Public Law Research Paper No. 11333184, May 14, 2008, http://ssrn.com/abstract=1133184. See also Ran Hirschl, *Towards Juristocracy: The Origins and Consequences of the New Constitutionalism* (Cambridge, MA: Harvard University Press, 2004), who makes the point that extending the power of the judiciary as a collective goal ("juristocracy") can only be achieved with a certain court reputation, such as impartial adjudication in the eyes of the public.

15. Tom Tyler, *Why People Obey the Law* (Princeton: Princeton University Press, 1998).

16. Richard McAdams, "The Expressive Power of Adjudication," *University of Illinois Law Review* 1043 (2005): 1043–121; Tom Ginsburg and Richard McAdams, "Adjudicating in Anarchy: An Expressive Theory of International Dispute Resolution," *William and Mary Law Review* 45 (2004): 1229–331; David S. Law, "A Theory of Judicial Review and Judicial Power," *Georgetown Law Journal* 97 (2009): 723–801.

17. Aharon Barak, *The Judge in Democracy* (Princeton: Princeton University Press, 2006).

18. Ibid.

19. Thomas Carothers, *Promoting the Rule of Law Abroad: In Search of Knowledge* (New York: Carnegie Endowment for International Peace, 2006).

20. See, for example, Edgardo Buscaglia, "Judicial Corruption in Developing Countries: Its Causes and Economic Consequences," Berkeley Program in Law and Economics Working Paper Series, 1999, 24–29; and Edgardo Buscaglia, "Judicial Corruption in Latin America," in *Essays in Law and Economics*, ed. Claus Ott and Georg Von Waggenheim (Amsterdam: Amsterdam Kluwer, 1997).

21. See, for example, Hernando De Soto, *The Other Path: The Economic Answer to Terrorism* (New York: Basic Books, 1989).

22. See Kate Malleson, "Selecting Judges in the Era of Devolution and Human Rights," in *Building the UK's New Supreme Court: National and Comparative Perspectives*, ed. Andrew Le Sueur (New York: Oxford University Press, 2004), who makes the point that a career judiciary in a common law system would create considerable adverse selection by attracting less talent, since the reputation for judicial independence would be reduced, even if recruitment would be more transparent.

23. For example, if reputation is based on social diversity, judicial professionalism, political ideology, and caseload size, then we should expect judges to promote an agenda that reinforces those factors. See G. A. Caldeira, "On the Reputation of State Supreme Courts," *Political Behaviour* 5 (1983): 83–108.

24. Previous work on individual reputation includes Thomas J. Miceli and Metin M. Cosgel, "Reputation and Judicial Decision-Making," *Journal of Economic Behaviour and Organization* 23 (1994): 31–51 (showing that individual reputation can restrain judicial discretion but also inspire it if future judges are expected to be persuaded by a decision and follow it, thereby enhancing the authoring judge's reputation); Sophie Harnay and Alain Marciano, "Judicial Conformity versus Dissidence: An Economic Analysis of Judicial Precedent," *International Review of Law and Economics* 23 (2003): 405 (explaining that an individual decision made by a judge reflects not only his personal preferences about a case but also the expected response of the judicial community to the decision); and Gilat Levy, "Careerist Judges," *RAND Journal of Economics* 36 (2005): 275–97 (showing that the possibility of appeal generates an equilibrium in which, on the one hand, careerist judges tend to be creative due to the assumption that contradicting previous decisions is a signal of ability and increases individual reputation and, on the other hand, there is an aversion to reversals because they reduce collective reputation).

25. Collective reputation has been discussed in the sociological and business literature on organizations. See Tom J. Brown, Peter A. Dacin, Michael G. Pratt, and David A. Whetten, "Identity, Intended Image, Construed Image and Reputation: An Interdisciplinary Framework and Suggested Terminology," *Journal of the Academy of Marketing Science* 34 (2006): 99–109; Peter A. Dacin and Tom J. Brown, "Corporate Identity and Corporate Associations: A Framework for Future Research," *Corporate Reputation Review* 5 (2002): 254–63; Susanne Scott and Vicki R. Lane, "A Stakeholder Approach to Organizational Identity," *Academy of Management Review* 25 (2000): 43–62; and Violina Rindova, "The Image Cascade and the Formation of Corporate Reputations," *Corporate Reputation Review* 1 (1997): 188–94.

26. For the general public, see, for example, Gregory A. Caldeira, "Neither the Purse nor the Sword: Confidence in the Supreme Court," *American Political*

Science Review 80 (1986): 1210–26; and Gregory A. Caldeira and James L. Gibson, "The Etiology of Public Support for the Supreme Court," *American Journal of Political Science* 36 (1992): 635–64. For administrative bodies and government audiences, see William N. Eskridge, "The Judicial Review Game," *Northwestern University Law Review* 88 (1993): 382–95; William N. Eskridge and John A. Ferejohn, "The Article I, Section 7 Game," *Georgetown Law Journal* 80 (1992): 523–64; and John A. Ferejohn and B. R. Weingast, "A Positive Theory of Statutory Interpretation," *International Review of Law and Economics* 12 (1992): 263–71. For the larger law school audience, see Schauer, "Incentives, Reputation." For an interesting example, see Marites Dañguilan Vitug, *Shadow of Doubt: Probing the Supreme Court* (Manila: Public Trust Media Group, 2010), 19, who describes Philippine Supreme Court justices viewing themselves as both individual operators and a collectivity.

27. The nonseparable component is extensively discussed by Barak, *Judge in Democracy*.
28. See Ronald Dworkin, "Law as Interpretation," *Texas Law Review* 60 (1982): 527–50.
29. Producers of the nonseparable component also include nonjudicial actors such as clerks or lawyers.
30. Oliver Williamson, *The Economic Institutions of Capitalism* (Boston: Free Press, 1985).
31. We will discuss variable pay for the judiciary in detail in chapter 7. A notable exception is Spain, where variable pay was introduced in 2003.
32. See Williamson, *Economic Institutions of Capitalism*.
33. Elaine Mak, *Judicial Decision-Making in a Globalized World* (Oxford: Hart, 2013).
34. See, for example, Richard A. Posner, *Cardozo: A Study in Reputation* (Chicago: University of Chicago Press, 1993).
35. See, for example, Ken Foskett, *Judging Thomas: The Life and Times of Clarence Thomas* (New York: William Morrow, 2005).
36. Richard Posner, *Law and Legal Theory in England and America* (New York: Oxford University Press, 1996).
37. For example, Sophie Boyron identifies a major concern in France with the "esprit de corps" of the judiciary, a professional culture driven by early socialization in the *Grande École*, then reinforced by collective decision making with a profound distrust for the individual judge and further enhanced by judicial trade unions that effectively impose judicial collective bargaining. Boyron argues that judicial accountability is also collective in France. See "The Independence of the Judiciary: A Question of Identity," in *Independence, Accountability and the Judiciary*, ed. Guy Canivet, Mads Andenas, and Duncan Fairgrieve (London: British Institute of International and Comparative Law, 2006). Another comparativist, Basil Markesinis, argues that French judges are trained to keep their ideas to themselves; see "A Matter of Style," *The Law Quarterly Review* 10 (1994): 607–28. In her book *French Legal Method* (New

York: Oxford University Press, 2002), Eva Steiner proposes that the French judiciary is educated and trained as a unit to adhere to a collegial form promoted by French courts.

38. See, among others, R. C. Van Caenegem, *European Law in the Past and the Future: Unity and Diversity over Two Millennia* (Cambridge, UK: Cambridge University Press, 2002), arguing that while in Britain the bench is paramount and the judges have a highly personal role, in the Continent, courts are faceless and the judges are described as fungible persons; and R. C. Van Caenegem, *Judges, Legislators and Professors: Chapters in European Legal History* (Cambridge, UK: Cambridge University Press, 1987), asserting that the legal system is dominated by judges in common law and by law professors in civil law. A tendency toward bureaucratization seems to be detected in the United States by Owen M. Fiss, "The Bureaucratization of the Judiciary," *Yale Law Journal* 92 (1983): 1442–67.

39. See John Henry Merryman and Rogelio Pérez-Perdomo, *The Civil Law Tradition: An Introduction to the Legal Systems of Europe and Latin America*, 3rd ed. (Stanford: Stanford University Press, 2007), observing the pressure for consensus in civil law jurisdictions due to legal tradition. See also John Henry Merryman, "How Others Do It: The French and the German Judiciaries," *Southern California Law Review* 61 (1988): 1865–76.

40. Georgakapolous, "Independence in the Career and Recognition Judiciary."

41. For example, the judiciary in the United Kingdom has been presented as a career judiciary, in which being a barrister is regarded as a first step into the judiciary, in a system more similar to that of the Continent than that of the United States. See, for example, Posner, *Law and Legal Theory*, chapter 1, discussing the British career judiciary.

42. On judicial elections, see, for example, Peter D. Webster, "Selection and Retention of Judges: Is There One Best Method?" *Florida State University Law Review* 23 (1995): 1–42; Frederick Andrew Hanssen, "Learning about Judicial Independence: Institutional Change in State Courts," *Journal of Legal Studies* 33 (2004): 431–62, at 462; and Lee Epstein, Jack Knight, and Olga Shvetsova, "Selecting Selection Systems," in *Judicial Independence at the Crossroads: An Interdisciplinary Approach*, ed. Stephen B. Burbank and Barry Friedman (Thousand Oaks, CA: Sage, 2002), 191–226.

43. See, generally, J. Mark Ramseyer and Eric B. Rasmusen, *Measuring Judicial Independence* (Chicago: University of Chicago Press, 2003), who focus on Japan.

44. Francisca Pou Giménez, "Constitutional Change and the Supreme Court Institutional Architecture: Decisional Indeterminacy as an Obstacle to Legitimacy" (paper presented at the CIDE Conference, Mexico City, March 11, 2013).

45. See evidence by A. E. Taha, "Publish or Paris? Evidence of How Judges Allocate Their Time," *American Law and Economics Review* 6 (2004): 1–27.

46. Ruth Bader Ginsburg, "Remarks on Writing Separately," *Washington Law Review* 65 (1990): 133–50, at 139.

47. Mark Graber, *A New Introduction to American Constitutionalism* (New York: Oxford University Press, 2013), 91.

48. See discussion about the quality of opinion writing by Donald C. Nugent, "Judicial Bias," *Cleveland State Law Review* 42 (1994): 1–59, at 4; and Geoffrey P. Miller, "Bad Judges," *Texas Law Review* 83 (2004): 431–86.

49. For the United States, see the evidence provided by Cass R. Sunstein, David A. Schkade, Lisa M. Ellman, and Andres Sawicki, *Are Judges Political? An Empirical Analysis of the Federal Judiciary* (Washington, DC: Brookings Institution, 2006), discussing these issues in chapter 5. See, generally, Kevin M. Stack, "Note: The Practice of Dissent in the Supreme Court," *Yale Law Journal* 105 (1996): 2235–59; Tracy E. George, "Developing a Positive Theory of Decisionmaking on U.S. Courts of Appeal," *Ohio State Law Journal* 58 (1998): 1635–77; and Lee Epstein, William M. Landes, and Richard A. Posner, "Why (and When) Judges Dissent: A Theoretical and Empirical Analysis," *Journal of Legal Analysis* 3 (2011): 101–37, doi:10.1093 /jla/3.1.101.

50. For the French case, see Steiner, *French Legal Method*. She traces the historical reasons for the inexistence of dissenting opinions and the doctrine supporting such practice. Historically, the absence of dissenting opinions is based on the secrecy rules introduced by Philippe VI (1328–50) and Charles VII (1422–61) to protect judges. This rule was abandoned in 1789 but reinstated in 1795. It now has a statutory basis in Article 448 of the Code of Civil Procedure and Article 355 of the Code of Criminal Procedure. The doctrinal justification is that dissenting opinions are seen as undermining legitimacy of the court and the stability of law (since they may lead to subsequent changes of the case law).

51. See William D. Popkin, *Evolution of the Judicial Opinion: Institutional and Individual Styles* (New York: New York University Press, 2007), 38–39; see also Mitchel Lasser, *Judicial Deliberations: A Comparative Analysis of Judicial Transparency and Legitimacy* (New York: Oxford University Press, 2004), who makes the point that by signing a decision, the judges assume individual responsibility, a principle disliked by the French. Such rejection of individual judicial responsibility is embodied by the Law on Judicial Organization from 1790, which restricted the high courts (the Parlement) from passing regulations or suspending royal legislation by refusal to record them in the official registry (essentially exercising a veto). However, Professor Lasser argues that American legal scholarship has misunderstood the bifurcated system existent in France. The idea that French judges are in no way individually responsible for shaping doctrines and developing laws is misplaced. They are, but not publicly. There is a bifurcation of legal reasoning and policy analysis into two argumentative dimensions: the *rapports* by

the reporting judge and the *conclusions* of the advocate general, on one side, and the *projets d'arrêt* prepared by the reporting judge, on the other side.

52. See Dan Simon and Nicholas Scurich, "Lay Judgments of Judicial Decision-Making," *Chicago-Kent Law Review* 88 (2013): 411–31.

53. Jeffrey Barnes, "The Continuing Debate about 'Plain Language' Legislation: A Law Reform Conundrum," *Statute Law Review* 27 (2006): 83–132.

54. Peter McCormick, *Supreme at Last: The Evolution of the Supreme Court of Canada* (Toronto: Lorimer, 2000), 143.

55. M. Todd Henderson, "From Seriatim to Consensus and Back Again: A Theory of Dissent," *Supreme Court Review* 2007 (2007): 283–330. See also John V. Orth, "The Truth about Justice Iredell's Dissent in *Chisholm v. Georgia* (1793)," *North Carolina Law Review* 73 (1994): 255–70.

56. Scott Gerber, ed., *Seriatim: The Supreme Court before John Marshall* (New York: New York University Press, 2000).

57. See Stanley H. Fuld, "The Voices of Dissent," *Columbia Law Review* 62 (1962): 923–29, at 928; and Robert Post, "The Supreme Court Opinion as Institutional Practice: Dissent, Legal Scholarship and Decisionmaking in the Taft Court," *Minnesota Law Review* 85 (2001): 1267–384, at 1349–57.

58. Lisa L. Milord, *The Development of the ABA Judicial Code* (Chicago: American Bar Association, Center for Professional Responsibility, 1992), 137.

59. Thomas G. Walker, Lee Epstein, and William J. Dixon, "On the Mysterious Demise of Consensual Norms in the United States Supreme Court," *Journal of Politics* 50 (1988): 361–89; Cass R. Sunstein, "Unanimity and Disagreement on the Supreme Court," working paper, Harvard Law School, July 2014.

60. Sunstein, "Unanimity and Disagreement."

61. See also Post, "Supreme Court Opinion."

62. Sunstein, "Unanimity and Disagreement"; Walker, Epstein, and Dixon, "On the Mysterious Demise," 379.

63. West Coast Hotel Co. v. Parrish, 300 U.S. 379 (1937).

64. Our account is consistent with those scholars, such as Professors Robert Post and Lani Guinier, who see the shift in Supreme Court opinion practices as facilitating new discourses with new audiences. See Post, "Supreme Court Opinion"; and Lani Guinier, "Foreword: Demosprudence through Dissent," *Harvard Law Review* 122 (2008): 4–138, at 21–23.

65. There is actually some evidence that judges believe this to be so. William D. Popkin, *Evolution of the Judicial Opinion: Institutional and Individual Styles* (New York: New York University Press, 2007), 122–26.

66. William J. Brennan Jr., "In Defense of Dissents," *Hastings Law Journal* 37 (1986): 427–38, 438; see also Ruth Bader Ginsburg, "Speaking in a Judicial Voice," *New York University Law Review* 67 (1992): 1185–209; and Ginsburg, "Remarks on Writing Separately."

67. Ira P. Robbins, "Hiding behind the Cloak of Invisibility," *Tulane Law Review* 86 (2012): 1197–242.

68. Jeffrey Rosen, "Roberts's Rules," *The Atlantic*, January 1, 2007, http://www
.theatlantic.com/magazine/archive/2007/01/robertss-rules/305559; Lee
Epstein, William Landes, and Richard Posner, *The Behavior of Federal Judges:
A Theoretical and Empirical Analysis* (Cambridge, MA: Harvard University
Press, 2013), 137.

69. See, generally, Linda Greenhouse, "Chief Justice Roberts in His Own Voice:
The Chief Justice's Self-Assignment of Majority Opinions," *Judicature*
97 (2013): 90–97; Elliot Slotnick, "Who Speaks for the Court? Majority
Opinion Assignment from Taft to Burger," *American Political Science Review*
23 (February 1979): 60–77; and Saul Brenner, "The Chief Justices' Self
Assignment of Majority Opinions in Salient Cases," *Social Science Journal* 30
(1978): 143–50.

70. John Paul Stevens, *Five Chiefs: A Supreme Court Memoir* (New York: Little,
Brown, 2011), 235.

71. Robert J. Hume, "The Use of Rhetorical Sources by the U.S. Supreme Court,"
Law and Society Review 40 (2006): 817–43.

72. Jeffrey Staton, *Judicial Power and Strategic Communication in Mexico*
(Cambridge, UK: Cambridge University Press, 2010).

73. Giménez, "Constitutional Change."

74. Lisa T. McElroy, "Cameras at the Supreme Court: A Rhetorical Analysis,"
BYU Law Review (2012): 1837–99.

75. Olga Frischmann, "Courts and Their Audiences: Organizational Identity,
Organizational Image, and Institutional Isomorphism of Courts" (PhD dis-
sertation, Tel Aviv University Faculty of Law, 2014).

76. On how judges use discretion in civil procedure to favor their own goals,
see Jonathan R. Macey, "Judicial Preferences, Public Choice, and the Rules
of Procedure," *Journal of Legal Studies* 23 (1994): 627–46; and Janet Cooper
Alexander, "Judges' Self-Interest and Procedural Rules: Comment on Macey,"
Journal of Legal Studies 23 (1994): 647–65.

77. United States v. Booker, 543 U.S. 220 (2005).

78. See, for example, Frederick F. Schauer, *Profiles, Probabilities and Stereotypes*
(Cambridge, MA: Belknap, 2005); Kathleen M. Sullivan, "The Supreme
Court, 1991 Term—Foreword: The Justices of Rules and Standards," *Harvard
Law Review* 106 (1992): 22–122; and Louis Kaplow, "Rules versus Standards:
An Economic Analysis" *Duke Law Journal* 42 (1992): 557–621, at 561–62.

79. Steven Shavell, "The Appeals Process as a Means of Error Correction,"
Journal of Legal Studies 24 (1995): 379–426.

80. See Stephen J. Choi and G. Mitu Gulati, "Ranking Judges According to
Citation Bias (as a Means to Reduce Bias)," *Notre Dame Law Review* 82
(2007): 1279–308; see also Richard Posner, "An Economic Analysis of the
Use of Citations in the Law," *American Law and Economics Review* 2 (2000):
381–406; William M. Landes, Lawrence Lessig, and Michael E. Solimine,
"Judicial Influence: A Citation Analysis of Federal Courts of Appeals
Judges," *Journal of Legal Studies* 27 (1998): 271–332; Stephen Choi and Mitu

Gulati, "A Tournament of Judges?" *California Law Review* 92 (2004): 299–322; Stephen Choi and Mitu Gulati, "Bias in Judicial Citations: A Window into the Behavior of Judges," *Journal of Legal Studies* 37 (2008): 87–129, at 92–93; and Frank Cross, James F. Spriggs, Timothy R. Johnson, and Paul J. Wahlbeck, "Citations in the U.S. Supreme Court: An Empirical Analysis of Their Use and Significance," *University of Illinois Law Review* 489 (2010): 489–575.

81. See, among others, Tonja Jacobi, "The Judicial Signaling Game: How Judges Shape Their Dockets," *Supreme Court Economic Review* 16 (2008): 1–38.

82. That is, "better" judges do not get "better" cases, whatever "better" might mean in this context.

83. David Kosar, "The Least Accountable Branch," *International Journal of Constitutional Law* 11, no. 1 (2013): 234–60, doi:10.1093/icon/mos056.

84. Anthony King, *The British Constitution* (New York: Oxford University Press, 2007), 135.

85. David S. Law, "Judicial Comparativism and Judicial Diplomacy," *University of Pennsylvania Law Review* 163 (2015): 927–1036.

86. Ramseyer and Rasmusen, *Measuring Judicial Independence*. Note the analysis of Epstein, Landes, and Posner, *Behavior of Federal Judges*, chapter 8, finding evidence that in the United States federal judiciary, some senior judges "audition" for the Supreme Court.

87. Martin Beckford, "More than 75 Judges Disciplined for Misconduct," *Daily Telegraph*, July 14, 2012, http://www.telegraph.co.uk/news/uknews/law-and-order/9399122/More-than-75-judges-disciplined-for-misconduct.html.

88. Mary Volcansek, ed., *Judicial Misconduct: A Cross-National Comparison* (Gainesville, University Press of Florida, 1996).

89. Jacqueline Lucienne Lafon, "France," in Volcansek, *Judicial Misconduct*, 34.

90. Ibid., 42–46.

91. The latest such judge was Samuel Kent, convicted in 2009 of lying to investigators about a sexual abuse case. After conviction, Kent resigned his seat but made it effective after one year, leading soon to Congressional impeachment.

92. Philipp-Marc Schmid, "Ist dieser Richter faul oder nur gründlich?," *Bild*, February 15, 2014, http://www.bild.de/regional/stuttgart/richter/ist-er-faul-oder-nur-gruendlich-34687036.bild.html.

93. Burbank, Plager, and Ablavsky, "Leaving the Bench."

94. Merryman and Pérez-Perdomo, *Civil Law Tradition*.

95. More examples are discussed in detail by Nuno Garoupa and Tom Ginsburg, "Judicial Reputation and Audiences: Perspectives from Comparative Law," *Columbia Journal of Transnational Law* 47 (2009): 451–90.

96. See Herbert Jacob, Erhard Blankenburg, Herbert M. Kritzer, Doris Marie Provine, and Joseph Sanders, *Courts, Law and Politics in Comparative Perspective* (New Haven: Yale University Press, 1996).

97. Ramseyer and Rasmusen, *Measuring Judicial Independence*.

98. John Owen Haley, "The Japanese Judiciary: Maintaining Integrity, Autonomy, and the Public Trust," Whitney R. Harris World Law Institute, Washington University School of Law, 2003, https://law.wustl.edu/harris/documents/2003-3HaleyJapaneseJudiciary.pdf.

99. John Owen Haley, *Authority without Power: Law and the Japanese Paradox* (New York: Oxford University Press, 1991). See also *I Just Didn't Do It*, a 2007 film directed and written by Masayuki Suo.

100. Ramseyer and Rasmusen, *Measuring Judicial Independence*.

101. Frank K. Upham, "Political Lackeys or Faithful Public Servants? Two Views of the Japanese Judiciary," *Law and Social Inquiry* 30, no. 2 (2005): 421–55.

102. Ramseyer and Rasmusen, *Measuring Judicial Independence*; J. Mark Ramseyer and Eric Bennett Rasmusen, "Why Are Japanese Judges So Conservative in Politically Charged Cases?" *American Political Science Review* 95, no. 2 (2001): 331–44; J. Mark Ramseyer and F. M. Rosenbluth, *Japan's Political Marketplace* (Cambridge, MA: Harvard University Press, 1993), 178; see also David S. Law, "The Anatomy of a Conservative Court: Judicial Review in Japan," *Texas Law Review* 87 (2009): 1545–93.

103. John O. Haley, "The Japanese Judiciary: Maintaining Integrity, Autonomy, and the Public Trust," in *Law in Japan: A Turning Point*, ed. Daniel H. Foote (Seattle: University of Washington Press, 2007), 99, 109; see also David M. O'Brien and Yasuo Ohkoshi, "Stifling Judicial Independence from Within: The Japanese Judiciary," in *Judicial Independence in the Age of Democracy: Critical Perspectives from around the World*, ed. Peter H. Russell and David M. O'Brien (Charlottesville: University of Virginia Press, 2001) 37, 59.

104. *Recommendations of the Justice System Reform Council: For a Justice System to Support Japan in the 21st Century*, Prime Minister of Japan and His Cabinet website, June 12, 2001, http://japan.kantei.go.jp/judiciary/2001/0612report.html.

105. Japan Const. art. 79(2): "The appointment of the judges of the Supreme Court shall be reviewed by the people at the first general election of members of the House of Representatives following their appointment, and shall be reviewed again at the first general election of members of the House of Representatives after a lapse of ten years, and in the same manner thereafter."

106. Kahei Rokumoto, "Judicial Reform in Japan," in *Justice System in Transformation*, ed. Dai-Kwon Choi and Kahei Rokumoto (Seoul: Seoul National University Press, 2007).

107. Changho Kim, "How Is the Japanese Supreme Court Changing? Empirical Analysis on the Recent Rise of Individual Opinions in the Japanese Supreme Court," University of Chicago Law School, unpublished paper on file with author.

108. Tokiyasu Fujita, *Saikosai Kaisoroku: Gakushahanji No Nananenhan* [Memoir of the Supreme Court: A scholar-justice's seven and a half years] (Tokyo: Yuhikaku, 2012), 157–61.

109. Ibid.
110. Kent Anderson and Mark Nolan, "Lay Participation in the Japanese Justice System: A Few Preliminary Thoughts Regarding the Lay Assessor System (Saiban-In Seido) from Domestic Historical and International Psychological Perspectives," *Vanderbilt Journal of Transnational Law* 37 (2004): 935–92.
111. Tate and Vallinder, *Global Expansion of Judicial Power.*

CHAPTER TWO

1. See Posner, "Judicial Behavior and Performance."
2. Ibid. See also Benito Arruñada and Veneta Andonova, "Common Law and Civil Law as Pro-Market Adaptations," *Washington University Journal of Law and Policy* 26 (2008): 81–130; and Benito Arruñada and Veneta Andonova, "Judges' Cognition and Market Order," *Review of Law and Economics* 4 (2008): 665–92.
3. See Posner, "Judicial Behavior and Performance."
4. Ibid.
5. Ibid. It is difficult, however, to compare rates of reversal across systems when the legal importance of precedent varies.
6. Legal economists have suggested possible rational explanations for the development of career judiciaries. See Arruñada and Andonova, "Common Law and Civil Law." More generally, see Edward Glaeser and Andrei Shleifer, "Legal Origins," *Quarterly Journal of Economics* 117, no. 4 (2002): 1193–229.
7. See Pierre Legrand, "European Legal Systems Are Not Converging," *International and Comparative Law Quarterly* 45, no. 1 (1996): 52–81; Pierre Legrand, "Against a European Civil Code," *Modern Law Review* 60, no. 1 (1997): 44–63; Pierre Legrand, *Fragments on Law-as-Culture* (Deventer: W. E. J. Tjeenk Willink, 1999); and Nuno Garoupa and Anthony Ogus, "A Strategic Interpretation of Legal Transplants," *Journal of Legal Studies* 35, no. 2 (2006): 339–63.
8. Vernon Palmer, *Mixed Jurisdictions Worldwide: The Third Legal Family* (Cambridge, UK: Cambridge University Press, 2007).
9. For a general discussion, see Alec Stone Sweet, *Governing with Judges: Constitutional Politics in Europe* (New York: Oxford University Press, 2000). Also see Hans Kelsen, "Judicial Review of Legislation: A Comparative Study of the Austrian and the American Constitution," *Journal of Politics* 4, no. 2 (1942): 183–200.
10. Austria Const. of 1920, art. 137–48.
11. This also applies to renewal of judicial terms. Generally speaking, constitutional judges have a fixed term in office, although Belgium and Austria, for example, have life tenure subject to mandatory retirement.
12. See Nuno Garoupa, "Empirical Legal Studies and Constitutional Courts," *Indian Journal of Constitutional Law* 4, no. 3 (2010): 1–30, http://ssrn.com/abstract=1635963.

13. See Lech Garlicki, "Constitutional Courts versus Supreme Courts," *International Journal of Constitutional Law* 5, no. 1 (2007): 44–68, doi:10.1093/icon/mol044.
14. Ibid.
15. See, generally, Amalia D. Kessler, "Marginalization and Myth: The Corporatist Roots of France's Forgotten Elective Judiciary," *American Journal of Comparative Law* 58, no. 3 (2010): 679–720.
16. Only the court recorder (*greffier*) has legal training. See John Bell, Sophie Boyron, and Simon Whittaker, *Principles of French Law* (New York: Oxford University Press, 2000).
17. Simple cases are heard by the president, and around 30 percent are heard by the three judge panel; see ibid.
18. Ibid.
19. For discussion, see Maria Angela Oliveira and Nuno Garoupa, "Choosing Judges in Brazil: Reassessing Legal Transplants from the U.S.," *American Journal of Comparative Law* 59, no. 2 (2011): 529–61.
20. See J. Mark Ramseyer and Minoru Nakazato, *Japanese Law: An Economic Approach* (Chicago: University of Chicago Press, 1999). But see also Haley, "Japanese Judiciary"; John O. Haley, "Litigation in Japan: A New Look at Old Problems," *Willamette Journal of International Law and Dispute Resolution* 10 (2002): 121–42 ("By nearly all accounts, Japan's judges are collectively the most politically autonomous and individually the most honest in the world, as well as among the most trusted."); John O. Haley, *The Spirit of Japanese Law* (Athens: University of Georgia Press, 1998); and Law, "Anatomy of a Conservative Court."
21. A similar mechanism applies to the intermediate rank, *maîtres de requêtes*: one quarter of the selected candidates should be from the *tour éxterieur*.
22. See the words of Nichoras Schipper (president of the Committee for Selection of Judges in 2003), "Lawyer-Turned-Judges in the Netherlands," Japan Federation of Bar Associations, 2003, http://www.nichibenren.or.jp/en/meetings/year/2003/20030202_2.html.
23. 5 U.S.C. § 556.
24. Universal Camera v. NLRB, 340 U.S. 474 (1951).
25. R. Terrence Harders, "Striking a Balance: Administrative Law Judge Independence and Accountability," *Journal of the National Association of Administrative Law Judiciary* 19, no. 1 (1999): 1–13. An exception is immigration law judges, who are "attorneys whom the Attorney General appoints as administrative judges" and are appointed to act "as the Attorney General's delegates in the cases that come before them." Immigration Judges, 8 CFR 1003.10.
26. See Jesse Etelson, "The New ALJ Examination: A Bright, Shining Lie Redux," *Administrative Law Review* 43, no. 2 (1991): 185–95, who critiques the exam structure.
27. Malcolm C. Rich, *The Central Panel System for Administrative Law Judges: A Survey of Seven States* (Chicago: American Judicature Society, 1983); Earl

Thomas, *Administrative Law Judges: The Corps Issue* (Washington, DC: National Conference of Administrative Law Judges, Judicial Administration Division, American Bar Association, 1987).

28. Not all British tribunals are established to hear cases against the administration. For example, employment tribunals hear cases brought by employees against employers, including for alleged discrimination.

29. United States v. Lewis, 63 M.J. 405 (C.A.A.F., 2006).

30. Douglass C. North and Barry R. Weingast, "Constitutions and Commitment: The Evolution of Institutions Governing Public Choice in Seventeenth-Century England," *Journal of Economic History* 49, no. 4 (1989): 803–32, http://www.jstor.org/stable/2122739.

31. See, among others, Landes and Posner, "Independent Judiciary in an Interest Group Perspective"; Tollison and Crain, "Constitutional Change in an Interest-Group Perspective"; Crain and Tollison, "Executive Branch in the Interest-Group Theory of Government"; and McNollgast, "Political Origins of the Administrative Procedure Act."

32. See Steven M. Teles, *The Rise of the Conservative Legal Movement: The Battle for Control of the Law* (Princeton: Princeton University Press, 2008), who describes how early membership in the federalist society serves as a costly signal among conservative jurists.

33. Hirschl, *Towards Juristocracy.*

34. J. Mark Ramseyer, "The Puzzling (In)dependence of Courts: A Comparative Approach," *Journal of Legal Studies* 23, no. 2 (1994): 721–47.

35. Merryman and Perez-Perdomo, *Civil Law Tradition.* For codification as a form of limiting the judiciary in a systematic and significant way (addressing preferences and cognitive biases), see Arruñada and Andonova, "Common Law and Civil Law" and "Judges' Cognition and Market Order."

36. Legislative precision and transparency in order to effectively restrain the judiciary were one of the goals of the *Code Napoléon.* See Jean-Louis Halperin, *The French Civil Code* (London: University College of London Press, 2006).

37. The illegitimacy of judicial lawmaking is codified by Article 5 of the *Code Napoléon* (judges are forbidden to pronounce, by way of general and legislative determination, on the causes submitted to them). On the importance of esprit de corps, see Eva Steiner, *French Law: A Comparative Approach* (New York: Oxford University Press, 2010).

38. It should be clear that we refer primarily to administrative adjudication and not to administrative law in the quasiconstitutional sense as suggested by Tom Ginsburg, "Written Constitutions and the Administrative State: On the Constitutional Character of Administrative Law," in *Comparative Administrative Law*, ed. Susan Rose-Ackerman and Peter Lindseth (Northampton: Edward Elgar, 2010). We also exclude here disputes between private parties, which can be addressed by administrative agencies in the United States but are not "administrative law" in the civil law sense.

39. The classification of lawmaking and social control also applies to more technical areas of the law such as intellectual property or antitrust law. Notwithstanding the general approach, some areas of the law could be more about lawmaking in one jurisdiction and more about social control in a different jurisdiction.

40. By no means are we the first to criticize or question the "purist" description. However, our reasoning is different. Most of the previous critiques focus on the inability of the purist description to explain a particular jurisdiction; in other words, the argument is that generalization does not inform the discussion of a particular case. We take the opposite approach. We suggest that generalization, in the sense of a broadly applicable theory, provides fundamental insights to understanding the observed configuration in particular jurisdictions. We simply believe that the generalized purist description fails to do so.

41. See discussion by Giuseppe Dari-Mattiacci, Nuno Garoupa, and Fernando Gómez-Pomar, "State Liability," *European Review of Private Law* 4, no. 4 (2010): 773–811.

42. In our sample, Israel, Malta, and South Africa are included as common law jurisdictions, while the Philippines and Jordan are civil law jurisdictions. The empirical results are robust to alternative classifications.

43. Further confirming that the vast majority of higher courts around the world are not packed by career judiciaries, as we have discussed previously.

44. "Worldwide Governance Indicators," World Bank, http://info.worldbank .org/governance/wgi/index.aspx#home.

45. "Federalism by Country," Forum of Federations, http://www.forumfed.org /en/federalism/by_country/index.php.

46. GDP per capita in thousands of US dollars. We have used the IMF dataset for all countries except Liechtenstein and Monaco. "World Development Report 2009," World Bank, http://web.worldbank.org/WBSITE/EXTERNAL /EXTDEC/EXTRESEARCH/EXTWDRS/0,,contentMDK:23062295~pagePK:47 8093~piPK:477627~theSitePK:477624,00.html.

47. Population estimates for 2010 in millions. "Population 2010," World Bank, http://siteresources.worldbank.org/DATASTATISTICS/Resources/POP.pdf.

48. "Doing Business," World Bank Group, http://www.doingbusiness.com.

49. Notice that the same observation does not apply to administrative review, since the choice of court jurisdiction in this matter is usually not a matter of constitutional law. In most civil law jurisdictions, it actually predates the current constitution by many decades. For example, the French Conseil d'État can be traced to before the Napoleonic revolution, while the current constitution dates from 1958.

50. We also performed the analysis with two other control variables: bureaucratic efficiency and ethnolinguistic fractionalization scores from Paolo Mauro, "Corruption and Growth," *Quarterly Journal of Economics* 110, no. 3 (1995): 681–712. However, these regressions are only possible with a much

reduced dataset (they exclude all the former socialist countries in Europe). The econometric results presented are largely robust to these alternative specifications.

51. In unreported robustness checks, we also ran a Poisson model, which is appropriate given that we are analyzing count data, and a negative binomial model with both delivering similar results.

52. We started with a two-stage probit least squares estimation (the routine *cdsimeq* in STATA 11), but the second stage regressions with instruments were affected by colinearity. This is not surprising, since this method is only recommended for a dataset with at least one hundred independent observations. We turned our attention to a 3SLS estimation that technically is less correct because two dependent variables, recognition mechanisms and constitutional powers, are binary. However, since we focus only on the regression with the continuous dependent variable, the estimation results are at least suggestive.

CHAPTER THREE

1. See Helena Smith, "Greece's Interim Government Sworn in before Fresh Election," *Guardian*, May 16, 2012, http://www.guardian.co.uk/world/2012 /may/16/greece-interim-government-sworn-in.

2. Vitug, *Shadow of Doubt*, 185 (describing the resignation of the Bolivian president and the appointment of the chief justice as caretaker).

3. "Former Presidents: Justice Abu Sayeed Chowdhury," The Bangabhaban: The President House of Bangladesh, accessed November 21, 2014, http:// www.bangabhaban.gov.bd/sayeed.html.

4. "The President, Previous Presidents," The President of the Islamic Republic of Pakistan, accessed November 21, 2014, http://www.presidentofpakistan .gov.pk/index.php?lang=en&opc=2&sel=4&pId=9.

5. President Getúlio Vargas lost popular support for his authoritarian government and was forced to resign in October 1945. He was replaced by Chief Justice José Linhares as acting president from October 1945 to January 1946.

6. Vitug, *Shadow of Doubt*, 176.

7. Ibid., 186–87.

8. For example, under Australian law, judges play a judicial function when they address a dispute to be resolved by application of law in order to establish facts and a binding resolution accepted by parties. See Patrick Emerton and H. P. Lee, "Judges and Non-Judicial Functions in Australia," in *Judiciaries in Comparative Perspective*, ed. H. P. Lee (Cambridge, UK: Cambridge University Press, 2011).

9. See Mistretta v. United States, 488 U.S. 361 (1989).

10. See, generally, ibid.; see also Kable v. DPP, (NSW, 1996) 189 CLR 51 (Austl.), showing the same point in the context of Australian law.

11. James P. Pfander and Daniel D. Birk, "Article III Judicial Power, the Adverse-Party Requirement, and Non-Contentious Jurisdiction," Northwestern Public Law Research Paper No. 14-13, April 13, 2014, http://papers.ssrn .com/sol3/papers.cfm?abstract_id=2424511.
12. For example, New Zealand law struggled with the meaning of *tribunal* until it was clarified in 2008. See Geoffrey Palmer, "Judges and Non-Judicial Functions in New Zealand," in Lee, *Judiciaries in Comparative Perspective.*
13. See Emerton and Lee, "Judges and Non-Judicial Functions in Australia."
14. In the United Kingdom, it has been clarified that judicial immunity applies only to judicial functions. See Abimbola A. Olowofoyeku, "Judges and Non-Judicial Functions in the United Kingdom," in Lee, *Judiciaries in Comparative Perspective.*
15. See Jeffrey M. Shaman, "Judges and Non-Judicial Functions in the United States," in Lee, *Judicaries in Comparative Perspective.*
16. The incompatibility test was conceived after the Heath case when a High Court judge was appointed to a special investigation unit in 2001. Later the Judicial Service Commission Amendment Act of 2008 was passed, opening the way for further limitations on nonjudicial functions in the future. See Cora Hoexter, "Judges and Non-Judicial Functions in South Africa," in Lee, *Judiciaries in Comparative Perspective.*
17. For example, in Canada there are no significant constitutional constraints and only some minor statutory limitations (Federal Judges Act of 1985). See Patrick Monahan and Byron Shaw, "The Impact of Extra-Judicial Service on the Canadian Judiciary: The Need for Reform," in Lee, *Judiciaries in Comparative Perspective.*
18. *Mistretta*, 488 U.S. at 404.
19. See Emerton and Lee, "Judges and Non-Judicial Functions in Australia." The landmark cases are *Drake v. Minister for Immigration & Ethnic Affairs* (1979), which questioned the appointment of a judge of the Federal Court of Australia to the Administrative Appeals Tribunal, and *Hilton v. Wells* (1985), which challenged a particular statute that allowed tapping by a warrant issued by a judge of certain specific courts, therefore raising questions concerning the distinction between *judge* and *court.* Later *Grollo v. Palmer* (1995) clarified the extent to which a function exercised by a judge is within *personae designatae.* In *Wilson v. Minister for Aboriginal and Torrens Strait Islander Affairs* (1996), the High Court of Australia decided that a judge of the Federal Court could not be involved in preparing a particular report in relation to a public policy issue that demanded taking sides. *Kable* 189 CLR 1 (Austl., 1996).
20. This is consistent with the Oxford English Dictionary, which defines *extra-judicial* as "lying outside the proceedings in court." *Oxford English Dictionary*, 2nd ed. (Oxford: Clarendon, 1989), 613.
21. On judicialization, see Alec Stone Sweet and Martin Shapiro, *On Law, Politics and Judicialization* (New York: Oxford University Press, 2003).

22. Belarus Const. of 1994, art. 147. Ecuador's 1967 constitution provided that the judges of the Supreme Court would sit with both houses of Congress to approve some constitutional amendments.

23. In Chile, the Supreme Court nominates five candidates for attorney general, from which the president chooses one to send to Congress. Chile Const. of 1982, as amended 1997, art. 80.c. A similar scheme obtains in Turkey, in which the nominee for prosecutor general must be a member of the High Court. Turkey Const. of 1982, art. 154.

24. Bolivia Const. of 1868, art. 37; Bolivia Const. of 1938, art.70; Bolivia Const. of 1945, art. 73; Bolivia Const. of 1961, art. 74; Brazil Const. of 1988, art. 61; Colombia Const. of 2005, arts. 154, 156; Cuba Const. of 1940, art. 135; Cuba Const. of 1976, art. 88; Dominican Republic Const. of 1878, art 38.2; Dominican Republic Const. of 2010, art. 96; Ecuador Const. of 2008, art. 134; El Salvador Const. of 1864, art. 41; El Salvador Const. of 1983, art. 133; Guatemala Const. of 1879, art. 56; Guatemala Const. of 1993, art. 174; Honduras Const. of 1880, art. 49; Honduras Const. of 1982, art. 213; Nicaragua Const. of 1911, art. 91; Nicaragua Const. of 1987, art. 140; Panama Const. of 1904, art. 98; Panama Const. of 2004, art. 165.2; Paraguay Const. of 1992, art. 203; Peru Const. of 1856, art. 63; Peru Const. of 1979, art. 190; Venezuela Const. of 1961, art. 165.

25. Russia Const. of 1993, art. 104.1; Azerbaijan Const. of 1995, art. 96.1; Kazakhstan Const. of 1993, art. 71; Kazakhstan Const. of 1995, art. 61; Mongolia Const. of 1960, art. 19; Turkmenistan Const. of 2003, art. 67; Turkmenistan Const. of 2008, art. 64; Tajikistan Const. of 1994, art. 60; Ukraine Const. of 1995, rt. 103; Uzbekistan Const. of 1992, art. 82; Afghanistan Const. of 1964, art. 73; Cambodia Const. of 1972, art. 53; Laos Const. of 1991, art. 45; Laos Const. of 2003, art. 59; Vietnam Const. of 1980, art. 86; Vietnam Const. of 1992, art. 87.

26. France Const. of 1958, art. 16; Gabon Const. of 1996, arts. 25–26, 52.

27. *Mistretta*, 488 U.S. at 407.

28. See, for example, Raphael Minder, "Spanish Judge Is Acquitted of Abusing His Authority," *New York Times*, February 28, 2012, http://www.nytimes.com/2012/02/28/world/europe/prominent-spanish-judge-cleared-of-abusing-powers.html.

29. For example, simple participation in constitutional conventions could change judicial preferences. See Edward N. Beiser, Jay S. Goodman, and Elmer E. Cornwell Jr., "Judicial Role in a Nonjudicial Setting: Some Empirical Manifestations and Consequences," *Law & Society Review* 5 (1971): 571–82. Notice, however, that in this empirical study there was a serious selection effect, since judges participating in those conventions had a political past.

30. See, for example, *Nonjudicial Activities of Supreme Court Justices and Other Federal Judges: Hearings before the Subcomm. on Separation of Powers of the S. Comm. on the Judiciary*, 91st Cong. 136 (1969).

31. Leslie B. Dubeck, "Understanding 'Judicial Lockjaw': The Debate over Extrajudicial Activity," *New York University Law Review* 82, no. 2 (2007): 569–600, 589.

32. See Bruce Allen Murphy, *The Brandeis/Frankfurter Connection: The Secret Political Activities of Two Supreme Court Justices* (New York: Oxford University Press, 1982), 267, who argues that Frankfurter believed William Douglas had presidential ambitions; and Peter Alan Bell, "Extrajudicial Activity of Supreme Court Justices," *Stanford Law Review* 22 (1970): 587–616.

33. "Model Code of Judicial Conduct: Canon 3," American Bar Association, accessed March 1, 2015, http://www.americanbar.org/groups/professional _responsibility/publications/model_code_of_judicial_conduct/model_code _of_judicial_conduct_canon_3.html.

34. Dubeck, "Understanding 'Judicial Lockjaw,'" 584, 587 (including more commentaries in the last seventy years and more speeches).

35. "Model Code of Judicial Conduct: Rule 3.4, Appointments to Governmental Positions," American Bar Association, 2011, http://www.americanbar.org /content/dam/aba/administrative/professional_responsibility/2011_mcjc _rule3_4.authcheckdam.pdf.

36. Canon 4(B), "Quasi-Judicial and Avocational Activities," *California Code of Judicial Ethics*, January 1, 2013, http://www.courts.ca.gov/documents /ca_code_judicial_ethics.pdf.

37. Canon 4(C)(3)(c), *California Code of Judicial Ethics*, January 1, 2013, http:// www.courts.ca.gov/documents/ca_code_judicial_ethics.pdf.

38. See, for example, Robert J. Martineau, "Disciplining Judges for Nonofficial Conduct: A Survey and Critique of the Law," *University of Baltimore Law Review* 10 (1980–81): 225, 238–41, who lists types of conduct for which judges have been disciplined.

39. Dubeck, "Understanding 'Judicial Lockjaw,'" (discussing debate).

40. Dubeck, "Understanding 'Judicial Lockjaw,'" 569.

41. Ibid., 572.

42. *Mistretta*, 488 U.S. at 361.

43. See "The Leveson Inquiry," National Archives, January 22, 2014, http:// webarchive.nationalarchives.gov.uk/20140122145147/http:/www .levesoninquiry.org.uk.

44. Warren Hoge, "Pinochet Lawyers Challenge Judge's Impartiality," *New York Times*, December 16, 1998, http://www.nytimes.com/1998/12/16/world /pinochet-lawyers-challenge-judge-s-impartiality.html.

45. See "The Hutton Inquiry," National Archives, January 28, 2009, http:// webarchive.nationalarchives.gov.uk/20090128221550/http://www.the -hutton-inquiry.org.uk.

46. Tim Buley, "Judges Chairing Public Inquiries: Observations on DCA Effective Inquiries," *Judicial Review* 9 (2004): 293–98.

47. *Effective Inquiries: A Consultation Paper Produced by the Department of Constitutional Affairs*, National Archives, May 6, 2004, http://webarchive

.nationalarchives.gov.uk/+/http:/www.dca.gov.uk/consult/inquiries
/inquiries.pdf.
48. Ibid., 21, para. 45.
49. See ibid., Annex B (including in a list of powers for possible future legislation the taking of evidence, cross-examination, legal representations, oaths,
and other quasijudicial procedures).
50. Jonathan Russell, "Olympus Appoints High Court Judge to Head 'Im-
proper Payments' Probe Panel," *Telegraph*, November 1, 2011, http://www
.telegraph.co.uk/finance/newsbysector/mediatechnologyandtelecoms
/electronics/8863139/Olympus-appoints-high-court-judge-to-head
-improper-payments-probe-panel.html.
51. Robert Hazell, "Judicial Independence and Accountability in the UK,"
University College London School of Public Policy, June 2014, https://
www.ucl.ac.uk/constitution-unit/research/judicial-independence
/Conference_Paper_Judicial_Independence_and_Accountability_in_the
_UK_jun14.
52. See "Code de l'organisation judiciaire" [Code for the organization of the
judiciary], Legifrance, accessed February 28, 2015, http://www.legifrance
.gouv.fr/affichCode.do?cidTexte=LEGITEXT000006071164&dateTexte
=20080505; see also "Ordonnance 58-1270 du 22 décembre 1958 portant
loi organique relative au statut de la magistrature" [Order 58-1270 of
December 22, 1958 concerning the organic law on the status of the judi-
ciary], Legifrance, http://www.legifrance.gouv.fr/affichTexte.do?cidTexte
=LEGITEXT000006069212&dateTexte=20090320.
53. See "Ordonnance 58-1270," bylaws, ch. I, art. 8.
54. Volcansek, *Judicial Misconduct*.
55. Section 104, sentence 2.
56. Judicial bylaws section 40.
57. "The German Judiciary Act," Bundesministerium der Justiz und für
Verbraucherschutz [Federal Ministry of Justice and Consumer Protection],
April 19, 1972 (last amended February 5, 2009), Bunesgesetzblatt, Teil I
(BGBL. I), 713, § 40, http://www.gesetze-im-internet.de/englisch_drig
/englisch_drig.html.
58. Ibid., § 41.
59. Ibid., judicial bylaws section 4.
60. Ibid., § 48(b).
61. Section 71 is to be read in conjunction with section 42 of the Federal Civil
Servants Act (Bundesbeamtengesetz; judicial bylaws section 76c).
62. "Israel Names Head of Commission for Flotilla Inquiry," *CNN News*,
June 13, 2012, http://articles.cnn.com/2010-06-13/world/israel.flotilla
.inquiry_1_gaza-strip-israeli-policy-israeli-raid?_s=PM:WORLD.
63. Adam M. Dodek, "Judicial Independence as a Public Policy Instrument,"
in *Judicial Independence in Context*, ed. Adam M. Dodek and Lorne Sossin
(Toronto: Irwin Law, 2010).

64. Tonda MacCharles, "Gomery Was Biased in Report, Judge Rules," *Toronto Star*, June 27, 2008, http://www.thestar.com/News/Canada/article/450179.

65. Canwest News Service, "Chief Justice Sheds Light on Morgentaler's Order of Canada Appointment," *Montreal Gazette*, August 16, 2008, http://www .canada.com/montrealgazette/news/story.html?id=7d8564bb-eca3-4404 -9d6b-f96c66b5416c.

66. Canadian Press, "Retired Judge to Head Alberta Queue-Jumping Health Inquiry," *CBC News*, March 5, 2012, http://www.cbc.ca/news/canada /edmonton/story/2012/03/05/calgary-health-inquiry-head-announced .html.

67. "Commissioners," Australian Law Reform Commission, accessed November 14, 2014, http://www.alrc.gov.au/about/commissioners.

68. "Members," Australian Competition Tribunal, accessed November 14, 2014, http://www.competitiontribunal.gov.au/about/members.

69. Emerton and Lee, "Judges and Non-Judicial Functions in Australia," 403.

70. "James Spiegelman Named as New ABC chairman," *Sydney Morning Herald*, March 8, 2012, http://news.smh.com.au/breaking-news-national/james-spigelman-named-as-new-abc-chairman-20120308-1ulfw.html.

71. R. S. French, "Executive Toys—Judges and Non-judicial Functions," *Journal of Judicial Administration* 19, no. 1 (2009): 5; see, generally, Emerton and Lee, "Judges and Non-Judicial Functions in Australia," 403. Some of the practices analyzed by Chief Justice French are, in our view, standard functions of executive oversight, such as issuing search warrants and orders for preventative detention. See Grollo v. Palmer, 184 CLR 348 (1995), on judges issuing covert warrants to authorize interception of communications.

72. Emerton and Lee, "Judges and Non-Judicial Functions in Australia," 414 (describing position of Victorian judiciary in 1923).

73. Fiona Wheeler, "Parachuting In: War and Extra-Judicial Activity by High Court Judges," *Federal Law Review* 38, no. 3 (2010): 485–502.

74. Huddart, Parker and Co Pty Ltd v. Moorehead, 8 CLR 330 (1909), 357. See Emerton and Lee, "Judges and Non-Judicial Functions in Australia," 405–6.

75. Wilson v. Minister for Aboriginal and Torres Strait Islander Affairs, 189 CLR 1 (1996).

76. Emerton and Lee, "Judges and Non-Judicial Functions in Australia," 410–12.

77. *Wilson*, 189 CLR 1 at 17–19.

78. See, for example, Nthambelini Gabara, "Judge Appointed to Probe Cricket SA Saga," *AllAfrica*, November 4, 2011, http://allafrica.com/stories /201111041280.html.

79. Denise Meyerson, "Extra-Judicial Service on the Part of Judges: Constitutional Impediments in Australia and South Africa," *Oxford University Commonwealth Law Journal* 3, no. 2 (2003): 181–200.

80. 2001 (1) SA 883, Constitutional Court of South Africa.

81. See Case Comment, "Bangladesh: Independent Judiciary—Consultation Required for Promotion of Judge to a Non-Judicial Post," *Commonwealth Human Rights Law Digest* 3 (1996): 380–83.

82. Quintus Perera, "Justice L K Wimalachandra Appointed as Commissioner for Tourism," *Asian Tribune*, February 24, 2008, http://www.asiantribune.com/?q=node/9733.

83. "Retd SC Judge to Head State HR Panel," *Times of India*, March 31, 2012, http://articles.timesofindia.indiatimes.com/2012-03-31/kolkata/31265952_1_retd-sc-judge-chief-justice-permanent-judge.

84. "Justice Sirpurkar Takes over as New Chairman of CATI," *New Kerala*, May 22, 2012, http://www.newkerala.com/news/newsplus/worldnews-25465.html#.T8KCgsWaTg0.

85. Maneesh Chhibber, "India Sent Former CJ to Probe Maldives Transfer of Power," *Indian Express*, May 22, 2012, http://www.indianexpress.com/news/india-sent-former-cj-to-probe-maldives-transfer-of-power/952108.

86. Arghya Sengupta, "A Case for Judicial Lockjaw," *Hindu*, February 22, 2012, http://www.thehindu.com/opinion/lead/article2935696.ece (discussing case of Justice Kumar Ganguly).

87. Zafar Abbas, "Pakistan Declassifies 1971 War Report," BBC News, December 31, 2000, http://news.bbc.co.uk/2/hi/south_asia/1094788.stm.

88. Hanif Khalid, "Abbottabad Commission Points Finger at PM, Others," *News International*, May 2, 2012, http://www.thenews.com.pk/Todays-News-13-14305-Abbottabad-Commission-points-finger-at-PM-others.

89. Salman Siddiqui, "Saleem Shahzad Murder: Commission Report Points Out Everything, but the Murderers," *Express Tribune*, January 13, 2012, http://tribune.com.pk/story/320957/saleem-shahzad-commission-report-released.

90. Qaiser Zulficar, "Dr. Arsalan Iftikhar Case: Verdict Clears Court, Judges of Wrongdoing," *Express Tribune*, June 15, 2012, http://tribune.com.pk/story/394065/dr-arsalan-iftikhar-case-verdict-clears-court-judges-of-wrongdoing.

91. "6 More Cabinet Appointments," *Daily Observer*, February 13, 2012, http://observer.gm/africa/gambia/article/6-more-cabinet-appointments.

92. "Cocaine Was Swapped before Being Tendered in Court—Justice Dordzie Committee," *Ghana News Agency*, January 11, 2012, http://www.ghananewsagency.org/details/Social/Cocaine-was-swapped-before-tendered-in-court-Justice-Dordzie-Committee/?ci=4&ai=37825.

93. Judicial bylaw, ch. II, art. 16.

94. Ibid.

95. In Portugal, see judicial bylaw, ch. II, art. 13, sec. 1.

96. *Ley Orgánica del Poder Judicial* in Argentina, *Ley Orgánica Constitucional del Poder Judicial* in Chile, *Ley Orgánica del Poder Judicial de la Federación* in Mexico, and *Lei Orgânica da Magistratura Nacional* in Brazil.

97. Mexico Const. arts.100, 101.

98. Mexico Const. art. 99.

99. "Oyarbide, molesto con la Policía por las versiones del hallazgo del explosivo," *La Razon*, May 23, 2012, http://www.larazon.com.ar/actualidad /Oyarbide-Policia-versiones-hallazgo-explosivo_0_352800155.html (Judge Norberto Oyarbide investigated the alleged conspiracy to kill Colombian former president Alvaro Uribe).
100. Paz Rodriguez Niell, "Apartan al Juez Rafecas de la causa que involucra a Boudou," *La Nacion*, April 27, 2012, http://www.lanacion.com.ar/1468623 -apartan-al-juez-rafecas-de-la-causa-que-involucra-a-boudou.
101. Brazil Const. art. 95.
102. Judicial bylaw, art. 36.
103. Vitug, *Shadow of Doubt*, 61.
104. Ibid., 80–81.

CHAPTER FOUR

1. There is a large body of literature on judicial independence and quality. See, for example, Richard Epstein, "The Independence of Judges: The Uses and Limitations of Public Choice," *Brigham Young University Law Review* (1990): 827–55; Paul Fenn and Eli Salzberger, "Judicial Independence: Some Evidence from the English Court of Appeal," *Journal of Law and Economics* 42, no. 2 (1999): 831–47; F. Andrew F. Hannsen, "Is There a Politically Optimal Level of Judicial Independence?" *American Economic Review* 94, no. 3 (2004): 712–29; Irving Kaufman, "The Essence of Judicial Independence," *Columbia Law Review* 80, no. 4 (1980): 671–701; Daniel Klerman and Paul Mahoney, "The Value of Judicial Independence: Evidence from 18th Century England," *American Law and Economics Review* 7, no. 1 (2005): 1–27; William Landes and Richard Posner, "The Independent Judiciary in an Interest-Group Perspective," *Journal of Law and Economics* 18, no. 3 (1975): 875–901, doi:10.1086/466849; Ramseyer, "Puzzling (In)dependence of Courts"; Eric B. Rasmusen and J. Mark Ramseyer, "Judicial Independence in Civil Law Regimes: Econometrics from Japan," *Journal of Law, Economics, and Organization* 13 (1997): 259–86; McNollgast, "Conditions for Judicial Independence," *Journal of Contemporary Legal Issues* 15, no. 1 (2006): 105–27; and William H. Rehnquist, "Seen in a Glass Darkly: The Future of the Federal Courts," *Wisconsin Law Review* 1993, no. 1 (1993): 1–12. For a more comparative perspective, see Josefina Calca de Temeltas, "Commentary: Comparative Constitutional Approaches to the Rule of Law and Judicial Independence," *Saint Louis University Law Journal* 40 (1996): 997–99. On accountability, see Kosar, "Least Accountable Branch."
2. Kurt E. Scheuerman, "Rethinking Judicial Elections," *Oregon Law Review* 72 (1993): 459–85 (providing overview of selection mechanisms); "Judicial Selection Materials," American Judicature Society, accessed February 28, 2015,

http://www.judicialselection.us/judicial_selection_materials/index
.cfm.
3. See, generally, Kate Malleson and Peter H. Russell, eds., *Appointing Judges in
an Age of Judicial Power* (Toronto: University of Toronto Press, 2006).
4. Malia Reddick, "Merit Selection: A Review of the Social Scientific
Literature," *Dickinson Law Review* 106 (2002): 729–45 (providing summary
of empirical evidence); Luke Bierman, "Preserving Power in Picking Judges:
Merit Selection for the New York Court of Appeals," *Albany Law Review*
60 (1996): 339–58 (advocating merit system for New York); Norman L.
Greene, "Perspectives on Judicial Selection Reform: The Need to Develop a
Model Appointive Selection Plan for Judges in Light of Experience," *Albany
Law Review* 68 (2005): 597–609 (merit system superior); Steven Zeidman,
"Judicial Politics: Making the Case for Merit Selection," *Albany Law Review*
68 (2005): 713–21; Lawrence H. Averill Jr., "Symposium on Arkansas Law:
The Arkansas Courts: Observations on the Wyoming Experience with Merit
Selection of Judges: A Model for Arkansas," *University of Arkansas Little Rock
Law Journal* 17 (1995): 281–327; Mark I. Harrison, Sara S. Greene, Keith
Swisher, and Meghan H. Grabel, "On the Validity and Vitality of Arizona's
Judicial Merit Selection System: Past, Present, and Future," *Fordham Urban
Law Journal* 34 (2007): 239–63; Victoria Cecil, "Merit Selection and Reten-
tion: The Great Compromise? Not Necessarily," *Court Review: The Journal of
the American Judges Association* 39, no. 3 (2002): 20–28; Jason J. Czarnezki,
"A Call for Change: Improving Judicial Selection Methods," *Marquette Law
Review* 89 (2005): 169–78; Lenore L. Prather, "Judicial Selection: What Is
Right for Mississippi?" *Mississippi College Law Review* 21, no. 2 (2002): 199–
207; Jona Goldschmidt, "Merit Selection: Current Status, Procedures, and
Issues," *University of Miami Law Review* 49, no. 1 (1994): 1–91 (providing
extensive history of merit selection and arguing for the merit plan); Joseph
A. Colquitt, "Rethinking Judicial Nominating Commissions: Independence,
Accountability, and Public Support," *Fordham Urban Law Journal* 34 (2007):
73–123; Mark A. Behrens and Cary Silverman, "The Case for Adopting
Appointive Judicial Selection Systems for State Court Judges," *Cornell
Journal of Law & Public Policy* 11 (2002): 273–314 (arguing for appointment
over election); Norman L. Greene, "The Judicial Independence Through
Fair Appointments Act," *Fordham Urban Law Journal* 34, no. 1 (2006): 13–34
(same); G. Alan Tarr, "Designing an Appointive System: The Key Issues,"
Fordham Urban Law Journal 34, no. 1 (2006): 291–314 (same); Jeffery D.
Jackson, "Beyond Quality: First Principles in Judicial Selection and Their
Application to a Commission-Based Selection System," *Fordham Urban
Law Journal* 34, no. 1 (2006): 125–61; Steven P. Croley, "The Majoritarian
Difficulty: Elective Judiciaries and the Rule of Law," *University of Chicago
Law Review* 62, no. 2 (1995): 689–794 (arguing that judicial elections un-
dermine rule of law); Paul R. Brace and Melinda Gann Hall, "The Interplay

of Preferences, Case Facts, Context, and Rules in the Politics of Judicial Choice," *Journal of Politics* 59, no. 4 (1997): 1206–31.

5. See Stephen J. Choi, G. Mitu Gulati, and Eric A. Posner, "Professionals and Politicians: The Uncertain Empirical Case for an Elected Rather than Appointed Judiciary," *Journal of Law, Economics and Organization* 26, no. 2 (2008): 290–336, who find that judges in partisan systems are more productive in terms of number of opinions but that appointed judges are cited more frequently.

6. Justice Sumption was judge of the Courts of Appeal of Jersey and Guernsey.

7. See Posner, *Law and Legal Theory*. See also Tom Bingham in Louis Blom-Cooper, Brice Dickson, and Gavin Drewry, *The Judicial House of Lords: 1876–2009* (Oxford: Oxford University Press, 2009), detailing that only eleven Law Lords in the period studied had no previous judicial experience. The appointment of Justice Sumption (Queen's Counsel but without much judicial experience) in May 2011 was extremely controversial.

8. See Burt Neuborne, "The Supreme Court of India," *International Journal of Constitutional Law* 1, no. 3 (2003): 476–510; and Venkat Iyer, "The Supreme Court of India," in *Judicial Activism in Common Law Supreme Courts*, ed. Brice Dickson (Oxford: Oxford University Press, 2007). Based on the Federal Court of India under the British, the Supreme Court of India was constituted in 1950. It had seven justices, six of whom (including the chief justice) had served in the British court. The composition of the Supreme Court of India has been expanded five times by constitutional amendments. The current composition is twenty-six justices. The selection of justices has been a matter of political tension. As for the appointment of the chief justice, there was supposed to be a norm that the senior justice becomes chief justice—a norm imposed by the court itself in 1951. Indira Gandhi violated the rule twice (1973 and 1976) to impose her candidate against senior justices (there were resignations at the court as a consequence). The seniority principle was reaffirmed in 1978 and since then has been followed. As for the selection of associate justices, the Indian constitution is ambiguous in the effort to avoid both the British and the American models. Appointments are to be achieved by consultations between the executive and the chief justice. Inevitably problems emerge when there is disagreement; the practice is for the executive to dominate. Three famous judicial cases have shaped the process (in 1982, 1994, and 1999) and minimize political influence by creating a powerful collegium of the five most senior justices (at the expense of the chief justice). This collegium has reinforced the trend to pick senior judges from the states' high courts. The system of collegium has recently been challenged before the Supreme Court of India. Satya Prakash, "Abolish Collegium System: Govt," *Hindustan Times*, April 4, 2011, http://www.hindustantimes.com/StoryPage /Print/681311.aspx.

9. See Daniel Klerman, "Non-Promotion and Judicial Independence," *Southern California Law Review* 72 (1998): 455–64.
10. Diffusion data on file with authors.
11. See Stephen B. Burbank and Barry Friedman, eds., *Judicial Independence at the Crossroads: An Interdisciplinary Approach* (Thousand Oaks, CA: Sage, 2002).
12. Martin Shapiro, *Courts: A Comparative and Political Analysis* (Chicago: University of Chicago Press, 1981).
13. See, for example, Sanford Levinson, "Identifying 'Independence,'" *Boston University Law Review* 86 (2006): 1297–308 (providing different concepts of judicial independence and arguing that there might be too much independence); Stephen B. Burbank, "The Architecture of Judicial Independence," *Southern California Law Review* 72 (1999): 315–51 (explaining judicial independence in contemporary American history); Archibald Cox, "The Independence of the Judiciary: History and Purposes," *University of Dayton Law Review* 21, no. 3 (1996): 565–84 (discussing historical reasons for judicial independence); John A. Ferejohn and Larry D. Kramer, "Independent Judges, Dependent Judiciary: Institutionalizing Judicial Restraint," *New York University Law Review* 77 (2002): 962–1038 (arguing that independence and accountability aim at a well-functioning system of adjudication); John Ferejohn, "Judicializing Politics, Politicizing Law," *Law and Contemporary Problems* 65, no. 3 (2002): 41–68; John Ferejohn, "Independent Judges, Dependent Judiciary: Explaining Judicial Independence," *Southern California Law Review* 72 (1999): 353–84 (discussing institutional protections for judges and the judiciary and explaining interest theories of judicial independence); Gordon Bermant and Russell R. Wheeler, "Federal Judges and the Judicial Branch: Their Independence and Accountability," *Mercer Law Review* 46 (1995): 835–61 (identifying different levels of independence, including decisional independence, personal independence, procedural independence, administrative independence, as well as different levels of accountability, namely internal versus external accountability); Frances Kahn Zemans, "The Accountable Judge: Guardian of Judicial Independence," *Southern California Law Review* 72 (1999): 625–55 (discussing institutional versus decisional independence); Rehnquist, "Seen in a Glass Darkly" (making the point that the shape of the court system is too important to be left to the judiciary); and Brace and Hall, "The Interplay of Preferences, Case Facts, Context, and Rules." See also Burbank and Friedman, *Judicial Independence at the Crossroads.*
14. See, for example, Kosar, "Least Accountable Branch"; Francesco Contini and Richard Mohr, "Reconciling Independence and Accountability in Judicial Systems," *Utrecht Law Review* 3, no. 2 (2007): 26–43; Wim Voermans, "Judicial Transparency Furthering Public Accountability for New Judiciaries," *Utrecht Law Review* 3, no. 1 (2007): 148–59; Daniela Piana, "From Judicial Independence to Judicial Accountabilities" (unpublished manuscript, 2009;

arguing that political insulation does not preclude accountability to other institutions that could be social in nature); and Michael Dowdle, *Public Accountability: Designs, Dilemmas and Experiences* (Cambridge, UK: Cambridge University Press, 2006).

15. See Stephen Burbank, "Judicial Independence, Judicial Accountability and Interbranch Relations," University of Pennsylvania Law Schools Working Paper No. 102, 2006, http://lsr.nellco.org/upenn/wps/papers/102, who argues that judicial independence in the United States is at a tipping point because of a characterization of judicial politics as ordinary politics.

16. Stephen M. Bainbridge, *Corporation Law and Economics* (St. Paul, MN: Foundation, 2002).

17. The intermediary is also, of course, an agent of the principal whose job is to control another agent. Notice that the intermediate body is paid by the principal, the taxpayers, as in the usual economic model.

18. See Martin M. Shapiro, *Who Guards the Guardians? Judicial Control of Administration* (Athens: University of Georgia Press, 1988), on administrative law.

19. Hanssen, "Learning about Judicial Independence."

20. Posner, "What Do Judges and Justices Maximize?"; Posner, "Judicial Behavior and Performance"; Posner, "The Role of the Judge in the Twenty-First Century." See also Easterbrook, "What's So Special about Judges?"; Cohen, "The Motives of Judges"; Schauer, "Incentives, Reputation, and the Inglorious Determinants of Judicial Behavior"; Foxall, "What Judges Maximize: Toward an Economic Psychology of the Judicial Utility Function"; Guthrie, Rachlinski, and Wistrich, "Blinking on the Bench." For a different perspective, see Baum, "What Judges Want"; and Baum, *Judges and Their Audiences*.

21. Measuring the performance of judges has been the object of some work but is still quite underdeveloped. Whereas quantitative measures (workload) and qualitative measures (reversal rates in appeal courts) are by now largely developed, complexity is still a problem (even the use of citations is still the object of discussion). See Choi and Gulati, "A Tournament of Judges?"; Stephen J. Choi and G. Mitu Gulati, "Choosing the Next Supreme Court Justice: An Empirical Ranking of Judicial Performance," *Southern California Law Review* 78 (2004): 23–117; and Steven G. Gey and Jim Rossi, "Empirical Measures of Judicial Performance: An Introduction to the Symposium," *Florida State University Law Review* 32 (2005): 1001–14.

22. In fact, the "laymen" in many types of council are lawyers, law professors, or legally educated individuals—hardly the standard example of independent laymen.

23. If the judges are supreme court judges, the council may tend to focus on the power struggle between government and supreme court and on maintaining a vertical hierarchy within the judiciary. However, if they are lower court judges, we should expect a relatively smaller role for the supreme court (which might be welcomed by the government). We have observed an increasing role of judicial associations (unions), which are motivated

by the need to coordinate the interests of junior judges to undermine the traditional vertical hierarchy.

24. Among others, see James R. Rogers, Roy B. Flemming, and Jon R. Bond, eds., *Institutional Games and the U.S. Supreme Court* (Charlottesville: University of Virginia Press, 2006); Timothy Besley and Abigail Payne, "Judicial Accountability and Economic Policy Outcomes: Evidence from Employment Discrimination Charges," London School of Economics Institute for Fiscal Studies Working Paper No. W03/11, 2003; Barry Friedman, "The Politics of Judicial Review," *Texas Law Review* 84 (2005): 257–337; Tracey E. George and Lee Epstein, "On the Nature of Supreme Court Decision Making," *American Political Science Review* 86, no. 2 (1992): 323–37; Tom Ginsburg, "Economic Analysis and the Design of Constitutional Courts," *Theoretical Inquiries in Law* 3 (2002): 49–85; Jonathan R. Macey, "Promoting Public-Regarding Legislation through Statutory Interpretation: An Interest Group Model," *Columbia Law Review* 86 (1986): 223–68; Jonathan R. Macey, "Competing Economic Views of the Constitution," *George Washington Law Review* 56 (1987): 50–80; and Alexander Tabarrok and Eric Helland, "Court Politics: The Political Economy of Tort Awards," *Journal of Law & Economics* 42 (1999): 157–88.

25. But see Linn Hammergren, "Do Judicial Councils Further Judicial Reform? Evidence from Latin America," Carnegie Endowment for International Peace Rule of Law Working Paper Series No. 28, June 2002; and Stefan Voigt and Nora El-Bialy, "Identifying the Determinants of Judicial Performance: Taxpayers' Money Well Spent?" working paper, 2013, http://ssrn.com/abstract=2241224.

26. Hanssen, "Learning about Judicial Independence."

27. We believe the primary rationale to be considered in assigning the task to a council is economies of scale and specialization vis-à-vis alternative managers, such as a ministry of justice (arguably better able to do things like purchasing supplies) or a supreme court (a body that typically has little time or expertise for management).

28. On the other hand, the politics of setting up the councils may vary greatly depending on local circumstances, in particular the historical balance of power between government and supreme court. For example, the extent to which the justices are easily captured by the government will result in different models of judicial council.

29. Hanssen's data from the United States suggests that the *timing* of the adoption of council-type mechanisms reflects these motivations.

30. A precursor for judicial councils can be seen in the use of formal nomination committees composed of various governmental officials. See, for example, Albania Const. of 1925 (judicial nominations from special committee of judges, prosecutors, and Minister of Justice). France had a council for disciplining justices dating back all the way to 1833.

31. The Italian council was made up of thirty-three members: twenty magistrates elected directly by the judges, ten lawyers or law professors nominated by Parliament, and the president, chief justice, and chief prosecutor all serving ex officio. It has been reformed recently to include only twenty-four members: sixteen ordinary magistrates and prosecutors and eight lawyers or law professors with fifteen years of experience in the legal profession, all of whom are appointed by Parliament. See Cheryl Thomas, *Judicial Appointments in Continental Europe*, Lord Chancellor's Department Research Series No. 6, 1997.

32. Hanssen, "Learning about Judicial Independence"; Goldschmidt, "Merit Selection."

33. New York faces a similar problem today, leading a judge to bring a lawsuit to allow her to run for a higher court without securing the blessing of party bosses. See Mark Hansen, "Questioning Conventional Behavior," *ABA Journal* 93 (2007): 21–22.

34. With respect to the federal judiciary, see Charles Gardner Geyh, "Customary Independence," in Burbank and Friedman, *Judicial Independence at the Crossroads*, 160, who discusses the historical foundations of the norms against court packing—namely, the Judiciary Act of 1789, the Midnight Judges Act of 1801 and its repeal in 1802, and Roosevelt's court-packing plan of 1937.

35. Roscoe Pound, "The Causes of Popular Dissatisfaction with the Administration of Justice," *Journal of the American Judicature Society* 20 (1937): 178–87.

36. Webster, "Selection and Retention of Judges"; Reddick, "Merit Selection" (noting only thirty-three judges lost retention elections in the entire United States between 1942 and 1978).

37. Hanssen, "Learning about Judicial Independence," 452.

38. Goldschmidt, "Merit Selection."

39. Hanssen, "Learning about Judicial Independence."

40. See, for example, Reddick, "Merit Selection" (reviewing the literature).

41. Hanssen, "Learning about Judicial Independence," 721.

42. For at least one indicator, states with the residual category of "other" appointment methods (typically legislative or gubernatorial appointment) have more political competition. See ibid., 720 ("In 95 percent of partisan election states the same party controlled both houses of the legislature, versus in 87 percent of merit plan states and 81 percent of other states.").

43. Ramseyer, "Puzzling (In)dependence of Courts." See also Tom Ginsburg, *Judicial Review in New Democracies: Constitutional Courts in Asian Cases* (Cambridge, UK: Cambridge University Press, 2003); Mathew C. Stephenson, "'When the Devil Turns . . .': The Political Foundations of Independent Judicial Review," *Journal of Legal Studies* 32 (2003): 59–89; Lee Epstein, Jack Knight, and Olga Shvestova, "Selecting Selection Systems," in Burbank and Friedman, *Judicial Independence at the Crossroads*, 191 (arguing that selection

systems are determined by political uncertainty and risk; empirical evidence seems to confirm that as political uncertainty has decreased, bolstering accountability has expanded as the main goal of judicial selection).

44. Webster, "Selection and Retention of Judges"; Henry R. Glick, "The Promise and Performance of the Missouri Plan: Judicial Selection in the Fifty States," *University of Miami Law Review* 32 (1978): 509–41. See also Choi, Gulati, and Posner, "Professionals and Politicians."

45. Reddick, "Merit Selection," 744.

46. See the discussion by Maria Angela Jardim de Santa Cruz Oliveira in "Reforming the Brazilian Supreme Federal Court: A Comparative Approach," *Washington University Global Studies Law Review* 5 (2006): 99–150.

47. Ibid.

48. Brazil Const., amend. 7, art. 120.

49. See Oliveira, "Reforming the Brazilian Supreme Federal Court."

50. Ibid.

51. Ibid.

52. Rogério B. Arantes, "Constitutionalism, the Expansion of Justice and the Judicialization of Politics in Brazil," in *The Judicialization of Politics in Latin America*, ed. Rachel Sieder, Line Schjolden, and Alan Angell (New York: Palgrave Macmillan, 2005).

53. See Oliveira, "Reforming the Brazilian Supreme Federal Court."

54. Brazil Const., amend. 45, art. 103B.

55. Ibid.

56. Ginsburg, *Judicial Review in New Democracies*; Ramseyer, "Puzzling (In)dependence of Courts."

57. Israel Basic Law: The Judicature, Courts Law 5744-1984 §§ 1–24. This replaced the Judges Act (1953) as the primary statute governing judicial appointments.

58. Ibid., § 4.

59. Levinson, "Identifying 'Independence,'" 1306; Eli M. Salzberger, "Judicial Appointments and Promotions in Israel: Constitution, Law and Politics," in Malleson and Russell, *Appointing Judges in an Age of Judicial Power*, 241, 248. Salzberger believes that the crucial factor is the majority of jurists on the committee and the majority of judges among the jurists.

60. Hirschl, *Towards Juristocracy*.

61. See Shimon Shetreet, "The Critical Challenge of Judicial Independence in Israel," in Russell and O'Brien, *Judicial Independence in the Age of Democracy*, 233, who points to changes in the rules of justiciability and standing; judges leading commissions of inquiry into corruption, administration, police acts, and oil drilling operations; and the judicial and legal consequences of security considerations.

62. Salzberger, "Judicial Appointments and Promotions in Israel," 242, 249. Salzberger characterizes Barak as shifting the court from a formalist conception of law to a more values-based jurisprudence.

63. Ibid., 252–53.
64. Binyamin Blum, "Doctrines without Borders: The 'New' Israeli Exclusionary Rule and the Dangers of Legal Transplantation," *Stanford Law Review* 60 (2008): 2121–72, at 2164; Amos N. Guiora and Erin M. Page, "Going Toe to Toe: President Barak's and Chief Justice Rehnquist's Theories of Judicial Activism," *Hastings International and Comparative Law Review* 29 (2005): 51–69.
65. Edna Adato and Israel Hayorn Staff, "MKs, Judicial Officials Hail Grunis Appointment as Chief Justice," Israel Hayom, February 12, 2012, http://www.israelhayom.com/site/newsletter_article.php?id=3085.
66. Lahav Harkov, "Judicial Selection Reforms Pass Initial Votes," *Jerusalem Post*, November 14, 2011, http://www.jpost.com/Diplomacy-and-Politics/Judicial-selection-reforms-pass-initial-votes.
67. Lazar Berman, "Bills Aimed at Checking Judicial Power Head to Knesset," *Times of Israel*, October 20, 2013, http://www.timesofisrael.com/bills-aimed-at-checking-judicial-power-head-to-knesset.
68. Jonathan Lis, "Knesset Approves Bill to Ensure Women's Spots on Judicial Selection Committee," *Haaretz*, January 21, 2014, http://www.haaretz.com/news/national/.premium-1.569674.
69. See Doris Marie Provine and Antoine Garapon, "The Selection of Judges in France: Searching for a New Legitimacy," in Russell and Malleson, *Appointing Judges in an Age of Judicial Power*, 176. See also John Bell, "Principles and Methods of Judicial Selection in France," *University of Southern California Law Review* 61 (1988): 1757–94.
70. Six members were elected by the National Assembly, four magistrates were chosen by their peers, and two members were appointed from the judiciary by the president of the republic.
71. This is the current republican constitution, which replaced a parliamentary government by a semipresidential system. In the Fifth Republic, most of the traditional powers of the minister of justice were reinstated.
72. These members were either appointed directly by the president of the republic (two members) or appointed after nomination from the courts and Conseil d'Etat (seven members total).
73. See Doris Marie Provine, "Courts in the Political Process in France," in *Courts, Law and Politics in Comparative Perspective*, ed. Herbert Jacob, Ekhard Blankenburg, Herbert M. Kritzer, Doris Marie Provine, and Joseph Sanders (New Haven: Yale University, 1996), 177, 203.
74. The French constitution grants the judges a status that guarantees their independence and security of tenure.
75. These are the president of the republic, the presidents of the two parliamentary chambers (the Senate and the National Assembly), and the General Assembly of the Conseil d'Etat.
76. According to the French Constitution, there must be ordinary legislation regulating the functioning of the council. See Law No. 94-100 of February 5, 1994, *Journal Officiel de la République Française* [J.O.; Official gazette

of France] (February 8, 1994), p. 2146; CC Decision No. 93-337 DC, January 27, 1994, J.O., p. 1776; Decree No. 94-199 of March 9, 1994, J.O. (March 10, 1994), p. 3779.

77. See Vincent Wright, "The Fifth Republic: From the *Droit de l'État* to the *État de droit?*" *West European Politics* 22, no. 4 (1999): 92–119, at 92, who reports several famous scandals that generated serious clashes between the French government and the judiciary, including the Ben Barka affair, the murder of the Prince of Broglie in 1977, the suicide of the Labor minister in 1979, and the famous *Canard Enchaîné* affair.

78. See Alec Stone Sweet, *The Birth of Judicial Politics in France: The Constitutional Council in Comparative Perspective* (New York: Oxford University Press, 1992), who explains that the process of empowerment of the French judiciary started in the early 1970s.

79. See Provine, "Courts in the Political Process in France," 204.

80. Ibid. (comparing famous American and French judges).

81. See Provine and Garapon, "Selection of Judges in France," 205.

82. France was ruled by right-wing administrations for more than twenty years. François Mitterrand became the first elected Socialist president of France in 1981, but after the loss of his party's majority in the French National Assembly in 1986, he had to live in *cohabitation* with the conservative government of Jacques Chirac. In the legislative elections of 1993, due to economic recession, consecutive scandals, and divisions on the left, Edouard Balladur became prime minister. This gave rise to the second *cohabitation* of Mitterrand's presidency. Jacques Chirac became president in 1995 and replaced Balladur with Alain Juppé. The third *cohabitation* started in 1997, when the president dissolved the National Assembly and Lionel Jospin became prime minister, constraining Chirac's political influence.

83. Thomas, *Judicial Appointments in Continental Europe*.

84. See Véronique Pujas and Martin Rhodes, "Party Finance and Political Scandals in Italy, Spain and France," *West European Politics* 22, no. 3 (1999): 41–63, who explain political corruption in Italy, Spain, and France and the role of the judiciary—in the French case, looking at the accumulated and distributed kickbacks during the Gaullist and Socialist governments.

85. See ibid., 59.

86. Valéry Turcey, "Le Conseil Superieur de la Magistrature Français: Bilan et Perspectives," *Revista del Poder Judicial* 75 (2004): 539–51.

87. Anja Seibert-Fohr, ed., *Judicial Independence in Transition* (Berlin: Springer, 2012), 278.

88. Ibid., at 280.

89. Ibid.

90. The French antipathy for a powerful and activist judiciary is discussed by Burt Neuborne, "Judicial Review and Separation of Powers in France and the United States," *New York University Law Review* 57, no. 3 (1982):

363–438; Michael H. Davis, "The Law/Politics Distinction, the French Conseil Constitutionnel and the U.S. Supreme Court," *American Journal of Comparative Law* 34 (1986): 45–92; and Stone Sweet, *Birth of Judicial Politics in France.*

91. The Italian Constitution came into force in January 1948.
92. Law No. 195 of March 24, 1958, *Gazzetta Ufficiale* (Gazz. Uff.; Mar. 27, 1958). See, generally, Mary L. Volcansek, "Judicial Selection in Italy: A Civil Service Model with Partisan Results," in Russell and Malleson, *Appointing Judges in an Age of Judicial Power,* 159.
93. Law No. 195 of March 24, 1958, reformed by Law No. 44 of March 28, 2002, Gazz. Uff. (March 29, 2002), sets the composition and functioning of the CSM.
94. Giuseppe Di Federico, "Independence and Accountability of the Judiciary in Italy: The Experience of a Former Transitional Country in a Comparative Perspective," in *Judicial Integrity,* ed. Andras Sajo (Boston: Brill Academic, 2004), 181, 184–85, http://siteresources.worldbank.org/INTECA/Resources /DiFedericopaper.pdf.
95. Since administrative jurisdiction is assigned to bodies separate from the ordinary courts, there is also a council for administrative judges, the *Consiglio di Presidenza della Magistratura Amministrativa.*
96. See Thomas, *Judicial Appointments in Continental Europe*; and Levinson, "Identifying 'Independence'" (stating that the Italian system exhibits a maximalist notion of judicial independence).
97. Ibid. If we refer to the role of the judicial associations, there are four that are crucial in elections to the CSM. Since 1990, no judicial representatives to the CSM have been elected without the backing of one of the following groups (from left to right on the political spectrum): *Magistratura democratica*; *Movimento per la giustizia*; *Unita per la Constitutzione*; and *Magistratura indipendente.* There is also another association, *Articolo 3-I Ghibellini,* but it has less influence. These five associations make up the *Associazione Nazionale Magistrati* (ANM).
98. Carlo Guarnieri, "Judicial Independence in Latin Countries in Western Europe," in Russell and O'Brien, *Judicial Independence in the Age of Democracy.*
99. Salary and benefits earned by magistrates are the highest in Italy for public service, for the purpose of guaranteeing all the conditions for true independence, regardless of individual judicial performance (under pressure from the judicial associations, judicial salaries have increased far beyond those of other civil servants).
100. See Patrizia Pederzoli and Carlo Guarnieri, "The Judicialization of Politics, Italian Style," *Journal of Modern Italian Studies* 2, no. 3 (1997): 321–36, at 331.
101. Patrizia Pederzoli, "The Reform of the Judiciary," in *Italian Politics: Quo Vadis?* ed. Carlo Guarnieri and James L. Newell (New York: Berghahn,

2005); David Nelken, "The Judges and Political Corruption in Italy," in *The Corruption of Politics and the Politics of Corruption*, ed. Michael Levi and David Nelken (Oxford: Blackwell, 1996).

102. A Google search of any of these names will reveal many newspaper articles referring to their work. See, generally, Nelken, "Judges and Political Corruption in Italy."

103. Guarnieri, "Judicial Independence in Latin Countries in Western Europe," 116–17.

104. Daniela Piana, "From Constitutional Body to Policy Arena: Politics, Inescapable Companion of the Italian Judicial Council," *Bulletin of Italian Politics* 2 (2010): 39–54, at 49.

105. Ibid. Also, Law No. 109/2008 amended a 2006 law on judicial discipline, to include affiliation to a political party and active participation in political activities in the list of disciplinary violations concerning the behavior of judges and prosecutors to be sanctioned. Seibert-Fohr, *Judicial Independence in Transition*, 380. However, it did not seem contradictory to the CSM that "the magistrates are still allowed to appear on party tickets in national, local, and European elections, to be elected and even assume positions of responsibility in the organization of the political party for which they were elected and return to the exercise of judicial functions after the end of their electoral mandate." Ibid., 381.

106. See Tim Koopmans, *Courts and Political Institutions: A Comparative View* (Cambridge, UK: Cambridge University Press, 2003), 76–84, who describes the growth in power of the Dutch judiciary.

107. Thomas, *Judicial Appointments in Continental Europe*.

108. Also note the existence of the Dutch Association of the Judiciary, *Nederlandse Vereniging voor Rechtspraak*. It defines itself as "the independent trade association and union of judges and public prosecutors." The NVvR advises the Ministry of Justice and participates in international organizations, and at the end of 2004, it had 3,244 members.

109. The creation of the Council for the Judiciary followed the Leemhuis Commission's advice to the minister of justice in the 1998 report *Updating the Administration of Justice*.

110. Three members come from the judiciary and two from senior positions at a government department.

111. See "The State of Our Democracy" (assessment report, Ministry of the Interior and Kingdom Relations, Netherlands, 2006).

112. Act of Settlement, 1700, 12 & 13 W. & M. 3, c. 2.

113. For example, Robert Stevens mentions several important episodes of political interference with the judiciary (including the decision of the Crown not to reappoint judges on the change of a monarch). He argues that the development of high formalism that protected the English judiciary from possible political interference made the judiciary increasingly irrelevant.

See Robert Stevens, *The English Judges: Their Role in the Changing Constitution* (Portland: Hart, 2005), 1–29.

114. See Johan Steyn, "The Case for a Supreme Court," *Law Quarterly Review* 118 (2002): 382–96 (who finds the argument in favor of maintaining this office unconvincing simply because, in practice, the lord chancellor delegates judicial business to the law lords).

115. See Herbert M. Kritzer, "Courts, Justice and Politics in England," in Jacob, Blankenburg, Kritzer, Provine, and Sanders, *Courts, Law and Politics in Comparative Perspective*, 81, 90–91. Less than 13 percent had parliamentary experience in the 1980s; between 1832 and 1906, it was 58 percent.

116. See Stevens, *English Judges*, 30–61, 100–194, who discusses the relationship of particular lord chancellors to politicization, arguing that Lord Kilmuir (1954–62) represented the first important shift (since he was a man of the traditionalist right of the Tories who opposed the abolishment of the death penalty); that Lord Gardiner (lord chancellor with Wilson's Labor governments from 1964 to 1970) served as the greatest reformist by advancing Labor's agenda; and that Lord Hailsham (lord chancellor with Edward Heath from 1970 to 1974 and with Margaret Thatcher's government from 1979 to 1987) marked the second important shift in politicization (in part through his controversial appointments to the bench), followed actively by Lord Mackay (lord chancellor with Thatcher's government from 1987 to 1992 and with Major's government until 1997), Lord Irvine (lord chancellor with Blair's government from 1997 to 2003), and Lord Falconer (lord chancellor with Blair's government from 2003 to 2007). Stevens's account leaves the impression of an increasing politicization of the role of lord chancellor. A similar thesis is presented by Steyn, "The Case for a Supreme Court," who argues that the vast increase in the nature and extent of the lord chancellor's executive responsibilities has increasingly politicized the office.

117. For example, senior judiciary members voted against the Irish Treaty (1922), criminal sentencing reforms (in the 1940s and 1950s), divorce law reforms (in the 1970s), a trade union and labor relations bill (1975), a police and criminal evidence bill (1984), a courts and legal services bill (1989), a human rights bill (1995), legislation concerning hunting (2001), and constitutional reform (2004). Occasionally, a law lord has introduced a bill (for example, in 1987, Lord Templeman introduced a bill on land registration). The convention that active and retired law lords are not supposed to discuss political matters is controversial.

118. See J. A. G. Griffith, *The Politics of the Judiciary*, 5th ed. (London: Harper Collins, 1997), 281–343, who argues that the myth of neutrality has undermined the building up of a strong judiciary. Griffith defends a political role for the judiciary in areas such as law and order or social issues. See also Stevens, *English Judges*, 76–99; and Robert J. Martineau, *Appellate Justices in*

England and the United States: A Comparative Analysis (Getzville: William S. Hein, 1990).

119. Uratemp Ventures Ltd v. Collins, [2001] UKHL 43.

120. See Andrew Le Sueur, "The Conception of the UK's New Supreme Court," in Le Sueur, *Building the UK's New Supreme Court*, 3 (observing a lack of sufficient transparency in such a system); and Kate Malleson, "Selecting Judges in the Era of Devolution and Human Rights," in Le Sueur, *Building the UK's New Supreme Court*, 295 (noting that a career judiciary in the United Kingdom could attract less reputation but more transparency).

121. See Griffith, *Politics of the Judiciary*, 65–102.

122. See Lord Woolf, "Judicial Review—The Tensions between the Executive and the Judiciary," *Law Quarterly Review* 114 (1998): 579–93, who recognizes that slowly executive-friendly judicial review has been replaced by a more intense review with higher standards of scrutiny and willingness to intervene, albeit in the absence of other constitutional safeguards. Lord Woolf was a master of the rolls, the senior civil judge in the Court of Appeal of England and Wales, from 1996 to 2000.

123. See J. A. G. Griffith, "The Common Law and the Political Constitution," *Law Quarterly Review* 117 (2001): 42–67, who makes the argument that there are two sovereignties: that of Parliament and that of the courts.

124. See a personal account by Lord Denning, a law lord and master of the rolls from 1962 to 1982, in *Lord Denning: The Discipline of Law* (Oxford: Oxford University Press, 1975). A controversial judge, Lord Denning maintained that the principles of common law as laid down by the judges were not suited for the late twentieth century. His most relevant personal contributions were on contract laws and negligence standards. For example, his defense of the rule of law doctrine in fundamental breach in 1978 (when he was then master of the rolls) was overturned by Lord Wilberforce (then a law lord) in favor of the rule of construction doctrine.

125. See Stevens, *English Judges*.

126. The contradictory decisions taken by different panels of three law lords were not easily understood by the public. For a detailed account, see Stevens, *English Judges*, 100–118. See also Robert Stevens, "Judicial Independence in England: A Loss of Innocence," in Russell and O'Brien, *Judicial Independence in the Age of Democracy*, 155.

127. McGonnell v. United Kingdom, European Court of Human Rights, 3rd Court Section (2000), http://hudoc.echr.coe.int/sites/fra/pages/search.aspx?i=001-58461.

128. Ibid.

129. Headed by Lord Denning. Griffith, "Common Law and the Political Constitution." Profumo was a minister of defense who shared a lover with a Russian military aide. This created a well-known scandal in the United Kingdom. See "Profumo Affair," Wikipedia, http://en.wikipedia.org/wiki/Profumo_affair.

130. Headed by Lord Wilberforce and Lord Widgery, respectively. Griffith, "Common Law and the Political Constitution."
131. Griffith, "Common Law and the Political Constitution," 14–29.
132. In the case of Scotland, judicial appointments were under review since September 1999, and an independent Judicial Appointments Board was established in June 2002.
133. See Diana Woodhouse, "The Constitutional Reform Act 2005: Defending Judicial Independence the English Way," *International Journal of Constitutional Law* 5, no. 1 (2007): 153–65.
134. Ibid.
135. Ibid.
136. The president of the Courts of England and Wales sits in the Court of Appeal, the High Court, and the Crown Court, among others, and is responsible for expressing the views of the judiciary and for welfare, training, and guidance of the English judiciary. He is not the president of the Supreme Court.
137. The new Supreme Court was launched in 2009 with the twelve former law lords (the lords of appeal in ordinary). An ad hoc Supreme Court selection committee presided over by the president of the Supreme Court was set up for future appointments.
138. The JAC started selecting judges in April 2006. Kate Malleson, *The Legal System* (Oxford: Oxford University Press, 2005), 245–46, argues that the JAC is effectively dominated by the judiciary. The fact that the council is chaired by a nonlawyer does not seem to counter a strong judicial membership. The traditional role of the lord chancellor in judicial appointments was the object of a study by Anthony Bradney, "The Judicial Activity of the Lord Chancellor 1946–1987: A Pellet," *Journal of Law & Society* 16 (1989): 360–72.
139. The JACO is responsible for investigating and making recommendations concerning complaints about the judicial appointments process and the handling of judicial conduct complaints and discipline. It is completely independent of the government and of the judiciary.
140. See, generally, Vernon Bogdanor, "Constitutional Reform in Britain: The Quiet Revolution," *Annual Review of Political Science* 8 (2005): 73–98.
141. See Margit Cohn, "Judicial Activism in the House of Lords: A Composite Constitutional Approach," *Public Law* (2007): 95–115. She considers a first example of the trend to more judicial activism the controversy surrounding the 2001 Anti-Terrorist, Crime and Security Act; the House of Lords considered the original bill inconsistent with the European Convention of Human Rights, forcing the government to make changes. More recent decisions have been perceived as a rising judicial activism. Other scholars go back to the Human Rights Act of 1998, which enhances judicial review by providing an augmented interpretative mandate. This has entrenched some of the Labor political ideas protected by courts through a more active judiciary. See, generally, Mark Tushnet, *Weak Courts, Strong Rights:*

Judicial Review and Social Welfare Rights in Comparative Constitutional Law (Princeton: Princeton University Press, 2008), 27–33.

142. See Robert Stevens, "Reform in Haste and Repent at Leisure: Iolanthe, the Lord High Executioner and Brave New World," *Legal Studies* 24 (2004): 1–34, at 14.

143. See Kate Malleson, "Modernizing the Constitution: Completing the Unfinished Business," *Legal Studies* 24 (2004): 119–33, at 120.

144. See, for example, Robert Stevens, "A Loss of Innocence? Judicial Independence and the Separation of Powers," *Oxford Journal of Legal Studies* 19 (1999): 365–402; and Matthew Flinders, "Mechanisms of Judicial Accountability in British Central Government," *Parliamentary Affairs* 54, no. 1 (2001): 54–71.

145. There is only one woman as lord of appeal in ordinary (Baroness Hale).

146. For an empirical analysis, see Jordi Blanes and Clare Leaver, "Are Tenured Judges Insulated from Political Pressure?," *Journal of Public Economics*, 95 (2011): 570–86. See Griffith, "Common Law and the Political Constitution," 18–21; and Kritzer, "Courts, Justice and Politics in England," 92.

147. Griffith, "Common Law and the Political Constitution," 63–259.

148. Seibert-Fohr, *Judicial Independence in Transition*, 156.

149. Ibid., 162.

150. Ibid., 161.

151. Concerns about the extent to which the present reform enhances judicial independence have been echoed by Sue Prince, "The Law and Politics: Upsetting the Judicial Apple-Cart," *Parliamentary Affairs* 57 (2004): 288–300.

152. Graham Gee, Robert Hazell, Kate Malleson, and Patrick O'Brien, *The Politics of Judicial Independence in the UK's Changing Constitution* (Cambridge, UK: Cambridge University Press, 2015).

153. Robert Hazell, "Judicial Independence and Accountability in the UK," University College London School of Public Policy, June 2014, https://www.ucl.ac.uk/constitution-unit/research/judicial-independence/Conference_Paper_Judicial_Independence_and_Accountability_in_the_UK_jun14.

154. See, for example, Rebecca Bill Chavez, "The Appointment and Removal Process for Judges in Argentina: The Role of Judicial Councils and Impeachment Juries in Promoting Judicial Independence," *Latin American Politics & Society* 49, no. 2 (2005): 33–58. Some refer to a distinction between a "Northern European Model" more focused on management concerns and a "Southern European Model" that is constitutionalized and focused on structural independence. Wim Voermans and Pim Albers, *Councils for the Judiciary in EU Countries*, European Commission for the Efficiency of Justice (CEPEJ), 2003. We reject this distinction as unhelpful and instead develop an index of powers and competences.

155. See Hammergren, "Do Judicial Councils Further Judicial Reform?" See also Pedro C. Magalhaes, "The Politics of Judicial Reform in Eastern Europe," *Comparative Politics* 32 (1999): 43–62 (discussing the judicial institutional design in Bulgaria, Hungary, and Poland and how it relates to the bargaining process between the different political actors); Pilar Domingo, "Judicial Independence: The Politics of the Supreme Court of Mexico," *Journal of Latin American Studies* 32, no. 3 (2000): 705–35 (arguing that specific constitutional reforms and the politics of co-optation subordinated the judiciary to the dominant party until 1994); Peter H. Solomon, "Putin's Judicial Reform: Making Judges Accountable as well as Independent," *East Europe Constitution Review* 11 (2002): 117–23 (discussing the reforms to the Judicial Qualification Commission); and Lauren Castaldi, "Judicial Independence Threatened in Venezuela: The Removal of Venezuelan Judges and the Complications of Rule of Law Reform," *Georgetown Journal of International Law Review* 37 (2006): 477–506 (discussing the current situation in Venezuela).
156. Art. 3.2.
157. Art. 3.1.
158. Subject to review by the Supreme Court; Art. 3.4.
159. Council of Europe Committee of Ministers to Member States on the Independence, Efficiency and Role of Judges Recommendation No. R (94) 12 (1994), art. I.2.c.
160. See Violane Autheman and Sandra Elena, "Global Best Practices—Judicial Councils: Lessons Learned from Europe and Latin America," ed. Keith Henderson, International Foundation for Electoral Systems Rule of Law White Paper Series, 2004, http://www.ifes.org/~/media/Files/Publications/White%20PaperReport/2004/22/WhitePaper_2_FINAL.pdf, who argue that judicial councils should be composed of a majority of judges elected by their peers and should be tasked with selection, promotion, discipline, and training.
161. These data are from the Comparative Constitutions Project, http://www.comparativeconstitutionsproject.org.
162. Hammergren, "Do Judicial Councils Further Judicial Reform?"
163. Data available from the Comparative Constitutions Project, http://www.comparativeconstitutionsproject.org.
164. Judicial independence on every measure is lower for these countries. Countries with constitutionalized judicial councils have a mean De Facto Independence (Voigt) score of .51, while those with nonconstitutionalized councils have a score of .41, though the n is too low to determine a significant difference in means. Using Howard and Carey's measure of judicial independence, the means are .47 and .16, respectively, significant at the .01 level.
165. The analysis follows that of Tom Ginsburg and Mila Versteeg, "Why Do Countries Adopt Constitutional Review?" *Journal of Law, Economics and*

Organization (2014), doi:10.1093/jleo/ewt008. A probit "onset" model is functionally similar to a duration model but does not directly examine duration. Because figure 4.3 suggests that the probability of adopting a judicial council increases over time, we have to account for duration dependence in our model. We model duration dependence in an ordinary logit or probit framework. See, for example, Janet M. Box-Steffensmeier, Suzanna de Boef, and Kevin Sweeney, "Multilevel, Stratified, Frailty Models and the Onset of Civil War," 2005, http://www.researchgate.net/publication /228383646_Multilevel_Stratified_Frailty_Models_and_the_Onset_of_Civil _War.

166. Wealth is modeled using GDP data from the Penn World Tables of the Center for International Comparisons of Production, Income and Prices, University of Pennsylvania, https://pwt.sas.upenn.edu/php_site/pwt_index .php.

167. This is a metameasure of de facto judicial independence that combines eight extant measures of de facto judicial independence into a single measure. See Drew Linzer and Jeffrey Staton, "A Measurement Model for Synthesizing Multiple Comparative Indicators: The Case of Judicial Independence" (paper presented at the 2011 Annual Meeting of the American Political Science Association, Seattle, September 2012). There has been some methodological criticism of this measure, so we tested our model on other measures such as those of Howard and Carey, and Feld and Voigt, with substantially similar results.

168. Ramseyer, "Puzzling (In)dependence of Courts"; Ginsburg and Versteeg, "Why Do Countries Adopt Constitutional Review?"

169. In an unreported specification in which dummy variables for regions are included, common law has a significant negative correlation with judicial council adoption, but we believe this result is driven by the presence of regional controls indicating that countries in South Asia, all of which are common law jurisdictions, are particularly likely to adopt a judicial council. This washes out part of the effect of the common law.

170. Ramseyer and Rasmusen, *Measuring Judicial Independence*.

171. See Tom Ginsburg and Nuno Garoupa, "Guarding the Guardians: Judicial Councils and Judicial Independence," *American Journal of Comparative Law* 57, no. 1 (2009): 201–32.

172. Voigt and El-Bialy, "Identifying the Determinants of Judicial Performance."

173. Kosar, "Least Accountable Branch."

174. Autheman and Elena, "Global Best Practices."

175. Autheman and Elena, "Global Best Practices," 4, provide a very interesting report of survey data from five Central American countries. Respondents in those countries that had a judicial council reported that the council had a negative impact on judicial independence. Respondents in those countries that did *not* have a judicial council felt that adopting a judicial council would increase judicial independence. These two results are not

contradictory from our point of view. First, the two sets of countries have different starting places and are likely to vary systematically. Second, the countries that have adopted judicial councils may have done so to enhance accountability rather than independence, in which case respondents are observing a successful institution.

176. Cristina Parau, "East Side Story: How Transnational Networks Contested EU Accession Conditionality," *Europe-Asia Studies* 62, no. 9 (2010): 1527–54.

CHAPTER FIVE

1. See Stone Sweet, *Birth of Judicial Politics in France*; and Alec Stone Sweet, "The Politics of Constitutional Review in France and Europe," *International Journal of Constitutional Review* 5 (2007): 69–92. The introduction of concrete review after the 2008 constitutional reform has increased the similarities between the French Conseil Constitutionnel and the other Kelsenian courts in Europe. Concrete review is now possible according to Article 61-1 of the French Constitution, as the Cour de Cassation and the Conseil d'Etat can refer to the Conseil Constitutionnel in matters of law.

2. Ginsburg and Versteeg, "Why Do Countries Adopt Constitutional Review?"

3. For a general discussion, see Stone Sweet, *Governing with Judges*. See also Kelsen, "Judicial Review of Legislation." The notion of a "negative legislator" is based on the idea that the court expels legislation from the system and therefore shares legislative power with the parliament.

4. See Tom Ginsburg and Zachary Elkins, "Ancillary Powers of Constitutional Courts," *Texas Law Review* 87 (2009): 1431–61.

5. See John Ferejohn and Pasquale Pasquino, "Constitutional Adjudication: Lessons from Europe," *Texas Law Review* 82 (2004): 1671–704.

6. Ibid.

7. Ibid.

8. Ibid.

9. For a general discussion, see Friedman, "Politics of Judicial Review"; and Matthew D. McCubbins and Daniel B. Rodriguez, "The Judiciary and the Role of Law: A Positive Political Theory Perspective," in *The Oxford Handbook of Political Economy*, ed. B. Weingast and D. Wittman (Oxford: Oxford University Press, 2006), doi:10.1093/oxfordhb/9780199548477.001.0001.

10. Epstein, Landes, and Posner, *Behavior of Federal Judges*; see also George and Epstein, "On the Nature of Supreme Court Decision Making"; and Jeffrey R. Lax and Charles M. Cameron, "Bargaining and Opinion Assignment on the US Supreme Court," *Journal of Law, Economics and Organization* 23 (2007): 276–302.

11. See Alec Stone Sweet, "Complex Coordinate Construction in France and Germany," in Tate and Vallinder, *Global Expansion of Judicial Power*, who explains the judicialization of the legislative process by consequence of

referrals to the court; the constitutional courts are no longer a "negative legislator" only, as they have and exercise creative legislative powers to recast policies, shape legislative solutions, and promote more precise terminology.

12. See Ferejohn and Pasquino, "Constitutional Adjudication."

13. Gunther Teubner, "Legal Irritants: Good Faith in British Law, or How Unifying Law Ends Up in New Differences," *Modern Law Review* 61, no. 1 (1998): 11–32.

14. See Garlicki, "Constitutional Courts versus Supreme Courts."

15. See, among others, Wojciech Sadurski, *Rights before Courts: A Study of Constitutional Courts in Postcommunist States of Central and Eastern Europe* (New York: Springer, 2008), who explains how constitutional courts pursue the monopoly over constitutional adjudication and how they search for institutional legitimacy in between the judicial and the legislative branches.

16. See discussion by Nuno Garoupa, "The Politicization of the Kelsenian Constitutional Courts: Empirical Evidence," in *Empirical Judicial Studies*, ed. K. C. Huang (Taipei: Academia Sinica, 2009).

17. See discussion by Epstein, Landes, and Posner, "Why (and When) Judges Dissent"; and Paul H. Edelman, David Klein, and Stefanie A. Lindquist, "Consensus, Disorder, and the Supreme Court: A Challenge to Attitudinalism," *Journal of Empirical Legal Studies* 9, no. 1 (2012): 129–48. We recognize that there are other factors besides audience selection that will influence dissent rates. Docket control, for example, will allow a court to focus on the most difficult and important cases, which presumably will produce higher rates of dissent. Internal turnover on a court may matter as well. See also Scott Meinke and Kevin Scott, "Collegial Influence and Judicial Voting Change: The Effect of Membership Change on US Supreme Court Justices," *Law and Society Review* 41 (2007): 909–38.

18. Ibid.

19. For example, Andrew F. Daughety and Jennifer F. Reinganum, "Speaking Up: A Model of Judicial Dissent and Discretionary Review," *Supreme Court Economic Review* 14 (2006): 1–41, model the following situation: justices in the Supreme Court decide whether or not to grant certiorari based on the extent to which the decision at appeal is closer to their preferences and whether there are reasoned dissents that provide information to reverse the decision at appeal. Judges at appeal have an incentive to write dissenting opinions when they disagree with the majority in order to force certiorari and increase the chance of an overruling at the higher level. The majority at the appeal court has an incentive to search for a compromise to avoid reasoned dissent and therefore an overturn by the Supreme Court. Strictly speaking, our framework is different, since (1) there is no appeal from the constitutional court to the supreme court; (2) there is no certiorari, since the so-called principle of legality prevails in most jurisdictions that we consider; and (3) there is no court hierarchy. Charles M. Cameron and Lewis A.

Kornhauser, "Modeling Collegial Courts III: Adjudication Equilibria," New York University School of Law Public Law Research Paper No. 12–52, 2010, http://papers.ssrn.com/sol3/papers.cfm?abstract_id=2153785, show that the final outcome might not be the position of the median justice, because it depends on the entire distribution of ideal points. The model also suggests the importance of opinion assignment. See also Lewis A. Kornhauser, "Modeling Collegial Courts I: Path-Dependence," *International Review of Law and Economics* 12 (1992): 169–85 (explaining that path-dependence in collegial courts results from the fact that no single judge controls lawmaking); and Lewis A. Kornhauser, "Modeling Collegial Courts II: Legal Doctrine," *Journal of Law, Economics and Organization* 8 (2003): 441–70 (pointing out that, due to collective decision making, case-by-case and issue-by-issue approaches can result in different outcomes; the development of legal doctrines is determined crucially by how collegial courts operate).

20. See Pablo T. Spiller and Rafael Gely, "Strategic Judicial Decision Making," NBER Working Paper 13321, 2007, http://www.nber.org/papers/w13321 .pdf, who present an extensive survey of judicial behavior. The authors argue that for civil law jurisdictions, because of a strong and unified polity, courts are inherently more deferent because exercising independence will trigger political conflict and retaliation. Courts are more likely to go against the government when there is a divided polity. Another important article is Pablo T. Spiller and Richard G. Vanden Bergh, "Toward a Positive Theory of State Supreme Court Decision Making," *Business Politics* 5 (2003): 1–39, at 7. They focus on the interaction between the state supreme courts and the political branch. The lack of tenure is addressed by taking into account the need to be reelected in retention elections. Such possibility seems to constrain judicial behavior.

21. An example of how this does not perfectly track the common law–civil law distinction is South Africa. The South African Constitutional Court was created in 1993 and inserted into a standard common law court structure (with a High Court and a Supreme Court of Appeal). Zimbabwe is another example; it adopted a constitutional court in 2013.

22. Robert Dahl, "Decision-Making in a Democracy: The Supreme Court as a National Policymaker," *Journal of Public Law* 6 (1958): 279–95; C. Hermann Pritchett, *The Roosevelt Court: A Study in Judicial Politics and Values, 1937–1947* (New York: Macmillan, 1948).

23. See Stefanie A. Lindquist and Frank B. Cross, *Measuring Judicial Activism* (Stanford: Stanford University Press, 2009).

24. If the procedure does not allow formal dissent, there may be informal mechanisms, such as the media coverage we see in France or Italy.

25. In authoritarian regimes, unanimous decisions can be perceived as being subservient to the government (loyal constitutional courts). In order to achieve a reasonable reputation for judicial independence, the constitutional court might need to show fragmentation. If a minority signals that

there is dissent, the court as a whole might develop a reputation for some degree of independence from the executive. In fact, at least in the final stages of authoritarian regimes, fragmentation could become dominant as a way to signal a more democratic court (for example, Chile after 1981 and Argentina before the transition to democracy). Fragmentation is a costly signal, since it is usually unwelcomed by the authoritarian regimes and reprisals might take place. See Gretchen Helmke and Mitchell S. Sanders, "Modeling Motivations: A Method for Inferring Judicial Goals from Behavior," *Journal of Politics* 68 (2006): 867–78, who define a policy-seeker court, where the example is Argentina (although that is not a specialized constitutional court). See also Gretchen Helmke, *Courts under Constraints: Judges, Generals, and Presidents in Argentina* (Cambridge, UK: Cambridge University Press, 2005), on Argentina; and Lisa Hilbink, "Agents of Anti-Politics: Courts in Pinochet's Chile," in *Rule by Law: The Politics of Courts in Authoritarian Regimes*, ed. Tom Ginsburg and Tamir Moustafa (Cambridge, UK: Cambridge University Press, 2008), on Chile.

26. See Ferejohn and Pasquino, "Constitutional Adjudication," who note that the disallowance or absence of dissents in many European constitutional courts reflects "the archaic civil law notion that the law is fixed, clear and discoverable and that all judges do is discover and apply it."

27. See discussion by Dieter Grimm, "The German Constitutional Court," in *How Constitutional Courts Make Decisions*, ed. Pasquale Pasquino and Barbara Randazzo (Milan: Giuffrè, 2009).

28. See discussion by Victor Ferreres Comella, "The Consequences of Central-izing Constitutional Review in a Special Court: Some Thoughts on Judicial Activism," *Texas Law Review* 82 (2004): 1703–36.

29. For example, in a recent case debated by the Italian Constitutional Court on the immunity of Prime Minister Berlusconi and other higher authorities of Italy, the Italian media widely reported that the "unanimous" decision of the court against the prime minister had six dissents (constitutional judges who supported the prime minister's legal argumentation). The re-cent publication by the French Constitutional Court of the internal debates over landmark cases from 1958 to 1983 also shows the extent of dissent in that court.

30. See Sadurski, *Rights before Courts*, who observes that legitimacy is politi-cally more complicated when the court is engaged in abstract rather than concrete review, even if the court has undisputed formal legitimacy.

31. Stone Sweet, *Governing with Judges*.

32. In Chile, for example, the Constitutional Court exercises abstract review, while the Supreme Court performs concrete review.

33. See Garlicki, "Constitutional Courts versus Supreme Courts."

34. Ibid.

35. See Stone Sweet, "Politics of Constitutional Review."

36. At the limit, developing a court-made constitution that supplements or even replaces the original text. See, for example, Garlicki, "Constitutional Courts versus Supreme Courts."

37. See the Spanish case, for example, Leslie Turano, "Spain: Quis Custodiet Ipsos Custodes? The Struggle for jurisdiction between the Tribunal Constitucional and the Tribunal Supremo," *International Journal of Constitutional Law* 4 (2006): 151–62.

38. See Stone Sweet, "Politics of Constitutional Review."

39. Ibid.

40. Ibid.

41. See, for example, Ran Hirschl, "The Judicialization of Mega-Politics and the Rise of Political Courts," *Annual Review of Political Science* 11 (2008): 93–118, who explains the political consequences of systematic unwelcomed judgments concerning contentious political issues and how that creates unstable courts.

42. See Mitchel de S.-O.-L.'E. Lasser, "Judicial Transformations: The Rights Revolution in the Courts of Europe," *European Constitutional Law Review* 6, no. 1 (2010): 163–70, doi:10.1017/S1574019610100108.

43. Ibid., discussing the external European influence on imposing "judicial review" and "fundamental rights and principles": the European Court of Human Rights (the jurisprudence on fair trial), the European Court of Justice, and the construction of EU law, including domestic interpretation of European law.

44. Ibid.

45. For example, Brazil has a constitutional court (*Supremo Tribunal Federal*) and an infraconstitutional court (*Supremo Tribunal de Justiça*). The hierarchical relationship between these two courts is established by the 1988 Brazilian Constitution.

46. On the European Union, see Joseph Weiler, "The Transformation of Europe," *Yale Law Journal* 100 (1991): 2403–83.

47. See Saul Brenner and Timothy M. Hagle, "Opinion Writing and Acclimation Effects," *Political Behavior* 18 (1996): 235–61.

48. "Worldwide Governance Indicators," World Bank, http://info.worldbank .org/governance/wgi/index.aspx#home.

49. One senate deals with basic rights, whereas the other senate looks at abstract review and major constitutional disputes. The full court exists but plays a secondary role. See Alfred Rinken, "The Federal Constitutional Court and the German Political System," in *Constitutional Courts in Comparison: The U.S. Supreme Court and the German Federal Constitutional Court*, ed. Ralf Rogowski and Thomas Gawron (New York: Berghahn, 2002).

50. See Georg Vanberg, *The Politics of Constitutional Review in Germany* (Cambridge, UK: Cambridge University Press, 2009).

51. See Rainier Nickel, "The German Federal Constitutional Court: Present State, Future Challenges," in Le Sueur, *Building the UK's New Supreme Court* (arguing those package deals lack transparency); and Grimm, "German Constitutional Court" (arguing that such package deals eliminate the possibility of electing extremists to the court and therefore reduce polarization).

52. See Donald P. Kommers, *Judicial Politics in West Germany: A Study of the Federal Constitutional Court* (Beverly Hills: Sage, 1976); and Vanberg, *Politics of Constitutional Review in Germany*.

53. See Grimm, "German Constitutional Court." In the early 1950s, the opposition Social Democrats favored the use of dissenting opinions, while the governing Christian Democrats were opposed. Consistent with our prediction, the movement for dissenting opinions emerged in the late 1960s once the German Constitutional Court was well established, strong enough to face the political audience, and sufficiently credible in the eyes of the other courts (and the general public).

54. Ibid.

55. See Garlicki, "Constitutional Courts versus Supreme Courts."

56. Ibid.

57. Ibid.

58. Ibid.

59. Another example, in the context of the German-speaking world, is Austria. The fourteen Austrian constitutional judges are chosen by the federal government (president, vice president, and six members) and both chambers of parliament (three members each), although all appointments are technically made by the president of Austria. The appointment mechanism has resulted in a de facto quota system allocation of seats. Judges are appointed for life (subject to a mandatory retirement age). Although a matter of discussion since Germany changed its policy in 1971, separate opinions are not allowed. The Austrian Constitutional Court has engaged in controversial decisions, but there are few instances of skirmishes with ordinary courts. See Alexander Somek, "Constitutional Theory as a Problem of Constitutional Law: On the Constitutional Court's Total Revision of Austrian Constitutional Law," *Israel Law Review* 32 (1998): 567–90.

60. See Stone Sweet, *Birth of Judicial Politics in France.* See also French Const. of 1958, arts. 37, 41.

61. French Const. of 1958, arts. 37, 41.

62. This was done as a natural reaction against the judges under the monarchy and the role of civil law in subordinating the courts to the legislature. However, France has a long tradition of legal control of executive action by the Conseil d'État, which by necessity has had to immerse itself in politics. See, among others, Neuborne, "Judicial Review and Separation of Powers"; Cynthia Vroom, "The Constitutional Protection of Individual Liberties in France: The Conseil Constitutionnel since 1971," *Tulane Law Review* 63 (1988): 265–333; and Martin M. Shapiro, "Judicial Review in

France," *Journal of Law & Politics* 6 (1989): 531–48. For example, in 1980, the Constitutional Court affirmed that the independence of the judiciary is a fundamental principle protected by the preamble of the 1958 Constitution.

63. See Davis, "Law/Politics Distinction"; Michael H. Davis, "A Government of Judges: An Historical Re-View," *American Journal of Comparative Law* 35 (1987): 559–80; and Denis Tallon, "The Constitution and the Courts in France," *American Journal of Comparative Law* 27, no. 4 (1979): 567–75.

64. French Const. of 1958, art. 56.

65. See John Bell, *French Constitutional Law* (New York: Oxford University Press, 1992), who argues that the goals of selection aim at achieving competence, legitimacy, and participation. In his view, this naturally results in procedural elitism in selection, where legal competences and judicial self-participation are purely instrumental.

66. See Raphael Franck, "Judicial Independence under a Divided Polity: A Study of the Rulings of the French Constitutional Court, 1959–2006," *Journal of Law, Economics and Organization* 25 (2009): 262–84.

67. See related discussion by Jean Louis Goutal, "Characteristics of Judicial Style in France, Britain and the USA," *American Journal of Comparative Law* 24, no. 1 (1976): 43–72. Notice that procedure is very different between the Conseil Constitutionnel and the ordinary courts in France, since in the latter, the statement must be offered in the context of a particular case. Ordinary courts hear cases; the council does not. It solves cases by legislative empowerment of different affected interests rather than intervening in particular situations.

68. The French *cohabitation* has been described as "majority divided government" in the American literature. See Cindy Skach, *Borrowing Constitutional Designs: Constitutional Law in Weimar Germany and the French Fifth Republic* (Princeton: Princeton University Press, 2005).

69. Concrete review has been introduced recently (July 2008). Under the terms of the new Article 61-1, the Cour de Cassation and the Conseil d'Etat can refer to the Conseil Constitutionnel in matters of law.

70. See Stone Sweet, *Birth of Judicial Politics in France*.

71. Ibid., discussing how decisions by the Conseil Constitutionnel are short and declarative, like the ones by the Cour de Cassation, as a way to make them look similar and more influential. The Conseil d'Etat was initially hostile but now accepts that case law dictated by the Conseil Constitutionnel is a source of law. See also Garlicki, "Constitutional Courts versus Supreme Courts."

72. See Sophie Boyron, *The Constitution of France: A Contextual Analysis* (Portland: Hart, 2013), 172–73.

73. Ibid.

74. See J. H. Merryman and V. Vigoriti, "When Courts Collide: Constitution and Cassation in Italy," *American Journal of Comparative Law* 15 (1967):

665–86; and Mary L. Volcansek, *Constitutional Politics in Italy* (New York: St. Martin's, 2000).

75. See Garlicki, "Constitutional Courts versus Supreme Courts."

76. Ibid. The Conseil Constitutionnel refused to apply a 1958 doctrine of the Cour de Cassation on summary investigations, and the latter decided that the new doctrine could only be applied prospectively and not retrospectively.

77. Ibid.

78. See discussion by Víctor Ferreres Comella, "The Rise of Specialized Constitutional Courts," in Tom Ginsburg and Rosalind Dixon, eds., *Comparative Constitutional Law* (Northampton: Edward Elgar, 2011), 274.

79. John Ferejohn and Pasquale Pasquino, "Constitutional Adjudication, Italian Style," in *Comparative Constitutional Design*, ed. Tom Ginsburg (Cambridge, UK: Cambridge University Press, 2013), 298–320.

80. See Turano, "Spain."

81. The *Estatut de Catalunya* was approved by the Spanish Parliament in 2005, and after a referendum in the region in 2006, it had to wait until July 2010 for the Spanish Constitutional Court's decision (after a petition from the conservative party that opposed this law).

82. For example, consider a recent case (STC 29/2008, of February 20, 2008) absolving two prominent Spanish financiers of a white-collar crime against the interpretation of the Spanish Supreme Court on the statute of limitation for criminal offenses.

83. See Sofia Amaral Garcia, Nuno Garoupa, and Veronica Grembi, "Judicial Independence and Party Politics in the Kelsenian Constitutional Courts: The Case of Portugal," *Journal of Empirical Legal Studies* 6 (2009): 381–404.

84. Ibid.

85. For example, in an important case (STC 810/93, of December 7, 1993), the Portuguese Constitutional Court decided that the judicial doctrines produced by the Supreme Court, even those "with general obligatory force" as stated by the civil code, are not a source of law. Therefore, such judicial doctrines are not binding; they do not establish (horizontal or vertical) precedent. However, in a concession to the Supreme Court, the Portuguese Constitutional Court recommended that the lower courts consider judicial doctrines for sake of legal stability and certainty. See Victor Ferreres Comella, *Constitutional Courts and Democratic Values: A European Perspective* (New Haven: Yale University Press, 2009), 173.

86. See Nuno Garoupa, Veronica Grembi, and Shirley Lin, "Explaining Constitutional Review in New Democracies: The Case of Taiwan," *Pacific Rim Law and Policy Review* 20, no. 1 (2011): 1–40.

87. In particular, Lee Teng-hui (1988–2000, KMT); Chen Shui-bian (2000–2008, DPP); and Ma Ying-jeou (since 2008, KMT).

88. Interpretation No. 242 (1989).

89. See Ginsburg, *Judicial Review in New Democracies*.
90. For example, Decision 627 on former president Chen Shui-bian's immunity from prosecution. See Justices of the Constitutional Court, Judicial Yuan, R.O.C., Interpretation No. 627, http://www.judicial.gov.tw/constitutional court/en/p03_01.asp?expno=627.
91. Republic of Korea Const., art. 111(1).
92. Constitutional Court Act, art. 47(1).
93. Rules implementing the Certified Judicial Scriveners Act Case, 2 KCCR 365, 89Hun-Ma178, October 15, 1990. Article 107(2) reads, "The Supreme Court shall have the power to make a final review of the constitutionality or legality of administrative decrees, regulations or dispositions, when their constitutionality or legality is a prerequisite to a trial."
94. See James M. West and Dae-Kyu Yoon, "The Constitutional Court of the Republic of Korea: Transforming the Jurisprudence at the Vortex," *American Journal of Comparative Law* 40 (1992): 73–119.
95. See discussion in Ginsburg, *Judicial Review in New Democracies*, 232.
96. This high-profile conflict led the *Korea Herald* to call for legislative resolution of the problem: "This complicated and subtle conflict between the two supreme juridical bodies calls for an intervention of the President and the National Assembly which can exercise their legislative prerogatives toward illuminating the balance of power and division of labour between the two highest courts." Editorial, *Korea Herald*, December 30, 1997.
97. Decree No. 1382 of 2000. This provision brought two changes. First, higher courts that rendered decisions that were to be reviewed under the protection of constitutional rights doctrine had to be noticed. Second, the Supreme Court had to review actions filed against its own decisions and then submitted to the Constitutional Court for revision. Nonetheless, the mandatory notice did not solve the existing nuisances, nor did Supreme Court judges accede to examine petitions to review their own decisions. Conflict persisted; several sanctions were imposed by the Supreme Council of the Judiciary on judges under prevarication grounds as a result of their refusal to comply with decisions rendered by the Constitutional Court.

CHAPTER SIX

1. See Note, "Cross Jurisdictional Forum Non Conveniens Preclusion," *Harvard Law Review* 121 (2008): 2178–99. For an important analysis of the governance implications of these kinds of decisions, see Christopher A. Whytock, "Domestic Courts and Global Governance," *Tulane Law Review* 84 (2009): 67–123.
2. Gilles Cuniberti, "Enhancing Judicial Reputation through Legal Transplants: Estoppel Travels to France," *American Journal of Comparative Law* 60 (2011): 383–400.

3. Slaughter, *New World Order*; see also Ran Hirschl, *Comparative Matters: The Renaissance of Comparative Constitutional Law* (New York: Oxford University Press, 2014).
4. See David S. Law and Wen-Chen Chang, "The Limits of Global Judicial Dialogue," *Washington Law Review* 86 (2011): 523–77, who document the grand justices on Taiwan and their extensive behind-the-scenes usage of foreign law.
5. See David S. Law, "Judicial Comparativism and Judicial Diplomacy," *University of Pennsylvania Law Review* 163 (2015), who describes the South Korean Constitutional Court.
6. Mak, *Judicial Decision-Making*, 206.
7. Roper v. Simmons, 543 U.S. 551 (2005).
8. Slaughter, *New World Order*, 65–82.
9. See *Knight v. Florida* (98-9741); Mak, *Judicial Decision-Making*, 210.
10. Hirschl, *Comparative Matters*. See also Basil Markesinis and Jörg Fedtke, *Judicial Recourse to Foreign Law: A New Source of Inspiration?* (London: Routledge-Cavendish, 2006).
11. Johanna Kalb, "The Judicial Role in New Democracies: A Strategic Account of Comparative Citation," *Yale Journal of International Law* 38 (2013): 423–65.
12. Martin Gelter and Mathias M. Siems, "Language, Legal Origins, and Culture before the Courts: Cross-Citations between Supreme Courts in Europe," *Supreme Court Economic Review* 21 (2013): 215–69.
13. Thompson v. Oklahoma, 487 U.S. 815, at 868–69, n. 4 (Scalia, J., dissenting).
14. Patrick Jonsson, "Court Dismisses Fears of 'Creeping Sharia Law' That Led to Oklahoma Ban," *Christian Science Monitor*, January 11, 2012, http://www.csmonitor.com/USA/2012/0111/Court-dismisses-fears-of-creeping-Sharia-law-that-led-to-Oklahoma-ban-video.
15. Eyal Benvenisti and George W. Downs, "National Courts, Domestic Democracy, and the Evolution of International Law," *European Journal of International Law* 20, no. 1 (2009): 59–72.
16. Mak, *Judicial Decision-Making*, 86.
17. "World Conference on Constitutional Justice," accessed May 13, 2014, http://www.venice.coe.int/wccj/wccj_e.asp.
18. Mak, *Judicial Decision-Making*, 85.
19. The "superjudge" concept comes from Kosar, "Least Accountable Branch."
20. For two different views on the legality of Garzon's actions, see Alicia Gil, "Spain as an Example of Total Oblivion with Partial Rehabilitation," and Javier Chinchón Álvarez, "The Challenges Posed to the Recent Investigation of Crimes Committed during the Spanish Civil War and Francoism," in *The Role of Courts in Transitional Justice: Voices from Latin America and Spain*, ed. Jessica Almqvist and Carlos Espósito (New York: Routledge, 2012).
21. Law, "Judicial Comparativism and Judicial Diplomacy," 36 (describing the South Korean Constitutional Court).

22. Ibid., 38.
23. "The Constitutional Court of Korea to Host the AACC's Inaugural Congress," Association of Asian Constitutional Courts and Equivalent Institutions, accessed March 10, 2015, http://www.aaccei.org/ccourt?act=noticeView &bbsId=3100&bbsSeqn=245.
24. Thomas Carothers, "The Rule of Law Revival," *Foreign Affairs* 77, no. 2 (1998): 95–106.
25. World Economic Forum, *Global Agenda Council on the Rule of Law*, accessed June 28, 2014, http://www3.weforum.org/docs/GAC12/IssueBrief /IB_RuleLaw.pdf.
26. Gianmaria Ajani, "By Chance and Prestige: Legal Transplants in Russia and Eastern Europe," *The American Journal of Comparative Law* 43, no. 1 (1995): 93–117.
27. Kathy Bergen, "Chicago Gains in Global Cities Ranking," *Chicago Breaking Business*, August 17, 2010, http://archive.chicagobreakingbusiness.com /2010/08/chicago-gains-in-global-cities-ranking.html.
28. "National Universities Rankings," *US News and World Report*, accessed June 9, 2011, http://colleges.usnews.rankingsandreviews.com/best-colleges /national-universities-rankings; "Academic Ranking of World Universities," accessed June 9, 2011, http://www.arwu.org.
29. "Newsweek's Green Rankings, 2014," *Newsweek*, http://www.newsweek .com/2014/06/13/newsweeks-green-rankings-2014-253482.html.
30. On ranking in general, see, generally, Kevin E. Davis, Benedict Kingsbury, and Sally Engle Merry, "Indicators as a Technology of Global Governance," *Law & Society Review* 46 (2012): 71–104.
31. Some of these are surveyed in Stephen Haggard, Andrew MacIntyre, and Lydia Tiede, "The Rule of Law and Economic Development," *Annual Review of Political Science* 29 (2008): 205–34, at 223. On the number, see Adeel Malik, "State of the Art in Governance Indicators," Human Development Report Office Occasional Paper, 2002, 19.
32. For example, Christopher Larkins provides the following objections: reliance on formal indicators rather than reality; the appropriate information is unclear for comparative purposes; problematic interpretation of significance of judicial outcomes; and the arbitrary nature of many findings due to subjectivity in numerical scoring. Christopher M. Larkins, "Judicial Independence and Democratization: A Theoretical and Conceptual Analysis," *American Journal of Comparative Law* 44, no. 4 (1996): 605–26. The rule of law indicator of the World Bank's Governance Indicators, which is seen as state of the art in many ways, lacks internal validity, as it purports to measure different concepts from year to year. See Marcus Kurtz and Andrew Schrank, "Growth and Governance: Models, Measures, and Mechanisms," *Journal of Politics* 69, no. 2 (2007): 538–54.
33. Tom Ginsburg, "Pitfalls of Measuring the Rule of Law," *Hague Journal of the Rule of Law* 3, no. 2 (2011): 269–80.

34. Veronica Taylor, "The Law Reform Olympics: Measuring the Effects of Law Reform in Transition Economies," in *Law Reform in Developing States*, ed. Tim Lindsey (New York: Routledge, 2006).

35. This section draws on Ginsburg, "Pitfalls of Measuring the Rule of Law."

36. Kevin Davis and Michael Cruse, "Taking the Measure of Law: The Case of the *Doing Business* Project," *Law and Social Inquiry* 32 (Fall 2007): 1095–119; Benito Arruñada, "Pitfalls to Avoid when Measuring Institutions: Is 'Doing Business' Damaging Business?" *The Economic Journal* 48, no. 3 (2010): 443–61.

37. See, generally, Cesare Romano, Karen Alter, and Yuval Shany, eds., *The Oxford Handbook of International Adjudication* (New York: Oxford University Press, 2014).

38. This problem is analyzed in Shai Dothan, *Reputation and Judicial Tactics: A Theory of National and International Courts* (Cambridge, UK: Cambridge University Press, 2014).

39. This figure is calculated by starting with the analysis of Leigh Swigart and Daniel Terrs, who analyzed a profile of "304 judges were serving on 21 of the most significant international judicial bodies." See "Who Are International Judges?" in Romano, Alter, and Shany, *Oxford Handbook of International Adjudication*, 612. Their analysis excluded nine international courts from Annex I of that volume, for which we identified 110 other judges. We subtracted, however, judges from the now-disbanded Southern African Development Community Tribunal.

40. Cuniberti reports that this possibility has changed some of the internal dynamics in the French judiciary, as two prominent judges were appointed by France to the ICSID list. Cuniberti, "Enhancing Judicial Reputation through Legal Transplants," 399.

41. Swigart and Kerrs, "Who Are International Judges?" 621.

42. Ruth Mackenzie, Cesare Romano, Philippe Sands, and Yuval Shany, *The Manual on International Courts and Tribunals*, 2nd ed. (New York: Oxford University Press, 2010).

43. Examples of current judges on the ICC who had worked at the International Criminal Tribunal for the former Yugoslavia or the International Criminal Tribunal for Rwanda include Fatoumata Dembélé Diarra of Mali, Chile Eboe-Osuji of Nigeria, Christine van den Wyngaert of Belgium, Howard Morrison of the United Kingdom, and Robert Fremr of the Czech Republic.

44. The last decade has seen the emergence of supranational adjudication in Africa, and one of the courts that allowed individual opinions has already gone defunct. The Southern African Development Community (SADC) Tribunal was set up in 2005 to adjudicate disputes related to trade. The tribunal included provision for individual opinions. In 2009, it issued a ruling in favor of evicted white farmers in Zimbabwe, leading to a counterattack on the court. It was suspended and ultimately disbanded in 2012. This is

perhaps a case of a court pursuing the legal audience of judges and lawyers but not paying sufficient attention to political constraints. See, generally, Karen Alter, *The New Terrain of International Law* (Princeton: Princeton University Press, 2014).

45. See Michel Rosenfeld, "Comparing Constitutional Review by the European Court of Justice and the U.S. Supreme Court," *International Journal of Constitutional Law* 4, no. 4 (2004): 618–51, who contrasts the style and rhetoric of the ECJ and the US Supreme Court. Another good case for consideration is the European Court of Human Rights.

46. Christoph Krenn and Armin Bogdandy, "On the Democratic Legitimacy of Europe's Judges: A Principled and Comparative Reconstruction of the Selection Procedures," in *Selecting Europe's Judges. A Critical Review of the Appointment Procedures to the European Courts*, ed. Michal Bobek (Oxford: Oxford University Press, 2015), 162–180.

47. Robin C. A. White, "Separate Opinions in the European Court of Human Rights," *Human Rights Law Review* 9 no. 1 (2009): 37–60.

48. Alec Stone Sweet, *The Judicial Construction of Europe* (New York: Oxford University Press, 2004).

49. See, generally, Karen J. Alter, *The European Court's Political Power* (New York: Oxford University Press, 2009).

50. See the discussion by Lasser, *Judicial Deliberations*; and Mitchell Lasser, *Judicial Transformations: The Rights Revolution in the Courts of Europe* (New York: Oxford University Press, 2009).

51. Alec Stone Sweet and Thomas Brunell, "Trustee Courts and the Judicialization of International Regimes: The Politics of Majoritarian Activism in the European Convention on Human Rights, the European Union, and the World Trade Organization," *Journal of Law and Courts* 1, no. 1 (2013): 61–88; see also Karen Alter, "Agent or Trustee: International Courts in Their Political Context," *European Journal of International Relations* 14 (2008): 33–63.

52. Stone Sweet and Brunell, "Trustee Courts and the Judicialization of International Regimes."

53. See, for example, Laurence R. Helfer and Anne-Marie Slaughter, "Toward a Theory of Effective Supranational Adjudication," *Yale Journal of Law* 107, no. 2 (1997): 273–391, at 273, who build a general theory of supranational adjudication from the European experience. Note a major exception is Alter, *New Terrain of International Law*.

54. Alexandra Huneeus, "Courts Resisting Courts: Lessons from the Inter-American Court's Struggle to Enforce Human Rights," *Cornell International Law Journal* 44, no. 3 (2013): 101–55.

55. Yves Dezalay and Bryant Garth, *Dealing in Virtue* (Chicago: University of Chicago Press, 1998).

56. New York Convention on the Enforcement of Arbitral Awards, 330 UNTS 38; 21 UST 2517; 7 ILM 1046 (1958).

57. Larry Ribstein and Erin O'Hare, *The Law Market* (New York: Oxford University Press, 2009).

58. Terence Halliday, Josh Pacewicz, and Susan Block-Lieb, "Who Governs? Delegations and Delegates in Global Trade Lawmaking," *Regulation and Governance* 7, no. 3 (2013): 279–98.

59. Jens Dammann and Henry Hansmann, "Globalizing Commercial Arbitration," *Cornell Law Review* 94, no. 1 (2008): 1–71.

60. Ibironke T. Odumosu, "The Antinomies of the (Continued) Relevance of ICSID to the Third World," *San Diego International Law Journal* 8 (May 2007): 345–86.

61. Susan Franck, "Development and Outcomes of Investment Treaty Arbitration," *Harvard International Law Journal* 50, no. 2 (2009): 435–89; Gus van Harten, "The Use of Quantitative Methods to Examine Possible Bias in Investment Arbitration" and "Reply" [to Franck, Garbin, and Perkins] in *Yearbook on International Investment Law & Policy*, ed. Karl P. Sauvant (Oxford: Oxford University Press, 2011); Olivia Chung, "The Lopsided International Investment Law Regime and Its Effect on the Future of Investor-State Arbitration," *Virginia Journal of International Law* 47 (2007): 953–73.

62. White Industries Australia v. India, Final Award, 2011, http://www.italaw .com/sites/default/files/case-documents/ita0906.pdf.

CHAPTER SEVEN

1. Cristina Parau and Richard Bellamy, "Introduction: Democracy, Courts and the Dilemmas of Representation," *Representation—The Journal of Representative Democracy* 49, no. 3 (2013): 255–66; Cristina Parau, "The Dormancy of Parliaments: The Invisible Cause of Judiciary Empowerment in Central and Eastern Europe," *Representation—The Journal of Representative Democracy* 49, no. 3 (2013): 267–80.

2. See Maria Ferrarese, "Penal Judiciary and Politics in Italy," *Global Jurist Topics* 1, no. 1 (2001), http://www.degruyter.com/view/j/gj.2001.1.2 /gj.2001.1.2.1030/gj.2001.1.2.1030.xml; Adam Reynolds, "Dimensions of Justice in Italy: A Practical Review," *Global Jurist Advances* 3, no. 1 (2003), http://www.degruyter.com/view/j/gj.2003.3.2/gj.2003.3.2.1083 /gj.2003.3.2.1083.xml.

3. The crowding-out effect is well known in the economic literature. See, among others, B. Frey and S. Neckermann, "Awards: A View from Psychological Economics," University of Zurich Institute for Empirical Research in Economics Working Paper No. 357, 2008; and R. McAdams and E. Rasmusen, "Norms in Law and Economics," in *2007 Handbook of Law and Economics*, ed. A. M. Polinsky and S. Shavell (Amsterdam: North Holland, 2007).

4. Daniel Klerman, "Jurisdictional Competition and the Evolution of the Common Law," *University of Chicago Law Review* 74, no. 4 (2007):

1179–226, at 1188; G. E. Aylmer, *The King's Servants: The Civil Service of Charles I, 1625–1642*, rev ed. (New York: Columbia University Press, 1974); G. E. Aylmer, *The State's Servants: The Civil Service of the English Republic, 1649–1660* (New York: Routledge and Kegan Paul, 1974).

5. Klerman, "Jurisdictional Competition and the Evolution of the Common Law."

6. Ibid., 1217.

7. James E. Pfander, "Judicial Compensation and the Definition of Judicial Power in the Early Republic," *Michigan Law Review* 107 no. 1 (2008): 1–52.

8. Ibid., 3. Pfander notes that other states allowed payment of fees into the nineteenth century.

9. Ibid., 12–15.

10. Ibid., 22.

11. Details can be found in Contini and Mohr, "Reconciling Independence and Accountability," 26. For a background on the Spanish judiciary and the transition from the Franco regime to democracy (in particular, noting that the judiciary has been more heterogeneous than expected and less of an instrument of a rigid governance), see Larkins, "Judicial Independence and Democratization."

12. We have seen some recent developments in measures of judicial performance, sometimes involving rankings of courts and judges.

13. Jens Dammann and Henry Hansmann, "Globalizing Commercial Litigation," *Cornell Law Review* 94 no. 1 (2008), http://scholarship.law .cornell.edu/cgi/viewcontent.cgi?article=3117&context=clr.

14. Tom Ginsburg, "International Substitutes for Domestic Institutions," *International Review of Law and Economics* 25, no. 1 (2005): 107–23.

15. Albert Hirschmann, *Exit Voice and Loyalty: Responses to Decline in Firms, Organizations, and States* (Cambridge, MA: Harvard University Press, 1970).

16. Jan van Zyl Smit, "Reforming the Kenyan Judiciary, 2003–2010: A Comparative Perspective," manuscript.

17. Paul Martin and Patrick Schmidt, "The New Public Face of Courts: State Judicial Systems and the Internet as a Political Resource," *Justice System Journal* 24 (2003): 118–36.

18. Graham Gee, Robert Hazell, Kate Malleson, and Patrick O'Brien, *The Politics of Judicial Independence in the UK's Changing Constitution* (Cambridge: Cambridge University Press, 2015). See also the lord chief justice's annual press conference on November 5, 2013, http://www.judiciary.gov.uk/media /media-releases/2013/lcj-press-conference-2013.

19. "Joseph Hall Quotes," BrainyQuote.com, accessed March 2, 2015, http:// www.brainyquote.com/quotes/quotes/j/josephhall126495.html.

Index

abortion, 30–31, 35, 90
accountability, 27–28; agency
  model and, 3, 105–10 (*see also*
  agency model); audiences and,
  49 (*see also* audiences); in Brazil,
  115–16; career model and, 66
  (*see also* career model); collective, 213n37 (*see also* collective
  reputation); in France, 120,
  213n37; hybrid systems and,
  66 (*see also* hybrid models);
  independence and, 98, 102–5,
  104f, 110–14, 126–27, 129, 131,
  138–40, 234n13, 248n175 (*see
  also* independence, judicial);
  individual, 18, 47, 192 (*see also*
  individual reputation); information and (*see* information); institutions and, 27–28, 234n14 (*see
  also* institutional structures); in
  Israel, 117–18; in Italy, 122; judicial councils and (*see* judicial
  councils); judicialization and,
  27–28, 49, 103, 104f, 134; levels
  of, 234n13; monitoring (*see*
  monitoring); in Netherlands,
  122–23; politicization and,
  27–28; recognition and, 66 (*see
  also* recognition model); reputation and, 18, 28, 31 (*see also*
  reputation); selection and, 98,
  237n43; transparency and, 192;
  in UK, 124–27 (*see also* United
  Kingdom); US and, 98 (*see also*
  United States). *See also specific
  countries and topics*

administrative law: adverse selection and, 64; career judiciary
  and, 51; civil law and, 222n38;
  constitutional law and, 51, 73,
  222n38; in France, 67; hybrid
  systems and, 73; judges in, 57–
  58; military judiciary, 58–59,
  64; monitoring and, 57, 64;
  recognition judiciaries and, 73;
  in US, 57–58. *See also specific
  topics*
adverse selection: administrative
  law and, 64; career judiciary
  and, 63, 64, 212n22; common
  law and, 212n22; corruption
  and, 63; defined, 60–61; ex ante
  screening, 63; higher courts
  and, 64; independence and,
  212n22; judicial councils and,
  110; moral hazard and, 62–65,
  66; nonjudicial functions and,
  82; recognition model and, 61,
  63, 64, 65, 74
Affordable Care Act, 1
Africa, 135t, 182t, 193, 195–96,
  260n39, 260n44. *See also specific
  countries*
agency model, 2, 3; audiences (*see*
  audiences); costs in, 4, 18, 60–
  67, 73, 74, 106, 138, 190; human capital in, 4, 9, 60; hybrid
  systems and, 52 (*see also* hybrid
  models); information and, xi,
  3, 19 (*see also* information); institutions and, 59–60, 65 (*see
  also* institutional structures);

Hirschl, Ran, 171
Hirschmann, Albert, 195
Holmes, Oliver Wendell, 14
human capital, 18–27, 80, 212; agency model and, 9, 60; collective reputation and, 24–25; costs of, 74; defined, 4; individual reputation and, 21, 24–25; nonjudicial functions, 83
Human Rights Act of 1998, 245n141
Huneeus, Alexandra, 183
hybrid models: accountability and, 66; administrative law and, 73; agency problems, 52, 67, 73, 74; ALJs and, 57; audiences and, 65–66; codification and, 66; common/civil law and, 11, 99; comparative literature, 52; constitutional law and, 73; disadvantages of, 66; incentives, 65–66; institutional structure and, 52, 65; legal reform and, 74; monitoring, 73; as norm, 52; optimality of, 53; pockets and, 52, 59–65, 73; procedural rules and, 66–67; purist models, 65; US and, 57

ICJ and. *See* International Court of Justice
IMF. *See* International Monetary Fund
incentives, 121, 188; accountability and, 27; agent model, 23, 26; appeals and, 37; career model and, 82, 99, 111; collective reputation and, 97; dissent and, 145; ex ante screening and, 25–27, 29; external audience and, 46; hybrid systems, 65; institutional structures and, 15, 49, 74, 188; judicial councils and, 106–11, 132; judicial systems and, 7, 8, 9, 21, 106, 107–8; moral hazard and, 82; seriatim opinions and, 27; size of judiciary and, 40–41; tenure and, 153. *See also specific countries and topics*
independence, judicial, 102, 193; accountability and, 102–5, 110, 127; adverse selection, 212n22; authoritarian regimes and, 251n25; civil law and, 251n20; collective reputation and, 21, 103; concepts of, 234n13; defined, 98; judicial councils and, 131, 136, 249n175; judicialization and, 103; literature on, 231n1; measures of, 247n164, 248n167; tenure and, 251n20; US and, 235n15
India, 71, 91; career model and, 63; investment arbitration, 185; nonjudicial

functions and, 92; Supreme Court of, 99, 233n8
individual reputation, 10, 16, 212n24; appeals and, 29, 37, 212n24; benefits of, 19; branding and, 39–40; career model and, 66 (*see also* career model); citations and, 38; civil law and, 44; collective reputation and, 29, 188, 191 (*see also* collective reputation); constitutional courts and, 145–47 (*see also* constitutional courts); dissent and, 33; dockets and, 38–39; ex post sharing and, 25, 26; external audiences and, 23, 66, 188; extrajurisdictional sitting, 193; fragmentation and, 147, 148; global audiences, 168; human capital and, 24–25; ICJ and, 180; individual opinions and, 31; information and, 17, 19, 26, 31; inquiries, 40; institutional environment and, 22; internal audiences and, 23; judicialization and, 27; liberal/conservative, 31; nonjudicial functions and, 80, 81; nonseparable product and, 17, 190; oral proceedings, 31; originalist/activist, 31; policy and, 44; precedent and, 32; private sector opportunities, 40; recognition model and, 29, 50 (*see also* recognition model); salaries and, 43; sentencing and, 36–37; size of judiciary and, 41; transparency and, 192; US and, 45 (*see also* United States). *See also specific countries and topics*
Indonesia, 12, 185
information: agency model and, xi, 3, 19 (*see also* agency model); asymmetry and, 3, 15, 19; audiences and, 188 (*see also* audiences); civil law and, 17; collective reputation and, 19, 26–27, 30; corruption and, 178; forum shopping, 192; individual reputation and, 17, 19, 26, 31; judges and, 4; metrics and, 178; monitoring and, 4, 27; noise, 23; reforms and, 188 (*see also* reforms). *See also specific topics*
institutional structures, 10–11; agency model and, 59–60, 65 (*see also* agency model); arbitration and, 184–85 (*see also* arbitration; *and specific organizations*); audiences and, 149–54; civil law (*see* civil law); collective reputation and, 22, 188 (*see also* collective reputation);